America's

POLKA
KING

America's POLKA KING

THE REAL STORY OF
Frankie Yankovic
AND HIS MUSIC

BOB DOLGAN

GRAY & COMPANY, PUBLISHERS
CLEVELAND

Gray & Company, Publishers
www.grayco.com

Library of Congress Cataloging-in-Publication Data

Dolgan, Bob.
America's polka king : the real story of Frankie Yankovic and his music / Bob Dolgan.
p. cm.
Includes discography (p.).
ISBN-13: 978-1-59851-026-3 (pbk.)
ISBN-10: 1-59851-026-6 (pbk.)
1. Yankovic, Frank.   2. Accordionists—Ohio—Cleveland—
Biography.   I. Title.
ML419.Y36D65 2006
788.8'6092—dc22
[B]

Printed in the United States of America
10 9 8 7 6 5 4 3 2 1

To Pauline and Joe

Contents

Preface

IN THIS BOOK, I have tried to tell the honest story of Frankie Yankovic, the foremost musician in American polka history. Some readers may feel it is too frank and revealing and that it may damage the Polka King's image and, therefore, the struggling polka culture. But I don't think so. Yankovic was a realist who never wanted to play it safe. As he said when I ghosted his autobiography almost thirty years ago, "Let's tell everything. People will like it better that way." In the time since that book was published, Yankovic won the first polka Grammy, a son died of a self-inflicted stab wound, and another son was imprisoned. He divorced his second wife and married his third, Ida, with whom he spent the rest of his life. This book tells the story of his three marriages and his complicated relationships with family members and musicians. Yankovic rose above all of his troubles, becoming an idol to polka fans in America, Canada, and Europe. He was a unique character, a man who probably would have succeeded in any area of show business if the world had never heard of polkas. He could be lovable, mean, generous, and petty, but always brave and audacious. Above all, he was an entertainer. There was only one Yankovic. There may never be another.

While telling his story, I wanted to give an overview of this underrated music, polka, especially the Cleveland style, which concentrates on melody rather than chaos. As Yankovic always said, "Polkas are the happiest music this side of heaven." Polkas may be fading from society as the older people die, but they still deserve respect. The music has meant so much to many people, especially those of Slovenian, German, Czech, and Polish descent. Being of Slovenian heritage, I grew up with polkas. When I was young, they were as much a part of me as my skin. They were everywhere. We sang the songs at home. You would go to the grocery store and hear them being played on the radio. We sang the Americanized version of the polkas in cars as we rode to baseball games. One went, "From water's edge to Waterloo, from Shaker Square to Brookside Zoo, you'll find the best location in the nation, when you travel down to good old Cleveland town."

Cleveland was known as Polka Town because of Yankovic and all the other accordionists in the city. A Yankovic hit song, written by William Lausche, was titled "Cleveland the Polka Town." It went, "I'm packing up my things, I'll soon be leaving; I'm going to polka town. It was there I met a girl one evening; now I'm Ohio-bound. Wedding bells will ring out in Cleveland. That's the place where I intend to settle down. And listen to the rhythm of the polka, in Cleveland the polka town."

Once, in the 1940s, our family and our friends the Tomsicks and the Plutts took three streetcars to get to a Slovenian picnic in a park at West 71st Street and Denison Avenue in Cleveland. On the way home, our foreign-born fathers harmonized in the streetcars, singing some of the Slovenian songs that Yankovic and others had turned into hits with English lyrics. The Irish conductors and the other riders, who did not know us or understand the foreign words, applauded the singing. We, of course, took it for granted. In our own little East Side world, we assumed everybody liked Slovenian music. We enjoyed it as much as we enjoyed Bing Crosby, Frank Sinatra, the Mills Brothers, the Andrews Sisters, Harry James, and Judy Garland.

Yankovic was closer to us because he was one of us. Our parents and neighbors knew him and could tell stories about him. The Clevelander traveled the world with his music for fifty years. He might have been considered square by some, but his life was as tumultuous as that of any rock star.

A few years ago music promoter Steve Popovich, who had a lot of show business contacts, approached several movie people, hoping to get a film made about Yankovic. It was a good idea.

Yankovic's life was filled with triumphs, defeats, crises, and controversies. He was an uninhibited original with a national reputation. His story, unlike many of the tales shown in movies and on television today, has a full plot: a beginning, a middle, and an end. However, Popovich could get nowhere. The closest he came to getting a nibble was from a producer who was interested if the story could be turned into a comedy. That was idiotic. Yankovic's life was no comedy. It was loaded with good times, but, if anything, it was more of a tragedy. But that is how Hollywood, and much of the public, has come to regard polkas in recent years. They look at the music as a fading relic, something not to be taken seriously. Fine. People are entitled to their own tastes. For this writer, rap and heavy metal music are more ridiculous. The great songwriter Irving Berlin must have turned over in his grave when that melodious new song *It's Hard Out Here for a Pimp* won the 2006 Academy Award. Say what you will about polkas, at least the listeners know they are hearing a melody. Yankovic, the Babe Ruth of the polka, always made sure the customers got their money's worth.

America's
POLKA
KING

Chapter One

"I Hate Yankovic"

GEORGIE COOK, THE GREAT banjo player, was the last surviving member of the Frankie Yankovic band that made "Just Because" and the "Blue Skirt Waltz" two of the few million-selling polka records in history.

He was about ninety years old and living in the Slovene Home for the Aged in Cleveland. I wanted to talk to him about Yankovic before he died, to get his comments on tape. In previous years I had chatted with him several times in social situations and he often told me of his dislike for Yankovic. Cook was a quiet, intelligent person, more subdued than the average rough-and-tumble polka musician of that time. After leaving Yankovic, he was the leader of his own successful polka band.

I went to the nursing home to see Cook. He was sitting in a wheelchair and had the same little smile on his face he always wore in his many years of performing onstage.

"Hello, George," I said. "How are you? It's good to see you."

There was no response from Cook. He just kept smiling. "George," I said. "You know me, don't you? I'm Bob Dolgan." Again there was no reply. He just kept staring and smiling.

I realized this was not going to be an easy interview. "George, what's wrong?" I said. "Don't you remember me? I'm Bob Dolgan. I'm a writer at *The Plain Dealer*. We used to talk." Still no reply. This went on for about five minutes.

I was just about to pick up my tape recorder and leave. Cook was obviously in a state of dementia. He had no idea who I was and maybe no idea who he was. I tried one last time. "What kind of a guy was Frankie Yankovic?" I asked.

Bingo. I had hit the magic button. Cook suddenly came to life. He was off and running. "I hate Yankovic with a passion!" he shouted. "He's no good. A lot of people liked me better than they liked him. That used to burn him like hell. In Milwaukee a whole gang of people were calling out my name, 'Georgie, Georgie,' making a fuss over me while I was playing. I was standing next to Yankovic as he played and made clinkers." (A clinker is a musician's term for hitting the wrong notes.) Cook sneered as he made the statement.

"He slapped me right on the face onstage in front of all those people," Cook continued. "I told him I'd report him to Local 4 [the musicians' union] and have him thrown out. I could have made trouble for him, but I didn't."

According to Cook, Yankovic slapped him on the face three times during their partnership of about five years, always making it look like an accident. One day, Cook decided not to take it any longer. He broke off an empty beer bottle and approached Yankovic, determined not to be bullied anymore.

"What did I do to you?" Cook yelled. "You're nothing. You're the boss of nothing." He did not finish the anecdote. Evidently, other people who were present quieted Cook down. "I played with him too long," he said. "But I needed the money, so I stayed with him."

I mentioned that Yankovic won the first polka Grammy award, getting the vote from fellow musicians. Cook scoffed. "He bought it," he said. "All those trophies. He bought everything." Cook stopped talking. He could not say any more, or elaborate on his charges. An attendant wheeled him back to his room.

Slovenian polka musicians and singers often come to the home to entertain the residents. Before his death, Cook would enjoy their performances, which would take place in the community room. There would normally be about seventy-five people listening to the music. If one of the entertainers played "Just Because," Cook would immediately ask an attendant to wheel him out of the room, holding a grudge against the Polka King to the end.

Chapter Two

Farewell to a King

FRANK YANKOVIC ALWAYS AROUSED strong passions. The public loved him. After his death on October 14, 1998, at age 83, he was honored in one of Cleveland's largest funerals. His body lay in state at Zele's Funeral Home in Collinwood, only a few blocks from his boyhood home.

Zele's contains four large chapels. Each can hold more than a hundred people for a wake. Usually only one of the rooms is used. When someone especially prominent dies, the wake can spill over into a second room.

When Yankovic died, the mourners filled all four chapels, one of the few times that had ever happened. "It was the largest funeral and wake I ever conducted," said Sutton Girod Jr., the veteran funeral director. "People came from all over the country."

Yankovic's third wife, Ida, received visitors. More than two hundred floral pieces filled the rooms. One refrigerator-sized bouquet came from Bobby Vinton, the rock idol who recorded "My Melody of Love," an ethnic record with polka overtones, late in his career. Another came from Wayne Newton, the Las Vegas singing star who had been a friend of Yankovic.

The Cleveland *Plain Dealer*, the state's largest daily newspaper with a circulation of a half million, went all out in its coverage of Yankovic's demise. The news of his death was carried in a huge, triple-byline story on the front page, authored by this writer, William Miller, and Brian Albrecht. The story carried over into an inside page and ran about fifty inches, the length reserved for first-line celebrities.

The lead paragraphs of the story said: "God plays a squeezebox, but he's got some serious competition now. Polka King Frankie

Yankovic, who kept Americans bouncing on the dance floor for decades, played life's last stanza yesterday. The bandleader, also described as a Frank Sinatra with an accordion, died yesterday at his home in New Port Richey, Fla."

Two pictures of Yankovic were at the top of the front page, with the caption "Frankie Yankovic 1915–1998." The bigger photo showed him smiling into the camera at a polka picnic. He was wearing the open-necked blue peasant shirt that he wore through his last thirty years onstage. Just below that picture was another shot of Yankovic playing the accordion. On the inside of the paper was another photo, taken in the 1940s, in which Yankovic is shown playing the accordion with two unidentified youngsters, a boy and a girl.

A *Plain Dealer* editorial said Yankovic "single-handedly preserved and popularized a musical genre that could have been drowned out long ago by its louder and often far less cheery cousins." An editorial-page cartoon by Jeff D'Arcy showed a broken accordion leaning off a stool, accompanied by the caption "The Day the Music Died."

Columnist Dick Feagler recalled that when he was a boy the accordion was not the scorned instrument it had become. He said half the boys in his neighborhood, including himself, took accordion lessons. Feagler said he preferred the polka to the anger and fury of contemporary rock music.

Music had always been present at the Yankovic family wakes at Zele's. When Frank's father, Andy, and his mother, Rose, died, the entire Yankovic band played before the caskets, turning out soulful Slovenian songs. When his sister, Rose, died, all the family's grandchildren sang.

The same thing happened when Frank died. His grandchildren sang "Just Because" and the "Blue Skirt Waltz," the songs he had made famous. Joey Miskulin, the fine accordionist who accompanied Yankovic longer than anybody, played. So did Bob Kravos, Yankovic's great-nephew, another splendid player.

The Associated Press, *Time*, and *People* magazine covered the funeral, along with all the local TV stations and suburban newspapers.

Yankovic was laid to rest in a blue casket. It was his favorite color, perhaps because of the success of the "Blue Skirt Waltz," which he always said was his most popular number. The crown he won as America's Polka King in 1948 was in the coffin. His accordions stood sentinel to the side of the casket. Tricia Yankovic, his tenth and last child, slipped a picture of herself and her baby into his hands in the coffin. Joey Miskulin closed the lid on the casket.

Emma Udovich, seventy, came to the funeral from her home in El Paso, Texas. "We would travel hours to see him in concert or at a dance, wherever he was," she told *The Plain Dealer*. "We are sad, of course, but we cannot be too sad because he lived one of the fullest lives anyone could live."

A man in his eighties flew in from Minnesota's Iron Range. He approached Ida and told her he and Yankovic were old friends. "We used to drink wine together," he said. It was the first time he had ever flown on an airplane. He knelt down before the coffin and sobbed.

"It was very sad," said Ann Birsa, a Chicagoan who was a longtime friend of Yankovic. "It was like tearing down a building, the end of an era." Eddie Blazonczyk, the Chicago Polish polka idol, was there. So was Jimmy Sturr of Florida, New York, the multiple Grammy Award winner who flourished in the Polish music style. "Frank Yankovic is truly America's polka king," Sturr was quoted as saying. "He's done more for polkas than the rest of us put together."

Yankovic's first wife, June, with whom he had eight children, did not come to the funeral for fear of causing a distraction. She had been married to Yankovic for twenty-eight years, during his heyday as a star. She deserted him in 1968, finding it impossible to stay with a husband who was on the road 325 days a year. June was now remarried to a Detroit automotive artist who worked for the Ford Motor Company. "She still had feelings for Dad," said one of her children. Yankovic had never forgiven her for leaving him.

Yankovic's second wife, Pat, mother of two of his children, visited the funeral home. She was twenty-eight years younger than Yankovic. She, too, found it too hard to live with a husband who was always on the road. They also divorced.

Bobby Yankovic, the King's youngest surviving son and a former member of his band, was another visitor. He was serving time in prison for robbery, something that had almost broken Yankovic's heart. Bobby was brought in the morning of the funeral, before anyone was there. He was wearing the orange suit of a convict and was accompanied by prison guards. He stayed for twenty minutes, looking at his father, then left with the guards and was taken back to prison.

The funeral was held at St. Mary's Church in Collinwood, where Yankovic had been married for the first time fifty-eight years before. Yankovic made his debut as a professional musician at a St. Mary's dance nearly seventy years earlier. The church was completely filled. About eight hundred people were there that Monday morning, October 19. Those who could not get in sat on the church steps. Half of the politicians in town attended, including Cleveland mayor Michael White, an African-American, and Congressman Dennis Kucinich.

Father John Kumse, a Catholic priest who was pastor of the church, conducted the mass. Father Frank Perkovich of Minnesota, called the Polka Mass Priest because he had popularized the singing of Slovenian folksongs at masses instead of the usual Catholic hymns, served as his concelebrant. It had been suggested that the Polka Mass be held in the church, but the idea was rejected.

Kumse gave the first eulogy. "This was where it all started, in this tight-knit, working-class neighborhood where people worked hard and played hard," Kumse said. "Yankovic had a special talent for entertainment. His greatest gift was that he knew how to make people happy, but no matter how high he rose he always remained that kid from Collinwood, from Polka Town. He was comfortable sitting next to the high and mighty as the well as the guy on the next stool in the barroom."

Mike Polensek, president of Cleveland City Council, called Yankovic a hero in the neighborhood. He was constantly asked to pass resolutions in Cleveland Council honoring Yankovic on his retirement. "I think I must have produced ten of them over the years." he said. But Yankovic would never retire.

Tony Petkovsek, the WELW Radio disc jockey who is a power in the polka community, paid tribute to the King. "He was truly the special polka man for all time in all of our lives," said Petkovsek in his eulogy. "Yankovic was a lifelong, round-the-clock campaigner who never quit. He was more than just the leading musician. He was the ultimate polka promoter."

Andrea McKinnie, one of Yankovic's daughters, read a letter from her imprisoned brother, Bobby. "He put many smiles on thousands of faces," Bobby wrote. "He always took care of his family and was always there to help us through life's ups and downs. I see what a wonderful legend he has become and I am truly grateful."

"My father now goes to one last show," said McKinnie. "I hope he is not thirsty, for in heaven there is no beer." That was a reference to one of Yankovic's hit songs, "In Heaven There Is No Beer."

The Plain Dealer again gave maximum coverage, with another front-page story and two pictures, plus a column by Elizabeth Auster, a young woman who probably never danced a polka in her life. She was astounded and impressed to hear faint music outside the church. "Could it be?" she wrote. "Could someone outside really be playing the boisterous polka music while inside the church hundreds of people were solemnly saying goodbye to the man they called The Polka King?"

Her guess was correct. At Petkovsek's urging, nine accordionists played Yankovic's most famous songs as the flag-draped coffin was wheeled outside to the hearse. The accordionists included Walter Ostanek, Canada's Polka King, Gaylord Klancnik and Jerry Robotka of Detroit, and Cleveland players Lou Trebar, Fred Ziwich, Joey Tomsick, Frank Moravcik, Dan Peters, and Tops Cardone.

The crowd began singing the songs. There were tears in people's eyes. "The music seemed like it was coming from heaven," said a woman in a babushka. "It was so sad, but it was a wonderful tribute," Birsa said. "This was perfect, exactly what Frank would have wanted," said Ida. "I'm speechless and so happy they are playing for my father," said McKinnie.

The music continued as Yankovic's coffin was carried to the hearse. Pallbearers included his grandchildren, John Yankovic, Frank Yankovic III, Brian Takita, and Patrick McKinnie, his nephew, Bob Kravos, his great-nephew, Bob Kravos Jr., nephew Dan Keba, his stepson, Frank Smodic Jr., his longtime drummer, Dave Wolnik, and Joey Miskulin.

The mourners were not finished. They knew their irrepressible Yankovic. They knew that he did not want tears, but laughs. They began dancing to the music on the sidewalk. Ida was grief-stricken, but one of the photos caught her in a joyous mood. She and Yankovic's niece, Dorothy Hock, are standing side by side, smiling at the performance.

About 250 cars were in the funeral cortege to Cleveland's Calvary Cemetery. Police stopped traffic all along the fifteen-mile route to allow the huge procession to pass through. Yankovic was buried in the family plot, alongside his parents, sisters, and Joe White, one of his longtime banjo players.

The accordionists jammed again at the cemetery. They were joined by Miskulin, Bob Kravos Jr., Frank Culkar, and his son, Anthony Culkar. The latter was five years old. "I always remember the little boy who played," Ida said years later.

"The music that made him a legend, here and across America, followed him all the way, as far is it could go," Auster wrote.

"God, how they played," recalled Birsa. "You'd have to be there to appreciate it. We were at Calvary a good hour." Afterward, the whole crowd repaired to Sterle's Slovenian Country House Restaurant, where Yankovic and Ida had held their wedding reception.

What caused this impressive tribute? Why did people get so emotional over an accordionist and the music that was so out of touch with contemporary life? In order to understand why and how it happened, you have to visit the culture from which he sprang. You cannot fully understand Cleveland unless you understand the accordion players.

Chapter Three

Princes of the Neighborhood

THE MUSIC WAS BORN in Slovenia, a small European nation of two million people, situated northeast of Italy and south of Austria. Its capital city is Ljubljana (Loveland.) Historian William Shirer once paid a marvelous compliment to Ljubljana. "Here is a city for the whole world to emulate," he wrote. "Its streets are filled with statues of thinkers and writers. There are no statues of military men." During the early part of the twentieth century, when Slovenia was a province of Austria-Hungary, about fifty thousand Slovenians migrated to Cleveland, hoping to improve their livelihoods. Except for Ljubljana, Cleveland soon had more Slovenians than any other city in the world. After World War I, Slovenia became part of Yugoslavia, then finally became an independent country in 1991.

Music dominated social life in Cleveland's Slovenian community. The people had a reputation for working hard and saving their money, but they always seemed to be playing accordions, dancing, or singing. As one wag said when discussing the three major nationalities of Yugoslavia, "Get three Croatians together and you have an argument. Get three Serbians together and you have a war. Get three Slovenians together and you have a choir."

The accordion players were the princes of the neighborhoods. Numerous families had clever, engaging sons who could perform miracles on the box when company arrived. They were the centers of attention, playing the old-country songs that people sang and danced to in their homes. Sitting around the kitchen table and warbling the time-tested melodies was a big thing.

There was something romantic about accordion players. There

was a devil-may-care attitude about them. It was easy to like them and idolize them. They smiled onstage. They looked handsome in their tuxedos and pompadours. They seemed clean-cut and friendly. Nobody epitomized this style better than Yankovic.

Most of the accordionists, including Yankovic, started out playing the diatonic accordion, also called a cheesebox and later a button box. The cheesebox was the easiest accordion to learn, since it was like playing only the white keys on the piano. There were no sharps or flats on its button keys. Therefore, not all songs, including American pop tunes, could be played on the instrument. Nevertheless, it had a charming, tinny sound and was perfect for playing most Slovenian songs.

The best cheeseboxes were made by Anton Mervar, who was born in the old country and began making accordions in 1915 in Cleveland. The sound that came out of his boxes was never matched by any other accordion maker, yet he never learned how to play the instrument himself. He was killed in a car crash in the 1950s, without divulging the secret to the divine sound he produced. At that time his accordions cost about a hundred dollars. Today they are valued at two thousand. Many a home has one of the ancient boxes in an attic, a silent souvenir of the culture that used to be.

Generally, after learning to play the cheesebox, serious accordionists graduated to the chromatic or piano versions of the accordion. They contained all notes and any song could be played on either.

Yankovic was an accomplished cheesebox player, but when he tried to learn the piano accordion, his progress was so slow he almost gave up. But he kept trying and finally solved the box's mysteries. This was unusual. In many Slovene households, there was a feeling that nobody should play the accordion (or do anything else) unless he was gifted and did not have to work too hard at it. There was a belief in "the natural," whether he be a lawyer or a doctor or a plumber. Someone who worked hard at the accordion might become an average player, but never outstanding. He should try something that came more easily to him.

Second to the accordionists in prestige were the singers. Each of the eight Slovenian halls in Cleveland had its own choir, performing concerts. Yankovic sang with the Soca choir, named for a Slovenian river, at the Holmes Avenue Hall. The most notable concerts were performed by the Glasbena Matica and Zarja choruses, which sang at the Slovenian National Home on St. Clair and East 65th, largest of the venues. The hall had been built by the neighborhood's citizens in 1924, with their own money, vigor, and expertise. It had cost $250,000. Today it would probably cost $5 million to build the huge auditorium, which seats a thousand, along with a stage, barroom, balcony, and kitchen. The Hall remains in use today and is often rented by diverse groups as a favorite for wedding receptions and parties.

Zarja (Dawn) was known for its lively, lighthearted singing and performing, capturing the essence of the culture's spirit. Glasbena Matica (Queen Bee of Song) was more formal. It performed operas such as *La Traviata*, *Carmen*, and *Rigoletto*, all sung with Slovenian words. Glasbena was directed by Anton Schubel, a former chorus singer in New York's Metropolitan Opera. Both Glasbena and Zarja are still thriving today.

Equally important were the dancers who packed the polka halls from the 1920s to the 1950s. They were not the old-timers who valiantly totter through the dances today in the aging days of the genre. In Yankovic's time, the halls were filled with people aged seventeen to twenty-five, beautiful young women and vigorous men. They all came to the dances hoping to be stricken by Cupid's arrow. Many people met their future spouses at these events.

Some of the dancers had the ability of professionals. They could whirl around the floor in a full pivot, the most difficult polka step, but the prettiest when executed in the correct manner. The full pivot has largely disappeared from today's polka havens, although you occasionally see it done. The dancers could do the half pivot, another vanished move, and the reverse turn. The polka tempo was also perfect for doing the jitterbug.

The young people had all learned to dance at home. The boys were mostly taught by their sisters and mothers. "You better learn to dance," a mother would say. "Otherwise, no girl will want you." As a result, even the clumsiest youths could do a serviceable polka. The Cleveland-style dance, which incorporated a slide and glide step, was smoother than the old lift-the-knee European style. Yankovic, a capable dancer, was a fixture in the halls, either on the floor or playing onstage.

The giant Slovenian National Home's dances were the most notable, with as many as five hundred youngsters whirling around the beautiful ballroom. "When you played there, you felt like you were in the big time," said Yankovic, a frequent performer in the hall, which featured two large mirrored pillars. Hardly anybody brought dates to the dances. The girls and boys would arrive for their dates with destiny on streetcars or buses. Or, heaven forbid, sometimes they would walk, another forgotten exercise. The regular couples congregated in the corners, dancing smugly with each other. The unattached young men would set up a long stag line on one side of the floor.

Girls would often dance with each other, pretending not to notice the stags, but hoping one of them would make an approach. Most often, two young men would break in on a couple of girls and they would separate into two couples. More than one marriage began this way.

Some boys needed to enhance their courage before asking girls to dance. They would go to the bar for a beer, then approach a girl they had their eyes on. If the girl turned the boy down, he would retreat to the stag line in humiliation or return to the bar. If the girl accepted the invitation, especially if she was beautiful, the boy would feel a pang of triumph, as though he had hit a line drive single in baseball, and the pair would glide around the floor as the envious stags watched. The most popular girls were the ones who danced with everyone who asked them. The standard ritual was for the bands to play three polkas, three waltzes, and three popular music numbers. Dancers of all nationalities came to the soirees. In those days, the standard way to begin a conversation was to say, "What nationality are you?"

The eight Cleveland Slovenian halls all staged weekly dances, often on both Friday and Saturday nights. The Aragon Ballroom on West 25th Street, which catered primarily to big band music, had polkas every Wednesday night. The huge, beautiful Euclid Beach Amusement Park ballroom had Thursday night polka dances in the summertime. St. Michael's Hall and the Polish Women's Hall both featured Slovenian polkas. Many of the polka dancers also attended dances in other parts of town in which big band music was played. The idea was to meet the opposite sex.

After the dances ended at midnight, couples would often pair off and do more polka dancing at taverns such as the Metropole, Gaiety Bar, Glen Park Café, the Uptown Grille, and Fritz's Tavern. For special dates and occasions the place to go was the Twilight Gardens in Eastlake. It was a safe, happy environment, marred only by the occasional fisticuffs over girls. The Metropole, on East 55th and St. Clair, was jocularly called "The Bucket of Blood." The Bank Bar on East 79th also saw its share of disturbances. Waltz King Lou Trebar, in what was doubtless an exaggeration, said that when he was playing at the Slovenian National Home in the 1930s he could look from the stage and see fights in all four corners of the hall. It was all done with fists, not knives or guns.

At the height of the polka boom from 1948 to 1954, which was instigated by Yankovic's million-selling records, Cleveland musicians could play every night of the week, never having to work at another job. Cleveland television stations carried shows such as *Polka Parade* and *Polka Varieties* (Sunday at 1 p.m. on WEWS Channel 5), and *Perme's Polka Party* (Saturday at 6 p.m.), sponsored by Frank Perme, a Collinwood furniture dealer. John

Saunders was the affable announcer. Accordionist Johnny Vadnal and his band played on *Polka Parade* every Sunday for several years. The band featured Johnny's brothers, Tony and Frank, and drummer Joe Stradiot. Tony, who played the bass, was one of Cleveland's finest singers. Frank played banjo and Stradiot also sang, besides providing comic relief and showmanship. Joe Black and then Paul Wilcox were the masters of ceremonies. When he was in town and not traveling all over the country, Yankovic often starred on the show.

Johnny Pecon and Lou Trebar, his talented sidekick, headed the Perme show. Pecon's sister, Nettie, was a popular singer on the program. Ernie Benedict and the Range Riders, featuring Frankie Zeitz and the singing Kendall Sisters, Dolly and Polly, had another lively TV show on Saturday mornings. Kenny Bass had a weeknight TV program, hosted by friendly Bob Forester. The *Old Dutch Revue*, featuring Polish bands such as Ray Budzilek, Chester Budny, and Henry Broze, was another Cleveland TV staple.

Paul Nakel had the first daily radio program on a major Cleveland station, WJMO, in the late 1940s. Bass, who was also a bandleader, soon followed with his own daily show on WSRS. This was at a time when Cleveland had only six radio stations, not the thirty or so of today. Yankovic appeared on all of the programs. One of the most famous of all the polka disc jockeys was Martin "Heinie Martin" Antoncic, who had a Sunday morning radio show on WGAR for decades, starting in the 1930s. Antoncic started Yankovic on his recording career. Tony Petkovsek, today's major polka disc jockey, has surpassed all of the previous DJs in power and influence. Petkovsek, now on WELW in Willoughby, has had a daily radio program since 1961 and is the foremost polka DJ in America. For more than forty years, he has conducted a Thanksgiving polka celebration that draws people from all over America to Cleveland. Petkovsek was the driving force behind the formation of the Cleveland-Style Polka Hall of Fame and has taken promotion of the music far beyond anything his predecessors ever dreamed of, including polka cruises and trips to every corner of the world.

Perry Como, the Andrews Sisters, and Arthur Godfrey, all major names in American pop music, caught the polka fever of the 1940s and 1950s, recording hit records. Actors such as James Stewart, Fred Astaire, Dean Martin, and Ward Bond played piano accordions in movies. The Three Sons, a major pop act, featured the accordion. It is still a mystery why the instrument became a target of jokes and scorn.

The first important Cleveland polka bandleader was Matt Hoyer, who lived in the Newburgh section off Broadway. Born in Slovenia, he played his chromatic accordion while sitting down. He remained true to the melodies of his native land, adding no embellishments. He was a fine player with excellent rhythm. Yankovic and Pecon grew up listening to his style. Pecon is considered the greatest of all polka accordionists. He did not read music until his later years, but he had perfect pitch and could play any tune after hearing it once. He once sat in with a jazz outfit that was so impressed with his skill it tried to hire him.

In the 1920s, a Cleveland dentist, Dr. William Lausche, Americanized the music, creating a sound that became the foundation for what is today called the Cleveland-style polka. Dr. Lausche, brother of the late Frank Lausche, the U.S. senator, Ohio governor, and Cleveland mayor, was obsessed with music, from Slovenian polkas to American jazz. He was constantly humming melodies as he worked on his patients' teeth. Born in America of Slovenian immigrant parents, he came up with new polka arrangements that were heavily influenced by jazz and pop music. He composed polka standards such as "Cleveland, the Polka Town," "The Girl I Left Behind," and "I've Got a Date with Molly." Lausche was a fine pianist. His brother, Charles, played the violin and another brother, Harold, played piano and guitar. The late dentist's daughter, Gloria Rado, recalls that their home was always filled with music.

Future Senator Lausche, a fine speaker and the most distin-guished Slovenian-American in history, could hold his own sing-ing, but he was the only one of the siblings who did not play a musical instrument. Lausche's sister, Josephine, and her friend, Mary Udovic, went to New York to sing on a series of Slovenian songs for Columbia Records in the 1920s. They were backed by a full thirty-two-piece orchestra that included violins. Dr. Lausche played piano. The records are true classics for polka lovers, but they did not make the Lausches rich. They were not thinking of money. They made the recordings because they loved the melo-dies. Lausche said the music belonged to the public.

Cleveland's young accordionists, like Yankovic, Pecon, and Trebar, quickly caught on to the Lausche style. Eddie Habat, a brash Collinwood teenager, is credited with taking the music an-other step forward, bringing it to the full Cleveland sound that survives today. That was in the late 1930s and early 1940s. Habat played aggressively, with a lot of emotion. He was inspired by big crowds, skillful dancers, and late nights. In his own words, he wanted to "kick ass" on the lively second parts, which followed the melody. When the second part was over, he would create a third part, moving up to a higher, sharper key that created elec-tricity in the dance halls, just as Artie Shaw and Benny Goodman did with the jitterbuggers. Habat, who died in May 2005, had a long career as a bandleader, recording for decades on the Decca label.

Bill Randle, the Clevelander who was the nation's most power-ful disc jockey in the 1950s (he heavily promoted Elvis Presley), surprisingly became entranced with polka music and the charac-ters who perform it. In the 1960s and 1970s, he was a regular at polka dances, getting to know the fans and musicians. Randle, foremost disc jockey in Cleveland history, loved the polka culture and considered the music and life far superior to what the rock world had become. To the end of his life in 2004, he often made complimentary comments about polka people on his programs.

Nominated several times for the Rock and Roll Hall of Fame, he refused induction. He was inducted into the Cleveland-Style Polka Hall of Fame.

With Yankovic playing mostly outside of Cleveland, the most popular local polka bands were those of Pecon and Trebar, Habat, Bass, and Vadnal. There were many others. They were well paid for their efforts, but they also seemed to be obsessed with the music. They would often gather in clubs and jam among themselves, drinking and laughing. There was something addictive about the music. They and their listeners were trapped by it. The music gave them everything they needed.

Everything changed with rock and roll. When Elvis Presley began performing in the mid-1950s, the young polka dancers flocked to the new sound in huge numbers. The polka dances that automatically drew 500 people at the Slovenian National Home suddenly dropped to crowds of 150.

Eventually the dances disappeared, although today they continue to be held after concerts, dinners, and weddings in the diminishing polka culture. Petkovsek, with his daily show, is often credited with being the sparkplug that has kept Slovenian music and social life alive. The remaining dancers are nostalgic over their lost society, where life was safe, predictable, and orderly. Rock and roll symbolized something else, something dynamic and furious, tinged with danger.

With the popularity of the polka on the wane, the polka bandleaders had to get regular jobs. The talented Pecon became custodian at Cleveland's City Hall. Habat became a house painter. Trebar had a white-collar job in City Hall. They continued to play one or two jobs on weekends for decades. Trebar, eighty-six, still performs on occasion with the Jeff Pecon Orchestra. Jeff, a former plant manager at Reliance Electric who is now in the computer business, is John's son, and a worthy successor to the old master. Many musicians say that Jeff is as talented musically as his father. He has the same facility, along with the ability to read music, and is a good singer. John Pecon Jr., a civil engineer, is the band's drummer. The group has been performing since their father's death in 1975, when Jeff and John Jr. were teenagers. When Jimmy Sturr heard the band for the first time, he told Jeff, "You've got the best Slovenian band I've ever heard," Amazingly, the band has been around longer than the original Pecon-Trebar outfit, which flourished for about twenty-five years, until Pecon became ill and retired in the early 1970s,

Today the polka music keeps ticking along, breathing heavily but still refusing to die. Today's accordionists are court reporters (George Staiduhar), firemen (Dan Wojtila), bakers (Don Wojtila), and owners of computer businesses (Ed Sumrada). The accordionists have learned to play keyboards and rock and roll, a necessity if they are to survive with the younger generation. When I see a good accordionist quietly playing a keyboard he looks to me like a Samson shorn of his powers, but that is the nature of the business. Newlyweds are willing to accommodate Mom and Pop and hire a polka band for a wedding, but usually they only want a few polkas played. The rest has to be rock.

Yankovic, however, never changed. He kept playing the polka all over America for another forty years after rock took over.

Chapter Four

Bootlegger's Son

FRANK YANKOVIC WAS BORN in the little town of Davis, West Virginia, where his Slovenian immigrant parents worked in a lumber camp. His mother, Rose, was a cook, supervising a kitchen staff that made meals for seventy-five lumberjacks. His father, Andy, was a blacksmith who supplemented his income by bootlegging whiskey, beer, and wine for the workers. He and Rose had met at the camp and were married in 1910. The bride was twenty-four and the groom thirty-one. Their first three children, Josephine, Rose, and Mary, were all born at the camp. The couple was overjoyed when they finally had a son, Frankie, who came along on July 28, 1915. Yankovic came into the world only a few steps away from where his father was cooking whiskey in the woods. The midwife remembered him as being a "real pink baby." When the police closed in on Andy's bootlegging activities, he fled to Cleveland to avoid prosecution. Rose and the children soon followed.

The family settled in the Collinwood neighborhood and survived the worldwide flu epidemic of 1918–1919, which killed thousands of Clevelanders. So many of their friends died that Rose and Andy seemed to be going to funerals almost every day. Rose kept her children healthy by hanging garlic around their necks in handkerchiefs soaked in camphorated oil, a remedy practiced by many mothers of the time.

Their first residence was a two-story, double-family house at 15702 Saranac Road. The Yankovics, who took in boarders, lived downstairs. Another boy, Frankie Valencic, lived upstairs with his family. He was called "Upstairs Frankie" while Yankovic was "Downstairs Frankie." One day the boys stole some cigarettes that

Rose always kept for the boarders. The boys went into the basement and hid in some empty wine barrels, smoking. Rose smelled
the smoke and investigated, finding the delinquents. That night
both Upstairs Frankie and Downstairs Frankie received strap-
pings with a belt from their fathers. Yankovic never smoked
again.

Handy Andy was first employed as a crane operator. Then he
bought a hardware store and built a nice brick house at 692 East
160th Street. It cost eleven thousand dollars and was the envy of
the neighborhood. Rose, the mother, was a practical, no-nonsense
woman who would get down on her knees to scrub the floors.
Judging from old photographs, she seldom smiled, but Frankie
was the apple of her eye. She was strict with her daughters, but
she pampered Frankie, affectionately calling him "porkychick"
(my little pork chop). She would pat him on the cheek and talk
to him as though he was a baby, making special meals just for
him. Yankovic especially liked to eat eggs, usually four or five in a
day. When he was nine years old, he suffered an appendix attack
and had surgery. The doctor said he became ill because he ate too
many eggs.

Frankie liked to play dominoes and checkers and loved dogs.
The family had a cocker spaniel for years, named "Clinker." In
later years Yankovic remembered him with a recording of "The
Clinker Polka." Frankie's major passion, however, was the movies.
He and his cousin, Frank Spilar, would go to the old Plaza and
Five Points theaters in Collinwood. His favorite actors were cowboy heroes Tom Mix, Buck Jones, and Hoot Gibson, along with
Rin Tin Tin, the wonder dog. Rose would give him ten cents to
see the shows, but warned him not to tell Andy where he got the
money. When he would come home, Andy would say, "Where the
hell you been all day? I got work for you."

A streak of bravado and mischief ran through the young boy's
personality. His cousin, Spilar, who was sixteen, had a beautiful
1924 Chevrolet. Frankie watched him closely as he drove, learning

how to shift gears. One day, when he was about ten, he got into the car and started driving down the street. He was still so small his head could barely be seen above the wheel. The police saw an apparently empty car rolling through the streets. When they caught up to the vehicle they were amazed to see the boy driving. They took him to the police station and called his father. Andy arrived, yelled at the boy, and gave him a memorable spanking.

Frankie and Spilar had another little trick. Frankie would go into the basement of his father's hardware store and position himself at a window with a BB gun. Spilar would stand upstairs and yell to him when a girl was approaching. Frankie would shoot BBs at her legs across the street. The boys thought it was funny, watching the girls look around, scratch their legs, and wonder what was happening.

It was a tougher era. Frankie played baseball in the neighborhood at Knuckles Field, so called because the games often ended in fights between the Italian and Slovenian boys. The Italians were called the Dagos and everybody else was called a Polack.

From an early age, Frankie worked in the hardware store, waiting on customers and learning how to install windowpanes, make electrical repairs, cut pipes, and sew leather for the harnesses of the few horses left in Collinwood. He also learned to cook ham and sausages, skin a pig, and hang the meat in the smokehouse in back of the house.

The boarders were the focal point of the Yankovic household. They were young Slovenian immigrants who had come to America looking for the pot of gold. Most of them planned to go back home someday, but the huge majority stayed in America. They might not have become rich, but they were still happy to be in the New World. Often there were seven or eight boarders in the house, paying twenty-five dollars a month for meals and sleeping quarters. Rose was said to be light-fingered with the loose change that might fall out of their trousers. Rose and Andy almost never turned down a prospective boarder. They stuffed as many as they could into one bed, young Frankie among them. The girls slept in their own rooms. Two of the daughters, Rose and Mary, eventually married boarders. Rose was wed to Tony Drenik and Mary to Herman Kravos. The boarders' favorite game was bocce, called "balinca" by the Slovenians. They played every night after work on the court in the Yankovics' backyard, gambling for drinks or money. Frankie was assigned to manicure the court. Every day during the summer, he would water it down with a fine spray, then carefully roll the sixty-foot-by-twelve-foot court until it was as smooth as a carpet.

Many of the men in the neighborhood watched the games, kibitzing and shouting. Andy and his brother, Joe, were great rivals. They would yell and swear over a few pennies in a game. Joe had been married in Slovenia and left his wife and three daughters to come to the U.S. He stayed here for twenty years, always sending money home to support them. Finally, he went back home. He died within a year.

Frankie idolized the boarders. They were young, physical men brimming with energy. They knew how to sing and joke with the ladies and were well dressed, wearing ties and hats. He loved to sit up late at night with them, watching them play cards and argue about who came from the best village in Slovenia or who cheated in balinca. Andy socialized with them as though he were a boarder himself. Like many people in America during the Prohibition era that began in 1920, Andy bootlegged, selling wine, beer, and whiskey to the men who lived under his roof and other visitors. Frankie, who watched his father cook whiskey and wine in copper kettles, also served the boarders when they called for drinks. My father, Joe, was one of the boarders. An old photo shows him playing the accordion during a family outing, with young Frankie sitting on the running board of a car.

In later years, it was said of Yankovic that he never forgot a name. I met him perhaps five times over a period of ten years when I was in my teens and twenties. Every time I saw him he had the same greeting, "I used to sleep in the same bed with your father and two other boarders." He always called me Joe.

Andy was caught three times for bootlegging, paying a fine of $115 each time. When the police came in to search the house for illegal whiskey, Frankie and his sisters were told to follow them, so they would not plant a bottle and later claim it as evidence. Often, Andy would be warned when the police were coming, and then he would hide the whiskey under the floor or roll barrels of beer into the nearby hardware store.

Max Zelodec, one of the boarders, taught Frankie to play the button box. Frankie admired the way he played on his Mervar accordion, with its tinny, contagious sound. Zelodec, who was about twenty years old, was a stocky, good-looking man who worked as a car mechanic. His playing was superb, often moving Andy to tears on a sentimental song.

Zelodec would also play at house weddings. Frankie would often accompany him, carrying Max's accordion and putting a towel on the back of his neck if he perspired too much in those days without air-conditioning. He noticed that Max was always respected by everybody. Between numbers, the musician would casually drink and joke with the audience. Frankie decided he wanted to be just like him. Even before he had an accordion, he would simulate playing one, moving his fingers and hands, pulling and squeezing the imaginary box in imitation of Zelodec.

He was only about nine years old when he asked Zelodec to give him some informal lessons on the cheesebox. Everything was done by ear. There were no notes or songbooks. When Max went to work during the day, Frankie would practice on his accordion. He got his own accordion when a bachelor who lived nearby died suddenly. The bachelor owed the Yankovics seventy-five dollars, so his landlady suggested Rose come over and look through his effects to see if there was anything she wanted. She found the accordion and brought it home. Frankie learned quickly, becoming an excellent player by the time he was a teenager.

Frankie's first playing job was at the Holmes Avenue Slovenian Hall when he was fifteen. He was paid five dollars to play at a lodge dance. Frank Skufca, one of his neighbors, accompanied him on the banjo. The dancers smilingly encouraged Yankovic, telling him if he played too slowly or too fast. Gene (Markic) March, who grew up with Yankovic, was at the dance. "The people liked him," March recalled. "In those days, if you played the accordion you were great. He played the old Slovenian stuff. I used to think they all sounded the same."

March wanted to be a professional pianist and played in smoky neighborhood taverns for three dollars a night. He hated the jobs, but it was the time of the Great Depression. Everybody was trying to make a dollar. Sometimes he would be paid in sausages.

Yankovic's father, Andy, was one of the few who had reservations about accordionists. "All accordion players are bums," he said once, probably meaning there was little money to be made playing the instrument. That statement might have been what drove Yankovic in later years. He was determined to prove to his father that he was wrong.

Rose, however, did everything she could to make her son happy. She knew he wanted a piano accordion. She heard that a Cleveland music teacher, Joe Russ, had one for sale. She and Frankie went to visit him at his home, accompanied by her daughter Mary and son-in-law Herman Kravos, who drove them. "How much do you want for the accordion?" Rose asked Russ. Told the price was eight hundred dollars, she peeled off five hundred dollars and offered it to Russ. "Take it or leave it," she said. He took it. You could buy a new car for five hundred dollars in those days. Rose made her two unmarried daughters, Josephine and Rose, who were living at home and working, chip in and help pay for the accordion. She also warned Frankie to learn to play well, since she had stuck her neck out for him.

Rose feared what Andy would say about the purchase. She told the boy they would have to keep the purchase secret and that he would not be allowed to practice at home. He would have to leave the box at his sister Mary's house down the street. Frankie accepted the terms gladly. He loved that accordion and practiced at every opportunity. Andy visited Mary every day. Whenever he arrived, Frankie would hide the accordion and run out of the house. "Where the hell is Frankie always running when I come here?" the mystified Andy exclaimed.

Frankie began taking lessons from Joe Notari, a teacher on East 55th and Broadway. The youngster would have to take two streetcars to get there, riding down St. Clair from Collinwood, then transferring at East 55th and taking another streetcar to Broadway. Things did not go well. Frankie, who had never read notes, simply could not play the assigned song, "Let Me Call You Sweetheart," no matter how much he practiced. After several lessons, the irritated teacher told him not to come back for the next lesson unless he learned the song. Yankovic tried and tried, fighting the keys through his tears, struggling with reading the notes. All of a sudden something clicked and he was able to hit the right keys. He did it slowly, but he did it. He felt a great sense of victory. It was a turning point in his life. He returned to play triumphantly for the teacher. Later, he took some more lessons from Joe Trolli, a neighborhood teacher who was to play a key role in his career. In all, Yankovic said he took about twenty-five piano accordion lessons in his life.

There was still the matter of revealing himself to his father. On Christmas Eve, with Andy feeling sentimental and happy among a group of guests and boarders, Frankie brought out his new accordion and played one of his father's favorite Slovenian waltzes. Andy was clearly touched. "I still like the cheesebox better but if you're going to play it, play it well," he said.

When he was sixteen, Yankovic quit school. He had gone to elementary school at St. Mary's and W. H. Brett and to Collinwood High. "The only thing I ever learned in school was to speak English," he recalled. When he began school he spoke mostly

Slovenian, like many other youngsters of the time. He liked shop classes, where he took woodworking and cabinet making, but he felt the other classes were meaningless. He found his teachers to be dry and boring, compared to the spirited boarders he was close to at home. He went to Cleveland Trade School for a short time, then quit altogether and had a series of twenty-five-cent-an-hour jobs. He was a driver and delivery man for Spang's Bakery, sometimes giving accordion lessons to children on his route. He also worked for Zalar's Bakery, the A.B. Box Co., and Murray-Ohio, which made bicycles. Later he worked in a foundry and as a pattern maker in a factory. More importantly, he began making a name for himself in the polka world.

Chapter Five

"I Found the Girl"

YANKOVIC'S FIRST BAND INCLUDED banjo man Frank Skufca, pianist Al (Nagle) Naglitch, drummer Lee Novak, and Bill Dunleavy on the saxaphone. They would play at weddings for five dollars and were glad to get the money. Yankovic got his first major exposure on Dr. James Malle's Sunday evening radio shows on WJAY in 1932. He played on the program for several years, his popularity burgeoning.

Yankovic's strength was in his charisma. He was among the first polka accordionists to stand while playing. He copied the style of another Cleveland box master, Jackie Zorc, smiling as he performed, rather than projecting a dour and serious mien. He bounced around the stage and sang. He was the best singer among the accordionists, rivaled only by Pecon, who had an excellent tenor. Yankovic's voice was not a threat to Sinatra, but he was extremely effective. "Singing is 75 percent personality," he said. He felt the same about playing the accordion.

Yankovic was not an adventurous polka musician. "He played the same songs over and over and was good at them," said Carl Paradiso, banjo player in one of his best bands. "When it came to learning a new song, it took him a while." Possibly because he did not have the facility of Pecon, Trebar, and Habat, or because he felt his fans did not want him to change, Yankovic stuck to the fundamentals. Like the old master Hoyer, he disdained saxophones, feeling they detracted from the accordion sound. After his first few years of performing, he never had a saxophone in his band. He preferred an instrument called the solovox, an electric organ keyboard that he played with one hand while playing the bass notes with his accordion.

Although he surrounded himself with top musicians, he was always the star. Nobody could upstage him. On the rare occasions somebody did, he made that musician's life miserable.

Yankovic soon became the most popular polka musician in town. With the encouragement of disc jockey Martin Antoncic, he put out two polka records in 1938, about ten years after the last Lausche-Udovic session. There had been no other Slovenian polka recordings since then. Antoncic took Yankovic and his band to the Cleveland Recording Company studio downtown, where they cut two 78 rpm discs, playing "The Silk Umbrella Polka," "Hooray, Slovenes," a waltz medley, and his father's favorite, "Always Jolly." They were all Slovenian folk tunes with American titles. Yankovic paid for the production of four thousand records and took them to Anton Mervar's music store. They sold out in two weeks. He was twenty-three and working as a pattern maker in a factory at the time.

His bandsmen had two outfits, wearing blue suits made of fine material or powder-blue jackets with black satin lapels. With his flair for performing, Yankovic consistently outdrew the fine bands headed by Pecon and Trebar, Shorty Callister, Louis Spehek, and even the sainted Matt Hoyer, who was past his peak. After the dances the band would head to polka joints like the Green Hat, owned by boxer Eddie Simms, who was his own host, comedian, and bouncer. On snowy nights after the bars closed Yankovic and the Yanks would sometimes go bobsledding down St. Clair Avenue.

Yankovic was always ambitious but at that time having fun ranked high on his agenda. He and his pals started "The Wrong Club," a group of about a hundred Slovene bachelors who lived for good times. They chose the name because it showed they were more interested in merrymaking than having meetings or collecting dues. They would assemble with their girlfriends for swimming, skating, and horseback riding. Once Yankovic got drunk and jumped out of a canoe into deep water at Nelson Ledges. There was one problem. He didn't know how to swim. He began sinking and was saved by Al Jalen, who later was his best man at his first wedding.

Always a practical joker, Yankovic used Lee Novak, a serious, bespectacled man, as his foil. At a horseback outing, he told the stable owner that Novak was a great rider. "Give him your wildest horse," Yankovic said. Novak had never even been on a horse. He tried to mount him from the right side, then was helped aboard. The horse immediately stood on his hind legs and took off at a gallop, with Novak holding on and screaming for help. The owner had to ride out and save him. Novak got even. When Yankovic got off his horse to answer the call of nature, Novak kicked his horse in the rear, causing it to take off. Yankovic had to walk back several miles to the stable.

Yankovic played and coached on a softball team. He joined the Soca singing society. He was a confident, aggressive young man, not afraid to fight. When another young man made fun of his porkpie hat, he and Yankovic started grappling. Yankovic ripped his opponent's shirt. Novak got between the two to calm things down.

Yankovic was always anxious to get married young. He had his share of experiences with various girls. The first serious candidate for nuptials was a seventeen-year-old girl. Yankovic was about twenty. They wanted to wed, but the affair broke up after he introduced her to his parents, apparently because of some sort of dispute between the two families. He asked another Cleveland girl to marry him. She was extremely beautiful and stood five feet, six inches, tall for those days. She rejected him. The most serious relationship was with a Collinwood girl, Ann Somrak, who resembled Alice Faye, the movie star. They had met at a wedding and the friendship blossomed as he delivered bread to her house while working for Spang Bakery. Her mother would invite

Yankovic in for a cup of coffee and they would all chat. Yankovic took her to the best restaurants and nightclubs, to cruises on Lake Erie and trips to Geauga Lake. She would accompany him to his playing jobs and he would come off the bandstand and dance with her. Her mother wanted her to marry Yankovic but in the end she turned him down because he was a musician. She felt it was too difficult a life. She married another suitor and had a nice family. All the women, by the way, said that Yankovic was always a perfect gentleman. Although he had struck out three times, Yankovic remained in the ball game, always looking for the right girl. He never moped around because of the broken romances. He had the same attitude as a ballplayer. You might go 0-for-3, but you don't get depressed because on the fourth at-bat you could hit a home run.

In 1939, he and his band were playing for a wedding reception in a Collinwood family's home. (In those days not everybody had money to rent a hall.) He was introduced to one of the guests, June Erwerthe, a pretty young woman. "I flipped when I saw her," he said. She was a five-foot, three-inch bundle of class and energy. She was of French, Irish, and Austrian ancestry and lived about five miles away, in the Hough area near downtown Cleveland. She had come to the wedding by streetcar with a girlfriend. Yankovic was struck by her careless vivacity and charm. As he played, he noticed she was a great dancer, with quick and agile moves. He asked her if he could give her a ride home after the wedding. June declined. "If you want to take me out, you have to come to my house and meet my parents," she said. Yankovic was smitten. They made a date. "I never felt anything go through my system like it did that night," he recalled. He was still living at home and shared a bed with Tony Drenik, one of the boarders, who would later marry his sister Rose. Yankovic was so excited that he woke up Drenik when he got into bed at 3 a.m. "I met an angel tonight," Yankovic said. "She's the girl I'm going to marry." Drenik was not overwhelmed. "That's good," he said. "Now go to sleep."

On one of their early dates, Yankovic took June to see the famed Glenn Miller Orchestra in downtown Cleveland. As the waves of applause poured over the audience, Yankovic said, "I wish I could do something like that."

"You can, if you really want to," said June. They were words she would live to regret.

They had the usual courtship, going out for hamburgers and malted milks, riding horses, going to movies. June and Frankie were a comely couple, riding around town in Yankovic's 1937 Chevrolet convertible. She would sit near the bandstand when he played at dances. Yankovic asked three of his closest friends, Patsy Krall, Al Jalen, and Ulrich Lube, to dance with her and keep her away from potential rivals. He was extremely jealous when she danced with strangers. She had studied the violin and had a good voice. She often sang on the bandstand with Yankovic. "You Must Have Been a Beautiful Baby" was her most popular number. They soon became engaged, although Yankovic's parents would have preferred that he marry a Slovenian girl. June impressed Andy one evening while he was sitting on the front porch. She arrived at the Yankovic home in a taxi. "My son's going to marry a rich woman," Andy exclaimed. "She rides taxis." The old man had never been in one in his life, even though he was fairly wealthy.

Yankovic's pals played a joke on the couple when he was performing at the opening of the SNPJ campgrounds in Kirtland in 1940. While they were standing at the bar during an intermission, they had a beautiful young woman approach and take the bottle of beer Yankovic was holding. She took a big swig, leered knowingly at him, and kissed him on the mouth. Yankovic had never seen her in his life. The infuriated June slapped him hard on the face and was screaming at him until the pals explained it was a gag.

June and Yankovic were married on July 15, 1940, in St. Mary's Catholic Church. Yankovic was twenty-five and he thought June was twenty. A few months later she confessed she was actually eighteen. She had lied because she didn't want him to think she was too young. He did not care. Following the wedding, the bridal party visited about twenty-five homes of friends and relatives, an old Slovenian custom, drinking and singing. Joe Lasicky, a future bandleader, played the accordion while they made the rounds. The reception was held in Yankovic's parents' house. The couple did not want a huge reception, fearing they would offend too many friends who were not invited. June and Yankovic went on a one-week honeymoon to Niagara Falls and Virginia. Life proceeded happily, with Yankovic continuing his factory work and adding to the income by giving lessons and playing with the band on weekends. Their first home was on East 172nd Street in Collinwood.

In 1941, with his first child, Linda, on the way, Yankovic decided to buy a Collinwood bar in partnership with his sister Josephine and her husband, Tom Milakovich. Andy loaned them six thousand dollars for the purchase, taking the money out of his safe in the kitchen. He did not trust banks. Too many of them had failed during the Depression. Andy counted out the bills on the kitchen table and they were in business. Yankovic had long wanted to buy a bar. He knew how lucrative they could be when he saw his musicians throw their hard-earned money across bars during and after jobs. He often told his band not to buy drinks for fans. "Let them buy drinks for you," he said. "Otherwise, you're working for nothing." Besides, he was practically raised to be a bar owner. His father had sold drinks when it was illegal. Now it was legal.

The new bar was a family operation. Yankovic was one of the bartenders, along with Milakovich and Herman Kravos, his brothers-in-law, and cousin Frank Spilar. June was a waitress. Yankovic also played onstage with his band, with June coming up to sing occasionally. The place was popular almost from the start. It became the hangout for musicians like Pecon, Habat, Vadnal and Bass. Habat was there from the time he was sixteen, playing his accordion and having fun. His brother, John, a schoolteacher, wanted Eddie, a smart boy, to go to college. On one particularly merry night, Eddie shouted, "Why should I go to college? Everything I want is right here." Andy would open the bar in the mornings, go to the bank to cash checks, and drink with the customers. Rose and her daughters would make lunches and clean up. It was a nice way to live. Yankovic thought he might spend the rest of his life there. That all changed when the Japanese bombed Pearl Harbor on December 7, 1941, throwing the U.S. into World War II.

Chapter Six

Yankovic Goes to War

WITH THE OUTBREAK OF war, the Depression finally ended. People flocked back to work, making tanks, ships, guns, bullets, and bombs. Laborers, who had been mostly out of work for a decade, suddenly had money. The factories were going full blast, men and women working six and seven days a week.

There was a huge demand for workers in defense plants. Patriotism was at a zenith. Everybody wanted to pull together to defeat Hitler's Germany and the Japanese. Yankovic, twenty-six, already had his hands full with his bar, but he had the drive to get even more work and cash. He went to Fisher Body and took a job as a machinist, working the third shift. He would leave the bar at 11 p.m. and work until 7 a.m. The factory had hired so many men, however, that it was disorganized. "We were standing around, doing nothing," Yankovic recalled. "The foremen didn't know what was going on. I didn't even know who my foreman was."

Yankovic, who always had a touch of larceny in his heart, concluded there was no point in standing around if there was no work. After a few days, he left the bar and punched in at the shop at 11, went home, and came back to punch out at 7 in the morning. The ruse worked for two or three months, with Yankovic collecting full pay. Eventually, the company figured out what was going on and he was fired.

Despite the awful bloodshed in the war, everybody at home was having more fun than they had in a long time. It was truly a boom time. Business was so good that the bar, which could accommodate 150 patrons, was getting too small. Yankovic decided to move into a bigger tavern across the street. "Financially, it worked out well," Yankovic recalled. "But I had second thoughts. It might have been better to stay in our original place. We were making a good buck and had no headaches. There was a bigger overhead in the new place and more pressure on everybody. Things might have been better if we stayed where we were."

Yankovic and his band began getting invitations to play at social events around Ohio, Michigan, and Pennsylvania. When Gene March, his old friend, got married in 1942, Yankovic could not attend because he had a playing date. But he promised to come to the reception at the Holmes Avenue Slovenian Hall when he finished. He and his band arrived after midnight and played without pay until 6 a.m. The reception finally broke up when the church bells could be heard ringing. Everybody was young then. Today weddings are pretty much over by 10 p.m. in the aging polka community.

Around that time, Yankovic said he began hearing rumors about June's social life, that she was having a fling with somebody else. She denied everything, but he could tell there was a change in their relationship. "Looking back, I don't think she ever really loved me," Yankovic said years later. "She loved the glamour of being married to a musician. I don't think she was ready to settle down at eighteen."

Divorce was out of the question while his mother was alive. Nobody in the family had ever been divorced. It would have broken her heart. In later years he felt that might have been the wisest course for the two of them. "People didn't get divorced in those days," he said. "I think the new way makes more sense. Why not get a divorce if you're not getting along?"

Yankovic was not drafted into the military immediately, probably because he was married and supporting a wife and two children. (Frank Jr. had arrived by then.) People would make wisecracks about his absence from the service. "Are you a goldbricker?" they would say, using a slang term for a person who was deceiving others and not carrying his share of the load. They pretended they were joking, but Yankovic knew they meant it. "I always cared what people thought about me," he said. "I wanted respect. So one day I went to the draft board and told them I didn't want to be exempt just because I had a family. I said I wanted to be called in."

He was inducted on March 17, 1943. The night before, he had one of those dramatic emotional experiences that always punctuated his life. A huge farewell party was held at his tavern. People stood three-deep at the bar and crowded the dance floor. Yankovic and his band played all night on the stage. June sang some songs with him. Yankovic knew it was going to be very hard to leave. He was still in love with her.

Just before the bar closed at 2:30 a.m., Yankovic called June onstage for a last number. They harmonized on a snappy polka tune, "Bye, Bye, My Baby."

They sang it cheerfully, even though their hearts were breaking. He played the second part with extra verve. Everybody was crying, including Yankovic.

He was sent to Fort Knox, Kentucky, and then to Camp Fannin, Texas, serving with the First Infantry Division. He got along well with the other soldiers but he hated getting up so early. "I would often skip breakfast so I could sleep for an extra hour," he recalled. He had brought his accordion along and often entertained the soldiers in the barracks. He also played in the officers' club, which enabled him to skip KP (peeling potatoes). One of the other soldiers became jealous and threw a cigarette under his bunk. When his barracks were inspected, the officer saw the butt and put Yankovic on KP. He peeled potatoes for ten hours. "I didn't say anything, but when it happened again, I went to the sergeant and told him I didn't even smoke," Yankovic recalled. "He read the riot act to the soldiers and that ended the trouble."

After basic training, Yankovic was given a two-week furlough prior to going overseas. He went home to Cleveland and decided to make some records while he had the chance. There was no telling how long the war might last. Some people were guessing it would go on for ten years. Yankovic rounded up pianist Naglitch, bass player John "Hokey" Hokavar, and banjo man Joe Miklavic and again went to Cleveland Recording Studios with Martin Antoncic. They recorded sixteen records and thirty-two songs, one on each side. There was no time to be perfect. If somebody made a mistake, they just kept going. "Leave the clinkers in," Yankovic said.

The records were another instant hit. Fred Wolf, head of the studio, was in charge of the sales and split the profits fifty–fifty with Yankovic. A shellac shortage was the only problem. The substance was used in the making of the records and it was in short supply because of the war. Customers were asked to bring in their old records so more could be made.

When the trip home ended, Yankovic and thousands of other soldiers were shipped to Scotland on the *Queen Elizabeth.* "We were packed in like sardines," said Yankovic, who was in the bottom deck with his berth pressed near the ceiling. At first, it looked like Yankovic was going to have an easy war. He arrived in France in late 1944. The Allies had already liberated that country and Yankovic's infantry division simply walked through France. The streets were mostly deserted. He remembered St. Lo was blown to bits, not a building standing. The few French people who were there welcomed the liberators.

The trouble started when they reached Aachen, a city in Germany, just over the French border. The Germans fought with all they had, defending their country. The chaos was worse than anything Yankovic had imagined, a frightening barrage of bullets, bombs, and shells. At night Yankovic did his share of sentry duty. "It was scary out there in the dark," he said. "You'd hear a squirrel coming down a tree and you'd be ready to shoot."

Yankovic found himself in a rough battle in the nearby Hurtgen Forest. On October 26, 1944, he wrote to Habat in a letter from "somewhere in Germany." "I went through hell the last four weeks," Yankovic wrote. "We slept on the ground in tents." He said the letter was written by candlelight in his tent. "There are blackouts every night from 6 p.m. to 6 a.m. We had rain almost every day and night." Throughout the correspondence with Habat, he said things such as "This Army life is hell. I wouldn't wish it on my worst enemy." In an aside, he said, "Tell Hokey (John Hokavar, his Cleveland bass player) to stay out of the Army."

On January 3, 1945, Yankovic sent Habat another letter. It was from a hospital in England. "I was sure glad to get your letter," Yankovic wrote. "I got 48 letters at once and it was the first mail I got since I came to the hospital on Nov. 13." He informed Habat that while he was on the front lines in Aachen, his feet froze. "The foxhole was always cold and wet," he wrote.

> I went to the medics and was taken to a hospital. They told me I got trench foot (a sore or inflammation caused by wet and cold). I'm coming along well and when my feet get back in shape I'll probably go back to my outfit. This was the first New Year's Eve I spent in bed as far back as I can remember. But I can't kick. It's better than being on the front lines. I sure miss the gang, but that will have to wait until we get through with the Germans.

He was feeling well enough to include a couple of bawdy comments in the letter.

In later years, Yankovic told several newspaper writers that his hands and feet were frozen while he was in the Battle of the Bulge. He said it happened when he and a dozen other soldiers were cut off from their outfit and that they had lain in the snow for more than twenty-four hours in zero-degree weather before they were found by medics. He said that doctors wanted to amputate his hands and feet because gangrene had set in. "They were turning black," he said. "My hands and feet were burning. They hurt so much I was afraid to move." He said that one doctor told him he would certainly die if his limbs were not amputated. Yankovic said he still refused. "I asked for a Bible and prayed," he told *Plain Dealer* reporter Jane Scott in 1986. He said he made a miraculous recovery through large doses of penicillin and other drugs.

In his letter to Habat, he said he went to the medics himself and said nothing about lying in the snow and being cut off from his outfit. Habat, a close friend, said Yankovic never mentioned anything about his hands being frozen, either in his letters or in conversations after the war. Other friends say Yankovic told them he had frozen fingertips and feet, but that he never said anything about amputation.

Yankovic was not in the Battle of the Bulge either. That conflict began on December 16, 1944. Yankovic entered the hospital more than a month earlier. He could have been confused about the Bulge because it was in the same general area as Aachen.

After the war, Yankovic amazed people with his love of steam baths. They could never be too hot for him. He would stay in them longer than anyone else. And he loved to soak up sun on the beach. Friends speculated it was a residual effect of his bout with frostbite. Around 1975, he underwent an operation to correct a toe that was curled under his foot, but it did not work. He said the toe was damaged by wet and cold in Aachen.

Following the horrors of the Hurtgen Forest, the war was over for Yankovic. His doctor was delighted with his recovery. According to Yankovic, he apologized profusely for recommending the amputations. Knowing he was a musician, the doctor brought him an accordion to play, which he said would be good therapy.

Yankovic spent the rest of his time in the army entertaining troops. He would go around the hospital playing popular wartime songs such as "Lili Marlene" and, of course, polkas. The young GIs, many of whom were of Anglo-Saxon descent, loved them. So did the English soldiers, who had never heard polkas before, at least not Yankovic-style polkas. He was assigned to Special Services and formed a five-man hillbilly band, with a piano, fiddle, bass violin, and harmonica backing him up. They emphasized comedy. Occasionally, Yankovic would dress like a girl to get some laughs. A photo shows him wearing a Scottish outfit, complete with kilts, entertaining troops in Glasgow. His troupe once performed for General Patton's famed Third Army.

He also played the accordion in a bigger concert band that did complete stage shows for the boys. The sergeant in charge of that band was Sidney Mills, whose uncle owned Mills Publishing in New York, one of the most important music publishers in the U.S. "Sidney took a liking to me and told me to make sure I looked him up after the war," Yankovic recalled. "Years later Mills Publishing put out all my songbooks." He collected royalties on them for over thirty years.

Yankovic was in Paris on April 12, 1945, when President Franklin D. Roosevelt died. He had been in office since 1932 and was a hero to working people. "We all felt bad," Yankovic said. "To millions of Americans who lived through the Depression, he was the greatest president we ever had."

When the European war ended on May 8, 1945, Yankovic was just outside Paris. Everybody was insane with happiness because the fighting was over and they were still alive. Yankovic and his men put on a particularly wild, no-holds-barred performance that night. (The war continued in the Pacific until the Japanese surrendered on August 14, 1945.)

Yankovic was once asked for his thoughts about war. "I'm not political-minded," he said. "I do my work and I figure the government has its job to do. I went in a private and came out a private. I did what I was told and didn't want anything else. But I can't see people who don't even know each other killing each other. Yet, the soldier has no choice. If he doesn't kill them, they'll kill him. It has to make you bitter. I had nightmares for a year after I came home."

Yankovic was discharged December 26, 1945, and went home to Cleveland, to June, to his children, to the polka life he loved.

Chapter Seven

"Just Because"

UNFORTUNATELY, YANKOVIC HAD AN unhappy homecoming. When he got off the train at Cleveland's Terminal Tower on December 26, 1945, June was not there to greet him. He was met by his parents and his lawyer, Anton Trivison. Yankovic had been worried about June much of the time he was in the service. She seldom wrote letters to him, perhaps one a month, he said. June was working in the bar and he kept getting letters from other people who said she was dancing up a storm and staying out late. Then her letters stopped entirely. "I didn't hear from her for six months," he said. "I wrote my parents and asked what was going on." Rose told Yankovic that June had taken the two infant children, Linda and Frank Jr., and moved home with her mother.

This had happened before. "Every time we had an argument, she would go running to her mother's house," Yankovic recalled. "Her mother was the type who would say, 'Honey, if anything happens between you and Frank you can always come home to me.' If she didn't have a place to escape to maybe things would have worked out better." Their arguments usually revolved around her social life and her housekeeping.

Yankovic called June as soon as he got home and went to his mother-in-law's house. They had a good heart-to-heart talk. She said she had not written to him because she was fed up with all the gossiping and the way the bar was being run. She said she felt like a fifth wheel there, that Yankovic's parents and sisters and manager, Sam Slapic, had taken things over and that she was ignored. She said she never wanted to work in a bar anyway. June and Yankovic came to a truce. She came home with the children.

Life got back into the old routine. June continued to help out in the bar and Yankovic resumed his musical career.

He was thirty years old. America was at the peak of its power and prestige. Soldiers and sailors home from the war were anxious to celebrate after four years of fighting. Everything was booming, including the polka. At that time one of Yankovic's best friends was Johnny Pecon, the great accordionist. Pecon was a tall and lanky blond man who was the same age as Yankovic. He had his accordion with him at all times, as though it was a part of his body and psyche. He loved to play and people loved to hear him play. He would play for anybody, anytime. Although he had never bothered to learn to read music, he had perfect pitch and flawless rhythm.

His favorite hangout was Yankovic's bar, where the good times never stopped. The music was continuous. So were the drinks. Pecon, wearing his sailor suit, sat in on the jam sessions as he if were just another boxman, rather than one of the best who ever lived. He and Yankovic's father, Andy, loved to drink together and tell jokes in Slovenian. "I think my father liked Johnny better than he liked me," Yankovic once said. "But we were like brothers. I was happy to see my best friend and my father get along so well." Sometimes Pecon and the others would sleep all night in the bar after the partying was over. Spilar would arrive to open the doors at 6 a.m. and they would be hollering for service and start all over again.

Pecon had the true artist's sense of surprise and entertainment. He did not tell anybody but his parents when he arrived home from the war. He was told a banquet was being held in the St. Vitus Church hall, where he had played many times before going into the service. Pecon called two old friends and musicians, bassist John "Hokey" Hokavar and guitarist Mickey Kling, and asked them to meet him in the church basement. He told them to keep his arrival secret. They went into the hall and sat down on the stage behind the closed curtain, Pecon having been given permission by the priests. After the dinner, the curtains were suddenly pulled apart and the crowd saw Pecon sitting there with his cohorts. They gave him a standing ovation.

The trio played several songs, including "Just Because," which he had learned while serving in the Seabees. It was the first time the song had ever been played as a polka tune in Cleveland. Somebody in the crowd started a grand march, with Pecon in the lead. The fun-loving Pecon, like a Pied Piper, led the march outside of the hall, where they walked around the building, everybody singing the simple words of "Just Because."

Pecon had picked up the song in the Pacific during the war. It was an old hillbilly number that had previously been written and recorded by the Shelton Brothers, Bob and Joe, in 1936. Another version of the song was done by the great guitarist Les Paul, who called himself "Rhubarb Red" before hitting it big with singer and wife Mary Ford in the 1950s. Both the Shelton Brothers and Rhubarb Red records flopped.

Yankovic never heard the song until he got out of the army, when Pecon played it in the bar. Yankovic liked the simplicity of the lyrics because he knew fans would find the song easy to learn. He asked Pecon and arranger Joe Trolli to create a polka-sounding bridge for the song. "You got a good second part, Joe?" Pecon asked. Trolli played an old Italian bit. "No, not like that," said Pecon. "Like this." He gave it an old Slovenian touch. It worked. It was a big favorite with audiences. Sometimes they requested it be played two or three times a night.

Pecon had decided to join Yankovic's band, marking one of the first times a polka group used two accordionists. Yankovic played the melodies and Pecon harmonized on his chromatic. Both men also harmonized on the vocals, with Pecon's tenor voice matching perfectly with Yankovic's baritone. Yankovic was traveling more and more. Pecon had joined him because of their friendship, his love of the music, and the chance to make more money. The Cleveland musicians who changed the polka world were all blue-collar

Slovenians who were delighted to find they could make a living playing polkas. It was much better than working in a factory. Habat, for example, was overjoyed when he was paid thirteen dollars to play his first dance at the Slovenian National Home in 1943. He proudly raced home to give his father the money.

By the late 1940s, Cleveland polka musicians could earn twenty dollars a night, seven nights a week. That doesn't sound like much today, but in an era when the average workingman made about sixty dollars a week, it was excellent remuneration. Yankovic's musicians were collecting double or triple what their peers received.

Joining Yankovic and Pecon in that postwar band were banjo player Georgie Cook, pianist Al (Nagle) Naglitch, and bass man Hokavar. Cook, a tremendous banjo player, also served as Yankovic's business manager and secretary, setting up schedules. Naglitch, a fine player who walked with a slight limp, had been with Yankovic since the 1930s. Yankovic had total confidence in his musical knowledge and ability. The burly, 190-pound Hokavar had won a state weightlifting championship, lifting over 350 pounds. He was a favorite of audiences because of the way he slapped and twirled the bass and was also a good singer. Sometimes they would be joined by drummer Whitey Lovsin, a handsome blond man who was always smiling and pursued good times relentlessly. He had been wounded in the war. When Hokavar wearied of traveling, he was replaced by Adolph "Church" Srnick, another colorful fellow who received his nickname because his father was the organist at St. Vitus, the largest Catholic Slovene parish in America.

In early 1946, Yankovic signed a contract with the Columbia Recording Company. The deal called for Yankovic to make four records a year (eight sides) on the old 78 rpm discs. According to Cleveland polka historian Don Sosnoski, Columbia had been looking to record a good polka band because of the popularity of the music after the war. Sosnoski said the Cleveland distributor for Columbia probably alerted the New York office, telling them Yankovic was a hot commodity. "His Jolly Label records were big sellers," said Sosnoski. "The distributor would have known that, just by talking to record people and from reading about Yankovic in the local papers." Sosnoski said RCA Victor and Decca also wanted to record Yankovic, but he went with Columbia because it offered the best deal. Columbia urged Yankovic to travel as much as possible with his band because it would promote record sales. Yankovic agreed. It was a fateful step, changing his life. He stayed with Columbia for twenty-six years.

It was about this time that Yankovic contacted his old army friend, Sidney Mills, whose uncle operated Mills Music Publishing in New York. Jack Mills signed Yankovic to another contract to produce songbooks. Yankovic, Trolli, and Pecon would take Slovenian folk songs, make modern arrangements, and add American titles. The books had Yankovic's picture on the cover and sold for one dollar. Each book contained twelve songs. Yankovic received 50 percent of the sales profits, Pecon 35 percent, and Trolli 15 percent. They were a big success, with the Mills company publishing seven sets of books. After Pecon left, seven more songbooks were published, with Yankovic and Trolli each getting 50 percent. Music teachers and students liked the books because of their easy arrangements.

Most of the songs had been around for years, but on occasion a new one would come along. That was the case with the "Rendezvous Waltz," written in 1947. It was a landmark song for Yankovic because it was his first vocal recording. The song came out of the Rendezvous Bar, a polka hangout located on West 25th Street in Cleveland. Yankovic and the Yanks were on their way to Chicago and stopped at the bar for some afternoon fun. The bar was owned by Mary Luzar and her husband, friends of many polka musicians. They were jamming and drinking when Mary asked Yankovic, "Why don't you write a song in honor of the Rendezvous Bar?"

Everybody thought that was a good idea. "Me and Pecon and Naglitch and the others started fooling around on the keys and pretty soon we had a nice melody," Yankovic remembered. "There were a lot of people in the bar and they all said they liked it. Then Mary said the song needed words. She got a pencil and with a little help from the boys wrote the lyrics right there at the bar. We recorded the song the next day in the Wrigley Building in Chicago and it wound up selling about fifty thousand copies. That was about standard for us then. We never dreamed of making a million-seller."

Columbia had to be convinced the lyrics were original. They sounded too professional. The company did not want a lyricist showing up who claimed royalties because they were his words. So the song was recorded twice, once with a vocal and once without. When Columbia was sure the words were original, it released the vocal. Mary Luzar's song was called "The Rendezvous Waltz."

In late 1947, Yankovic and the band went to New York for a recording session. Pecon, Cook, Naglitch, and Srnick were with him. "That Night in May," another polka classic, was put on one side. Yankovic told the Columbia executive in charge he wanted to record "Just Because" on the other side. The executive scoffed, "Why go again with that old turkey? Let's try something else."

Yankovic argued with him, telling him how popular it was with audiences. The executive still refused to give permission. He and Yankovic got into a shouting match. Yankovic threw some sheet music on the floor and kicked a chair. "No matter how hard I tried, I couldn't get through to this guy," Yankovic remembered. "Finally, I said, 'I'll make a deal with you. I'll buy the first ten thousand records myself.' I knew I could sell them off the bandstand. That convinced him. Columbia wasn't taking the chance anymore. I was. He gave us the go-ahead. I told the boys to play it as perfect as possible the first time. We only had a couple of minutes left in the record session."

They quieted down and played the song, which relates the story of a man who tells his fickle, gold-digging girl that he is breaking up with her. Yankovic and Pecon harmonized on the vocal.

They were making polka history.

Chapter Eight

The Million-Sellers

THE RECORD TOOK OFF like a comet. It received its biggest boost in Boston, which had seldom been interested in polka music. For some reason Columbia started its promotion in a Beantown music store. Of the first twenty-six customers who heard the song, twenty-five bought it. Bob Clayton, a Boston disc jockey, began playing it. Within two minutes of the first time he put it on the air, some sixty phone calls came in, requesting it to be played again. He played it six more times that first day. Some twenty-five thousand copies were sold in Boston the first week.

Columbia realized it had a hit on its hands and began promoting it nationwide. It put up a huge forty-five-foot sign over its New York headquarters, reading LISTEN TO THE SENSATIONAL "JUST BECAUSE" BY FRANKIE YANKOVIC AND HIS YANKS ON COLUMBIA RECORDS. In Albany, New York, 1,725 records were sold in one day. The spectacular showing was repeated all over the country. It was not long before the record sold 1 million copies. Eventually, it would sell about 2.5 million, including reissues.

Yankovic was suddenly in the big time. People flocked to ballrooms to see the Yanks. George Devine, owner of the Million Dollar Ballroom in Milwaukee, told the nationally famous big band leader Guy Lombardo, "You think you can draw a crowd? Well, I got a little five-piece band [Yankovic's] that can outdraw all you guys." The Yanks had set the gate record at the ballroom.

Yankovic won the America's Polka King title before a crowd of eight thousand in Milwaukee's City Auditorium in June 1948. The contest was promoted by the major recording companies, who each had their top polka band represented. The other contestants were bands headed by Louie Bashell, Romy Grosz, Sammy Madden, Lawrence Duchow and his Red Ravens, and the Six Fat Dutchmen, headed by tuba-thumping Harold Loefflemacher.

The *Milwaukee Journal* said the Yankovic band looked as relaxed as sleeping babies when they took the stand. Pecon, Cook, Srnick, and Lovsin were the other musicians. The Yanks were all good mixers and had been socializing in the barroom before their turn on the stage. They were already riding the fame of "Just Because," and when they went up to play the crowd surged close to the stage. They started out with the "Three Yanks" polka, a song named in honor of Yankovic's first three children. When they finished, the crowd insisted they play it again. They had to do it three times, with the crowd clapping along. Then they played "Just Because." When the votes were counted, Yankovic and the band won by an eight to one margin.

Yankovic was given a huge cup for the victory. He and the band celebrated by drinking whiskey, wine, and beer out of it. Yankovic also won the competition the next two years. After that, the contest ceased because the record companies withdrew sponsorship. Too many minor bands, which had produced records on their own, wanted to compete. The major record companies did not want to see their stars beaten out by comparatively unknown bands.

"Frank Yankovic is the only man to win a contest naming America's Polka King," Walter Ostanek said. "There were other bands that called themselves 'kings' in one way or another. I'm called Canada's Polka King. Jimmy Sturr now calls himself the Polka King. But those were titles that were given to us. Frank is the only man to actually win his crown." (Johnny Vadnal won the title of Cleveland's Polka King in a local radio contest in which listeners voted in 1949. He also won a Midwest Polka King title in a Michigan band contest.)

Yankovic was proud of the title "America's Polka King" and took it seriously. In the 1960s, when a Euclid newspaperman wrote a story implying that Pecon was the most important accordionist in polka history, Yankovic asked for a retraction. When it did not appear, he sued the newspaper for $1 million. Eventually, Yankovic withdrew the suit. The legal expenses were not worth it.

In later years, Yankovic expressed regret that he did not hire a professional booking manager to take advantage of his new celebrity in the late 1940s. "I never cashed in on 'Just Because' the way I should have," he said. "If I knew then what I know now, we would have made money galore. I had a hot band. Everybody wanted us. I was happy to be in such demand, but I only charged my usual rate. I should have tripled my price or taken a percentage of the gate. We were collecting three hundred or five hundred dollars a night and the ballroom operators were getting ten thousand. If I had an agent we could have been booked into every top nightclub in America and racked up all kinds of money. But I was one generation removed from the boat. I was green."

In 1949, he hit another home run with the "Blue Skirt Waltz." He was playing at Ciro's in Philadelphia when Jack Mills called and told him he had bought a catalogue of old Bohemian (Czech) melodies. Mills sent the sheet music to Yankovic to see if he liked any of them. Yankovic chose "The Red Skirt Waltz," but said it needed lyrics.

That was no problem. Mills had the great songwriter Mitchell Parish on his staff. Parish had written the lyrics to popular classics such as "Stardust" and "Stairway to the Stars." He quickly came up with the words and changed the title to the "Blue Skirt Waltz" for rhyming purposes. Yankovic suggested it would be a good idea to get two women to share in the singing and Columbia hired the Malavsky sisters, who had been performing at Jewish events in New York as the Marlin Sisters. Pecon, Cook, Naglitch, and bassist Stan Slejko backed up Yankovic on the record. They put a polka, "Charley Was a Boxer," on one side of the disc. Yankovic and Pecon and the women then alternated in the singing of "Blue Skirt Waltz," about a man who meets and dances with a mysterious lady in blue; she disappears after their brief encounter, and he pines for her return.

"Blue Skirt Waltz" was another smash, selling more than a million copies. *Redbook* magazine reported it was the second-biggest seller in the nation that year, trailing only Gene Autry's "Rudolph the Red-Nosed Reindeer." Yankovic's records sold 1.5 million copies in 1949.

(Victor Greene, in a book titled *Passion for Polka*, said that "Blue Skirt" was Columbia's second-biggest seller behind "Rudolph," not the nation's second-biggest. However, since "Rudolph" is one of the top sellers of all time, "Blue Skirt" might very well have been number two in the U.S.)

Shortly after recording "Blue Skirt," road-weary pianist Naglitch left Yankovic and joined the Cleveland band headed by Habat and Pete Sokach, called "The Tune Mixers." Drummer Al Tercek and bassist Kenny Bass were also in the group, which had a contract with Decca Records. Naglitch told his new band members about Yankovic's recording of "Blue Skirt Waltz" and gave them the lyrics. Decca rushed out with the record before Yankovic's version hit the stores and it sold briskly in the competitive market. With the success of Yankovic, the nation's record companies understood that polkas could sell. Clevelander Johnny Vadnal was soon recording with RCA Victor. Not too much later, Pecon would be signed up by Capitol Records and Bass by Epic Records. They all lived within a few blocks of each other in Collinwood. Bass's excellent bands were led by accordionists Joe Luzar and Dick Sodja.

Yankovic was now a celebrity. The *Cleveland Press* said his 1948 income was $78,000, astronomical in a time when only one-tenth of 1 percent of the nation's workers made $10,000 a year. *The Plain Dealer*, which called him "The Aladdin of the Accordion," said he grossed $160,000 in 1949. "He is a rich young man at 34," said the *Cleveland Press*. "His polka majesty is a wide-eyed, friendly guy who might be taken for 24."

Time magazine said, "Yankovic's band has been known to out-draw name bands such as Vaughn Monroe and Guy Lombardo by 2 to 1. Frankie makes music that sounds good to people who would not have listened twice to the old-style polka bands with their hard-blowing brass and woodwinds."

Redbook cooed:

> Inasmuch as the Yankovic band plays one-nighters almost exclusively, and to vast crowds, its profit is probably bigger than any ensemble in show business. Musically, it has its points. The most important is its terrific beat, which is chiefly attributable to its banjoist (Cook), who is in a class with the men who played the instrument with some of the great jazz bands of other years. This beat may be the principal reason none of the hundreds of imitators of the Yankovic style has ever been able to approach its popularity.

Polka historian Bob Roth, of Elgin, Illinois, said, "This band had a great sound, which was never duplicated in future years, not even by Yankovic himself. The Yankovic/Pecon accordions blended perfectly. Most later accordionists learned to play fill [counterpoint] by copying Pecon. We all owe a great debt to Johnny for being our first teacher in learning to play fill. Georgie Cook was a banjoist that no one since has been able to exactly copy. Georgie played a driving banjo and was responsible for the tempo. He used to amaze me in that he could slide up or down on the fretboard and end up on the right chord. The other big part of the band's secret was the sound of the solovoxes played by Yankovic and Naglitch."

Roth, an accordionist, had been indifferent to the polkas he heard around Chicago. But when he heard the Cleveland sound, as exemplified by Yankovic's great band, he was astounded. "They knocked my socks off," he said. He later played for a time with Yankovic.

The newly rich Yankovic had his hands insured for $50,000 with Lloyd's of London, strictly a publicity stunt. He bought a spacious colonial in South Euclid for $31,500; it was eventually worth $275,000 as he added more rooms. The *Cleveland Press* called it "A Castle Fit for a King." It was made of stone, brick, and aluminum and was nestled against a forested hill on a 375-foot-deep lot. It had a five-sided swimming pool warmed by radiant heat, allowing it to be used into the late autumn.

Yankovic purchased a fourteen-passenger Lockheed Loadstar airplane for $6,000 and hired a pilot. A mechanic asked him how much gas he wanted in it. "Fill it up," said the uninhibited Yankovic. When he received the huge gas bill, he was staggered. He flew the band and a gang of friends to an engagement in Hibbing, Minn. When they landed the whole town, including the mayor, was there to greet them. They had a polka party on the runway. He only had the plane a few days when he was told the license expired and that he had to get a new one. No problem, he thought. However, before the license could be granted the plane had to be inspected by the Federal Aviation Board. The board found all sorts of defects. Yankovic paid $20,000 in repairs, with no end in sight. He sold the plane for salvage, getting $2,000.

Most of the time, the car was his home. "I want to see how far the polka can go," he told *Time* magazine in 1950. "There is no reason it shouldn't be as popular as the rumba."

Yankovic always contended that "Blue Skirt" was more popular than "Just Because." "We get more requests for it," he said. "But we play both on every job. I never get tired of playing either one." He sometimes ruminated on why he never made another gold record, feeling that his "Charm of Your Beautiful Dark Eyes," "Beloved Be Faithful," and "Blue Eyes Crying in the Rain" were just as good.

It has often been stated that "Just Because" and "Blue Skirt" are the only two million-sellers in American polka history, but that is not quite true. Polka historians Don Sosnoski, of Cleveland,

and Chuck Debevec, of Minnesota, agree the Andrews Sisters had million-sellers with the "Beer Barrel Polka" and the "Pennsylvania Polka" before Yankovic. They also say Arthur Godfrey's "Too Fat Polka" and Perry Como's "Hoop Dee Doo," which came after Yankovic's hits, sold a million. Will Glahe, a German, also had a million-seller in the U.S. with his version of "The Beer Barrel Polka" in the 1930s. Frank Wojnarowski, the Polish-American star, is said to have had a gold record, although historian Sosnoski says that is doubtful. Nevertheless, Yankovic's two smash hits are members of a highly exclusive group. And he and the Andrews Sisters are the only performers to get polka gold twice in America.

Chapter Nine

"Nobody Will Ever Match That Sound"

ONCE HE BEGAN CASHING in, Yankovic started having problems. In May 1949 he agreed to pay a tax settlement of $11,312.88 to the U.S. government. The IRS claimed he understated his bar income for 1942, 1943, 1945, and 1946. Yankovic, of course, was in the army much of that time and the bar was being operated by friends and relatives. "We're sorry we had to come after you," an IRS man told Yankovic. "We know you were in the army. But the license is in your name."

He was sorry to lose Naglitch, who was replaced by Collinwood pianist Frank Piccorillo, who had considered himself above polkas. "I was strictly a jazz player," Piccorillo recalled. "I wanted to play with Artie Shaw. I hated polkas. But I heard Yankovic's band and they sounded good. They didn't sound old-fashioned."

Pecon, inducing Piccorillo to join him with Yankovic, said, "Stay with this guy. We're going places."

Money helped Piccorillo make up his mind. He had been playing at Leo's Tavern in Cleveland for $40 a week, working six nights. He had also played in a ten-cents-a-dance hall. Dancers had to pay a dime to get on the floor for a song. When the song was over, they had to leave the floor, then pay another dime to dance to the next tune. When Yankovic offered him $50 a night ($350 a week) he gladly took the job. "He paid us every Monday in cash," Piccorillo recalled.

Piccorillo recognized that Yankovic was not as deft as many musicians, but he respected him. "He would make all kinds of mistakes, but he was good," Piccorillo said. "The important thing was he had a style that was all his own. When he played you knew it was him and nobody else."

Yankovic's biggest setback came when Pecon and Cook left. They were his two most talented musicians and the men closest to him. The parting was not pretty. It had been in the works for some time. "The boys in the band started getting the idea I was making too much money," said Yankovic, who was getting the majority of the record profits as the bandleader. "They felt they deserved as much as I did. They weren't satisfied with the standard sidemen's fees." Aside from the continuous travel, Pecon probably resented the fact that Yankovic was getting rich from "Just Because," a song that he had brought to the Polka King's attention. Yankovic, thrilled with his new riches, had developed the habit of flaunting thousand-dollar bills, carrying one in his pocket and flashing it at every opportunity. "See what you can make if you know how to play," he chortled to a friend while waving the thousand-dollar bill. The friend said, "You just got lucky." Yankovic did not talk to him for three years.

Yankovic later contended that he did not profit as much as people thought on "Just Because." "The record sold for only seventy-five cents and I got four cents a record," he said. "I only made about fifty thousand dollars on it. The biggest royalty check I ever got was twenty-six thousand dollars for 'Just Because' and some other songs."

According to Yankovic, Pecon and Cook began grumbling, making demands, and dictating. Nothing was right anymore. They complained that the trips were too long, the hotels were lousy, and that Yankovic drove too fast. "We were snapping at each other all the time," Yankovic recalled. He tried to appease Pecon and Cook by giving them bonuses of three hundred and five hundred dollars from his royalty checks. Pecon's feelings were doubtlessly aggravated by a failed bar venture he had gone into with Yankovic.

In late 1949, matters came to a head. Yankovic felt Pecon had let his emotions affect him onstage. Never an overly demonstrative musician, Pecon let his playing speak for him. Yankovic felt he was looking too gloomy and drinking too much. "People came

to see us put on a floor show," Yankovic said. They were performing at the Village Barn in New York and staying at the Presidents
Hotel. They met in Yankovic's room and discussed the situation.
Yankovic said, "Johnny, it doesn't seem to be working out anymore. Maybe you don't want to stay with the band." Yankovic contended they split as friends. Others say Pecon was fired. Whatever
the case, Pecon never spoke to Yankovic again, nor did he discuss
their differences publicly.

Pecon went back to Cleveland, got married, quit drinking, and
started a highly successful group, with Lou Trebar as his accordion
partner. It was probably the finest Cleveland-style polka band of
all time, also featuring Eddie Platt on saxophone, Whitey Lovsin
on drums, Adolph "Church" Srnick on bass, and Johnny Kafer on
piano. Lovsin, Srnick, and Kafer, all genial men who liked to socialize, died in youthful middle age. Later, Paul Yanchar sang and
played sax. Mirk Yama was on bass and Al Markic played banjo.
Yanchar was the best singer Pecon ever had and is still at it today.
The band played almost exclusively around Cleveland. Some of
their hit recordings included "Argentina Waltz," "So You Think
You're Smart," "Zip Polka," and "Jack on St. Clair." Pecon was a
fun-loving man, but he was strict when it came to music. If one of
his sidemen hit a wrong note or inserted a flourish he did not like,
he was liable to say, "Who are you going to be playing with tomorrow?" When a hero-worshipping fan said to him, "When you play,
my feet start to itch," Pecon replied, "Try a little foot powder."

Over the years, Yankovic constantly tried to patch things up
with Pecon. "He snubbed me many times," the Polka King said.
"I'd walk up to him with my hand outstretched and he never
even looked at me. It was the same the few times we played on
the same bandstand (a number or two on special occasions). It
was the same with Cook. We never exchanged another word. I
thought for sure Pecon would come to the wake when my father
died. They had been so close. But he never showed up."

Yankovic was playing in Wisconsin when he got word that

Andy was seriously ill. He hired a private plane and rushed home. When he saw how Andy looked, he passed out. He continued playing his engagements, flying back to Cleveland every day, until his father died at age seventy. "Dad died too soon," said Yankovic. "He felt good but he was always afraid to die, so he went to a doctor for a checkup. The doctor told him he had cirrhosis of the liver and that he had to stop drinking. From then on, his health deteriorated. I think it was too much of a shock to his system to make him quit like that after all those years of drinking."

On the final night of the wake, Yankovic played some of his father's favorite songs. When he played "Beyond the Lake" (Gor Cez Jezero), many people cried. Yankovic's nieces, Dorothy and Rose, who had recorded with the King when they were little girls, also sang.

Cook stayed with Yankovic a few more months after Pecon's exit, but then he too departed. He headed his own popular Cleveland band for many years. Piccorillo also quit. The travel was too much, his wife was expecting, and Yankovic was a hard man to get along with. One winter night Yankovic was driving and the others were sleeping. So Yankovic opened the car window. "It was freezing," Piccorillo said. "He was mad because he was driving and we were taking it easy, so he wanted us to suffer. Another time he stranded us in Appleton, Wisconsin. If you got mad at him, he'd get more mad at you, put you on the defensive, make you feel like you were the jerk. Frank was a swell guy when I started with him. He was kind of fat and jolly then. When he lost weight, it changed him."

Years later, Piccorillo survived a triple bypass operation. The doctor congratulated him and said, "You must have nine lives." Piccorillo said, "I've got eighteen lives. I used up nine with Yankovic."

Yankovic continued to try to reconnect with Pecon. He went to the funeral home each day when Pecon's mother died but was ignored. When Pecon became ill and spent four months in a hospital, Yankovic wanted to visit him, but felt it might do more harm than good. Pecon died in 1975 at the age of sixty. Shortly before his death, twenty-eight polka bands honored him at a huge party in the Slovenian Society Home (Recher Hall) in Euclid.

Yankovic knew what he had lost when he and Pecon split. "It's a shame Johnny and I had to wind up the way we did," he said twenty-five years later. "Nobody will ever match that sound we had. Our accordions and voices blended in a unique way. The old records sound better than the new."

Fred Kuhar of Wickliffe, retired president of Curtis Industries, a $100 million company, is second to no one in his admiration of Pecon's playing. An accordionist himself and a student of polka history, Kuhar knows that Pecon was a genius of the Cleveland-style polka. However, he understands what made Yankovic a national success. "He was a showman," said Kuhar. "He understood the business probably better than anybody. He related to people and made them feel at home." Yankovic knew that talent was not enough. Where other polka bands stayed off by themselves during intermissions, he would be mingling with the customers, selling himself, selling his band, selling the polka.

Joe Fedorchak, the outstanding Youngstown accordionist, said, "When we were young, we all wanted to be like Yankovic. He was voted man of the year in Kuzman's (a Youngstown lounge) and when he came in he walked all around the hall, talking to people. He had everybody in his pocket. My mother told him he cost her a lot of sleep because I was always practicing the accordion at three in the morning."

Kuhar added, "Yankovic had access to major record distributors, which is more important than the quality of the records. And he always surrounded himself with good musicians."

Richie Vadnal played the accordion alongside Yankovic. He has a pithy answer to the question: Why did Yankovic stand out among all other polka musicians? "He was willing to do anything," said Vadnal. "He wasn't afraid of anything."

Chapter Ten

Going Hollywood

YANKOVIC WAS NOT GOING to give up and die just because he had lost two of the finest players in polka history. Some friends suggested he take off for a few weeks to reorganize his group, but he did not like that. "It would have meant canceling bookings and disappointing fans," he said with characteristic determination. "I decided to keep going and try out new players on the run. After all, when we played in Pocatello, Idaho, or Trinidad, Colorado, the people there didn't know if Pecon was a banjo player or Cook was an accordionist. The only one they knew was Yankovic." He was the show.

During his short stops at home, he found the men he wanted in accordionist Anthony "Tops" Cardone, pianist Buddy Griebel, banjo player Carl Paradiso, and bassist Al Leslie. They were all Cleveland musicians who had been recommended to Yankovic. None of them had ever played polkas. They were all in the pop field. Yankovic gave them quick auditions and hired them. He liked the fact they could all read music.

"These men were professionals," he said. "With them, you didn't have to worry about hitting a wrong note or not being able to read. They also developed terrific arrangements. They were versatile and talented." Yankovic was to call them his finest all-around show band. Cardone may not have played the polka with Pecon's electricity or feel, but he was a superior showman. "He sold himself with a million-dollar smile," Yankovic said. "In this field, it isn't music that counts so much. Ninety percent depends on your personality."

At first, Cardone was not sure if he should take the job because of all the travel. Yankovic suggested he take a nine-day trip with him to Wisconsin. He paid him $500, triple what he was making in Cleveland. "Tops was impressed with the fine treatment we received," Yankovic said. "It opened his eyes. People picked up our dinner tabs and bought us gifts. Tops enjoyed it so much he stayed for six years." Cardone said he averaged about $600 a week during his stay with Yankovic, from 1949 to 1954. The King was charging at least $500 a performance in those days, while the top Cleveland polka bands were getting $200.

Paradiso, a guitarist and singer who had been a solo performer, had never played the banjo. "Don't worry," Yankovic said. "I'll get you a banjo. We'll work it out." He also bought the bald-headed Paradiso a nice wig. Paradiso was an excellent singer, one of the best to ever warble in a Yankovic band. The tenor often paired up with Yankovic on duets. "He was good to sing with," remembered Paradiso. "Sometimes I sang the melody and sometimes he did. He was a good harmonizer, had a strong voice." Yankovic had a phenomenal memory for lyrics, Cardone recalled.

The new band members, who all sang, were not crazy about the traveling, but they liked the money they were making. Since Yankovic would pick up all the road expenses, except for meals, they could send almost all their pay home to their families. Leslie limited himself to twenty-five dollars a week for meals. One week, when a lot of fans were buying him meals, he spent only two dollars and fifty cents. Paradiso was able to buy a nice house in Euclid with his earnings. Fifty years later he was still living in it. In 2006, still hale and hearty in his eighties, he was enjoying retirement as a starter at Airport Greens golf course in Willoughby Hills, and shooting his age. Cardone died in 2002 at age eighty-one. Griebel has lasted the longest. In 2006, he was still playing the piano in Cleveland clubs, and very well too.

The new men, who had been playing in quiet cocktail lounges, were stunned by the crowds Yankovic drew. "I couldn't believe it when we went to the Million Dollar Ballroom in Milwaukee," said Paradiso. "They had thousands of people there. We were all signing autographs. When we went to Youngstown people crowded all around us when we walked in. They wanted to know when we were coming back to play again. We hadn't even played a number and they wanted to know when we were coming back."

By this time, Yankovic had made a change in his performing style. He no longer wore a suit and tie onstage. He and the band began wearing expensive peasant outfits and boots. This gave them an identity, just as Xavier Cugat had with Latin costumes and cowboy Gene Autry had with his Western outfits. It was a style Yankovic would maintain for the rest of his career. The idea might have first begun when they played for a month at the Village Barn in New York, where management created a farm atmosphere, with cans hanging from the ceiling and a chicken or two on the piano. Yankovic and Cardone further enhanced their peasant image, kicking their legs high or doing deep knee bends as they played, prancing about the stage, smiling all the time.

One of the highlights of Yankovic's career came in 1950, when the band performed at Hollywood's Mocambo nightclub, the playground of movie stars. He got the job through Art Michaud, an agent who had handled Tommy Dorsey, Henry Busse, and other top bands. Yankovic hated giving away a percentage of the money to an agent. He thought he could do the negotiating himself. But he admitted Michaud was worth it.

Before he headed West, he received a big sendoff from his old neighborhood friends at the Skyway Lounge in Cleveland. Huge floral pieces read, "Good Luck, Frank." and "Local Boy Makes Good."

Yankovic was booked to play at the Mocambo for eight straight Monday and Thursday nights. It was the first of his many brushes with the big-timers of the entertainment world. On opening night, as a publicity stunt, Yankovic and the band arrived at the nightclub in a cart that was pulled down Sunset Boulevard by a donkey. Yankovic did not mind being laughed at if there was money in it. Rosalind Russell, a major star, sat on the donkey for a photo. Ann Sheridan and Bob Hope were also there as publicity foils. Academy Award winner Jane Wyman, who had recently divorced future president Ronald Reagan, breaking his heart, came to the bandstand to talk to Yankovic and the band. "How long have you been playing this kind of music?" she asked, with genuine interest. They liked her.

Yankovic was nervous before the first number. "I was actually scared," he said. "Hollywood was the absolute center of the entertainment world, with some of the most famous people in the world. I knew there weren't going to be any polka people there." He was not sure if these celebrities would enjoy polkas. Then he said, "The heck with it. Let's play what got us here." They went into their standard repertoire and, lo and behold, all the movie stars took the floor and had a merry time. Yankovic had them in the soft palm of his hand from the start. The *Los Angeles Herald-Express* reported the performance this way:

> The Hollywood stay-up-late crowd woke up seeing spots before their eyes after the dottiest night in the history of Sunset Strip. That old-time skip and jump, the polka, got the revival treatment at the Mocambo and all the people were invited to turn out in polka-dotted ties and dresses. Frank Yankovic, America's polka king, and his band rolled out the barrel and everybody had a lot of fun. To the strains of 'Hoop Dee Doo,' 'You Are My Sunshine,' and 'The Milwaukee Polka' people like Diana Lynn, Lou Nova, Betty Hutton, Joi Lansing, Ann Sheridan, Jane Wyman and Lorraine Cugat panted and puffed around the dance floor. Then they joined hands in a big circle like a bunch of farmhands after a hard day of plowing the South Forty.

The Yanks also played pop music. Milton Berle told Yankovic, "You guys play good, but you're even better with American music."

Uncle Miltie, the biggest star on television, asked them why they were wearing pajamas onstage. The eight-week Mocambo run always drew good crowds. The band also played at Los Angeles's Aragon Ballroom and at the Lick Pier in Santa Monica during its stay. The Yanks made some five-minute movie shorts for Universal Pictures. Yankovic would drop in on an unknown young disc jockey, Steve Allen, nearly every night in L.A., chatting with him on the program. Allen would soon become one of the most famous men on national TV, hosting the *Tonight Show*.

The band was invited to perform at the palatial house of movie star Joseph Cotten on New Year's Eve. Five other bands took turns playing. Paradiso danced with Jennifer Jones and Cardone danced with Gene Tierney. Both were popular movie stars. Griebel and Mrs. Cotten played a duet on twin grand pianos. Movie legends such as Lana Turner, Cecil B. DeMille, and Gilbert Roland were there.

Paradiso and Roland, former husband of movie star Constance Bennett, had a long conversation. "He was a lot of fun," Paradiso recalled. "He tried to sing, but he couldn't hack it." It was a lively party, with a lot of drinking. It did not break up until 7 a.m.

The band made a recording of "You Are My Sunshine" with Doris Day, with Paradiso harmonizing. Everybody liked the easygoing, shapely Day, who became one of the most important movie stars in history. She was dressed in blue jeans and a checkered shirt and had her hair pulled back. During the recording she had words with Marty Melcher, her manager, who would later become her husband. Melcher objected to Day standing in the same booth with Paradiso as they recorded. "He thought we were too close together," Paradiso recalled. "He made us sing in separate booths." When the session was over, she autographed Paradiso's banjo. When Paradiso left the band years later, Yankovic took the banjo back. "I wish I had it today," Paradiso said. "That autograph would be worth a lot of money."

Yankovic grumbled about Melcher's record selections. "He insisted we do the 'Comb and Paper Polka' and the 'Pumpernickle Polka,'" Yankovic said. "The only one that was any good was 'You Are My Sunshine.'" According to Don Sosnoski, Day had recorded "Hoop Dee Doo" a few weeks earlier. It was not a smash. Had she done it with Yankovic it very well might have become the King's third million-seller. Yankovic's biggest hit with the Cardone bunch was "The Tick-Tock Polka," taken from an old Italian folk tune that Cardone had found. Yankovic had it Americanized with the words, "Tick, tick, tick, tock, goes the clock on the wall as we're dancing the evening away . . ." Sosnoski says the record also sold more than a million records but did not get a gold because the sales were made in two years, rather than the required one.

The band continued its madcap schedule, playing all over the country, mostly in one-nighters. They usually traveled in big, black Packards or Cadillacs that looked like limousines. "We would sleep in the cars and try to get into a hotel once a day to clean up and do laundry," Yankovic said. "We always used nylon shirts and underwear so we could wash them fast and not have to iron. We often had to miss a meal to make a playing date."

Once they were supposed to play in Minominee, Wisconsin, but mistakenly went to Minominee, Minnesota, about two hundred miles away. Yankovic called the ballroom owner and apologetically said they went to the wrong state. "That's all right," the owner said. "Get here as fast as you can. We'll wait for you."

"We piled into the Packard and I took the wheel," Yankovic said. "I had the guts. I didn't let anything get in my way if I was in a hurry. If I had to go a hundred, I'd go a hundred. The band was on pins and needles, but we got there, over two hours late." They were greeted by enthusiastic cheers from the crowd and performed overtime. In Wisconsin, true Yankovic country, the band played against the legendary Duke Ellington Orchestra in a polka versus jazz contest. Yankovic won, of course. Ellington was big about it. "You've got the liveliest music I ever heard," he told Yankovic. "I wish I could turn people on like you do." The gentlemanly Duke was being nice. His classics, such as "Sophisticated Lady" and "Satin Doll," are known all over the world.

The Yankovic band also made appearances with TV stars Arthur Godfrey and Jackie Gleason, and singers Patti Page and Lauritz Melchior in that period. "I once offered to teach Bob Hope to dance the polka," Yankovic said. "He said he was still trying to learn the Charleston." In 1952, Yankovic was paid $2,500 to play at the Wagon Wheel in Lake Tahoe.

The nonstop travel, along with the fact that the men were always together, could lead to frayed nerves. One time Paradiso and Cardone, who could shoot par in golf, were invited to play at a country club. When Yankovic, who shot in the high eighties, found out, he called a rehearsal so they could not get on the links. He was angry because he was not invited. Yankovic often snapped at Leslie and Griebel. "He always had to have at least one guy to pick on," Cardone said. If the talented Griebel played too elaborately, Yankovic would immediately object. He wanted him to stick to the basics. Griebel could not have minded too much. Yankovic was his best man when the pianist was married.

One night in Twin Falls, Idaho, Leslie couldn't get his amplifier working. Yankovic yelled at him to hurry up. Leslie grabbed him by the lapels in anger and it looked as though they might fight. Somebody got between them. Yankovic just smiled at Leslie in a confident manner and stepped away. "I forgot about it in five minutes," said Yankovic. "It didn't mean anything."

The men took turns driving in the frantic race from town to town. One day in the upper Midwest a swath of Canadian Soldiers (a winged insect that seasonally swarms across the Great Lakes from Canada) covered the windshield while Paradiso was at the wheel. He turned on the windshield wipers, which just made the vision worse. They had to stop the car to wipe off all the bugs, but they just kept coming for a stretch of about a hundred miles. Every few minutes they had to get out of the car and clean the windows. It was a harrowing experience.

Once Yankovic had to fly from St. Louis to Duluth on business. The musicians were to drive the same route and meet him to perform that night. The weather was fine when they left St. Louis, but as they proceeded north they ran into a snowstorm. They didn't arrive at the ballroom until 11 p.m. When they came in, Yankovic was playing with three other musicians he had picked up in the emergency.

The fearless Yankovic was stopped for speeding many times. He would try to talk the policeman out of giving him a ticket, saying, "I'm Frank Yankovic. How would you like to have one of my albums?" One cop was unimpressed. He wrote out a ticket anyway. Yankovic was so furious he went to the top of the hill where he had been stopped and made a sign with the words SPEED TRAP AHEAD. He stood there with the sign for half an hour, exacting revenge.

"I would take chances, pass on hills and curves at high speed," Yankovic admitted. "It's a wonder we weren't all killed."

They almost met their demise at a railroad crossing, when Yankovic tried to beat a train across the tracks. He made it, but the train nicked the trailer in which the musicians had their instruments and scattered them across the countryside. Cardone was furious and made the sign of the cross. He screamed at the humbled Yankovic and said he was quitting. The others felt the same. Yankovic talked them into a compromise in which he agreed not to drive anymore. He never took the wheel again for the remainder of their time together, about four years.

With all the driving, mishaps were inevitable for even the most careful chauffeur. Leslie once hit a deer while going seventy miles an hour in Wisconsin. Cardone hit two horses in Pennsylvania, killing one of them. Another time, Leslie fell asleep and woke up with the car on the wrong side of the road, just in time to miss hitting a semi head-on while everybody was asleep. The entire band would have been killed.

No matter where they played, they packed in the crowds. One

of their most unusual jobs was in Bimidji, Minnesota, where they played in a forty-foot-by-seventy-foot room warmed by a coal stove. Another time they played at an Indian reservation in Wolf's Point, Montana. From all reports the Indians could do a mean polka. "We'd play in Duluth, Minnesota, on Sunday and have to be in Regina, Saskatchewan, on Monday, eight hundred miles," Yankovic said. In Leadville, Colorado, the band noticed the dancers tired quickly. The Yanks also became fatigued from their jumping, kicking, and deep knee bends. Then they realized why. Leadville was thousands of feet above sea level and the thin air made it hard to breathe.

Yankovic was grateful to his musicians and knew they were sacrificing a lot for their families. He tried to make road life as palatable as possible. On days off, he would take them to resorts, where they could relax for a day and play some golf. One Christmas he bought Cardone a diamond ring. He gave Leslie the trailer he had been wanting for his speedboat. Another Christmas, he bought each musician a musical instrument of his choice. Griebel took a clarinet. He took them to an expensive men's store, had them fitted, and bought them tailor-made sport coats. Whenever they played in New York, he would fly out June and all their wives and put them in a nice hotel. He would buy a corsage for each woman and take the party to 21, the famed restaurant, for dinner.

After six years with Yankovic, Cardone decided to leave the band. Like everyone else, he was sick of the road. Only Yankovic could handle the grind. Cardone gave Yankovic three months' notice, sending the king into a rage. "He made my life miserable for more than two months," Cardone recalled. "Sometimes you'd want to kick his teeth out. But the last two weeks he treated me like a king. We stayed friends."

The other band members left about the same time as Cardone. After their last job together, Yankovic quietly asked them if he could drive home for old times' sake. They agreed. It was a way of saying good-bye.

Chapter Eleven

"He Fired Me Three Times"

IT WAS NOW ELVIS Presley's time. Rock and roll took over American music in the mid-1950s, but Yankovic ignored the changes and just kept going. Having lost two great bands in the last decade, he knew it was a pattern that would probably never change. Since mature musicians found the rigors of life on the road too hard to withstand for long, he began turning to youth. Now forty, he hired ambitious, grateful youngsters who would be thrilled with the opportunity to travel, see the country, and, most of all, to perform with the King.

Richie Vadnal, eighteen, was one of his early second accordionists after Cardone departed. Vadnal was the younger brother of Cleveland polka star Johnny Vadnal. He was a handsome, friendly young man who was sure to appeal to the polka crowd. Yankovic had known the boy since he was twelve. Vadnal asked Cardone for advice. "Stand right next to Frank on the stage," Cardone said. "Watch his fingers. When he starts, you start. Stop when he does. In between, anything goes. If anything goes wrong, or if he makes a mistake, just keep going, even if he looks at you."

Yankovic almost never had rehearsals. He felt his bands did not need any because they were playing all the time, using the same material over and over. He did not worry about playing perfectly in the halls because people were dancing, talking, and having good times. They were not critiquing. They were glad to see the King, no matter who was performing with him.

Banjo player Ron Sluga, nineteen, became one of Yankovic's most popular sidemen. Sluga had graduated from Euclid High School in 1954. Yankovic heard him playing with the Kenny Bass band and invited the young musician to go on the road with him. They had never met before. Like Vadnal, Sluga jumped at the chance. The pay was good, thirty dollars a gig, with seven shows a week. "I thought I was rich," said Sluga. "I was making ten thousand dollars a year, more than guys who had engineering degrees. Jazz players would be envious of us. We were drawing bigger crowds and making more money than they were." Sluga bought a new powder-blue Mercury convertible from a car dealer who sponsored Yankovic's TV show, paying cash. Later Sluga was collecting fifty dollars a performance.

Vadnal was getting thirty-five dollars a show as the second accordionist. Yankovic was businesslike about keeping the proper tax records, perhaps because of his previous troubles with the IRS. "Every time he paid you he gave you a statement," Vadnal recalled. "We got paid each week. At the end of the year you got a W-2 form."

Sluga, who has been a full-time professional musician all his life and was nominated for a Grammy in 2006, learned the fundamentals of show business from Yankovic. "He told us that no matter how good you are, you don't have a job without the people," recalled Sluga. "He was entertaining from the time we got to a job until we left. He contacted people visually. He knew the right songs to play. If nobody was dancing, he'd stop the music and say, 'This isn't a concert. It's a dance. I want everybody to get up and dance.' He wanted us to show we were having a good time on stage. Other bands might have been having a good time, but they didn't show it."

Unlike most polka bands, which took two breaks during a four-hour performance, Yankovic took only one. He would play a solid three hours, take a half-hour break, then come back and finish. During the intermission, he did not want the musicians drinking together in the bar. He wanted them to chat with the audience. If they were late getting back to the stage, he would play by himself. "He worked very hard at it," said Sluga, who earned the Cleveland-Style Polka Hall of Fame's Lifetime Achievement Award in 2005. "He wanted to be the biggest star. He wanted attention at all times. When somebody else got it, he'd be jealous. But he was an icon. My time with him was the highlight of my career. If you were with Yankovic, everybody loved you."

Once Vadnal got into an accident in his 1955 Buick Roadmaster. He told Yankovic, who did not bat an eye. He gave Vadnal the phone number of a friend, who made the repairs. The friend did not charge a penny for the work. Another time, Yankovic gave a bag of shoes that needed repair to a cobbler when the band was on the road. "I'll be back next month," Yankovic told the man. When Yankovic returned to the city for another performance, the cobbler brought him the bag of repaired shoes. "What do I owe you?" Yankovic asked. "Nothing," the man said. "Buy me a drink." People all over the country did things for Yankovic just because they wanted to be known as his friends.

The travel was brutal and unrelenting. Sluga provided an example from the band's itinerary in 1956, typed by Yankovic:

May 25, New Philadelphia, OH, F.O.E. Hall
May 26, Oil City, Pa. Pulaski Club
May 27, Kane, Pa., Moose Ballroom
May 28, Strabane, Pa., SNPJ Hall
May 29, Washington, Pa., Armory
May 30-31, Home (Cleveland)
June 1, Youngstown, OH
June 2, Fruitport, Mich., Fruitport Pavilion
June 3, Gary, Ind.
June 4, Chicago, Pilsen Park
June 5, Milwaukee, Schmidt's Ballroom
June 6, Cedar, Mich., Sugar Loaf Tavern
June 7, Chicago, Club Irene
June 8, Racine, Wisc., Golf Bowl
June 9, Waterloo, Iowa, Electric Park

June 10, Austin, Minn., TERP Ballroom

June 11, Milwaukee, Muskegon Beach

June 12, Milwaukee, Nightingale Ballroom

June 13, Off

June 14, Cloquet, Minn., Labor Temple

June 15, Clintonville, Wisc., Rustic Resort

June 16, Eau Claire, Wisc., Fournier's Ballroom

June 17, Mankato, Minn., KATO Ballroom

June 18, Bismarck, N.D.

June 19, Off

June 20-21, Regina, Saskatoon, Canada, Trianon Ballroom

June 22, Kenosee Lake, Saskatoon, Canada, Clarke Resort

June 23, McGrand, North Dakota, Bachelors Grove

June 24, St. Cloud, Minn., Fairgrounds

June 25, Milwaukee, Phillies Ballroom

June 26, Wausaw, Wisc., Schmidt's Ballroom

June 27, Black River Falls, Freeman Hotel

June 28, LaCrosse, Wisc.

June 29, Plane, Wisc.

June 30, Michigan City, Indiana

July 1, Monroe, Wisc., Turner Hall

July 2-3, Muskego, Wisc., Muskego Beach Ballrroom

July 4, Chicago, Club Irene

July 5, Port Stanley, Ont., Canada, Memorial Bldg.

July 6, Youngstown, OH, Park

July 7, Wallaceburg, Ont. Canada, CB Club

July 8, Fruitport, Mich., Fruitport Pavilion

July 9, Waukegan, Ill, private wedding

July 10, Milwaukee, Campbell's Sport Club

July 11-12 Off

That totaled forty-three jobs in forty-seven days in ten states, two countries, and thirty-two cities and towns, with more than one visit to some of them. Only a man with the iron will and energy of Yankovic could have brought it off, month after month, year after year, smiling onstage all the time. Yankovic always said, by the way, that Canadian audiences were the best. He made many sojourns there, all the way from Manitoba to Ontario. A few times he even took his band to Alaska, once appearing in a Quonset hut. His standard appearance price in that era was about seven hundred dollars. On occasion, he received a thousand dollars.

In between his travels, Yankovic somehow fitted in a weekly TV show on WGN in Chicago. Yankovic introduced Sluga to the TV audience as "Mr. Banjo." The handsome youth's big number was "Kiss Me, Darling," with English words sung over an old Slovenian melody.

Sluga would spin around while singing and playing, radiating youthful vigor. Audiences went wild over his performances. Sluga suddenly had a fan club. He was receiving bushels of mail at the TV station, more than Yankovic was getting. Young girls were sending him their pictures and asking him for dates. Crowds of girls would be waiting for him when he came out of the TV studio. At dances, they would be crowding around the stage and screaming, "Ronnie, Ronnie." Sluga dated some of the groupies. They would go to a daytime movie, or to the zoo. Sluga was too young to drink. When he went to the bar, he was given a glass of milk. Sluga was such a big hit that he had a chance to audition with the Kingston Trio, which sang folk songs. Sluga passed up the opportunity, feeling Yankovic was a bigger star than the Kingstons. Later on, of course, the Kingston Trio became world famous.

Instead of being happy that he had a player of Sluga's star appeal in his band, Yankovic seethed. As he had with Cook years earlier, he began giving Sluga trouble. Once he kicked out his amplifier and took over the stage, playing the accordion with his frowning, charismatic smile, as Sluga struggled to plug in the amplifier so he could be heard.

"He fired me three times," Sluga recalled. Once Yankovic was overruled by the TV show producer, who insisted Sluga was too important to the program to be dropped. A few times Yankovic stranded Sluga after jobs, packing the musicians and instruments into the car and taking off for the next destination. If another musician protested, Yankovic would say, "That's okay. He'll find us." Yankovic was obviously hoping Sluga would get tired of the hostile treatment and quit. Sometimes Vadnal was caught in the feud. After one job, Yankovic looked angry and gave Vadnal and Sluga hurried instructions on how to get to the next gig. "Take twenty-two to seventeen to four," he said, mentioning some route numbers. "Then he took off," Vadnal said. "He was driving eighty miles an hour. We got lost and didn't get there until a half hour before we were supposed to play. He just said, 'Where were you guys?'"

"He wanted the attention at all times," said Sluga. "When somebody else got it, he'd get jealous. Maybe he wouldn't talk to you for a couple of days. He was good to his fans, but bad to his musicians. Whatever he did, we still loved the guy. We had a lot of fun with him too. He was so popular. The halls were always packed. We'd go into a little town and there was nothing there. You didn't think anybody lived there. Then all of a sudden the hall would be packed, like they all came down from a mountain."

That was one of the secrets of Yankovic's success. He played in towns and cities that were starved for entertainment and polka music. When he arrived, he was the only show in town. Had he stayed in Cleveland all the time, where there were many more bands, the competition would have been much more fierce.

Yankovic was always typing letters in his car, sending them to fans around the country. "I don't relax until my mail is taken care of," he told columnist James Neff of *The Plain Dealer*. "My mail is No. 1 in my life." Vadnal was amazed to watch him type all day in the backseat, then go onstage and play all night. He never used capital letters and never worried if he made typing mistakes. He knew his fans would be glad to hear from him. He and the band members usually stayed in the fans' houses, rather than hotels.

For Yankovic, it was no big deal to bunk in someone's home. He had learned all about that in the old days when his parents had boarders. This was just an extension of that life.

The band would come into a hall and Yankovic would tell his musicians where they were to sleep that night. He would say to Vadnal, "Rich, you're sleeping at Jones's house."

"Who's Jones?" Vadnal would ask.

"He's that guy over there in the white shirt," Yankovic would say. "Go introduce yourself. I told him about you."

Vadnal would walk over and say hello to his landlord for a night. "Oh, hi, Richie," Jones would say. "C'mon, sit down. You're sleeping at our house tonight." Sometimes the five band members each slept in a different house. They would be well fed and sleep in clean quarters. It was better than putting up in an impersonal hotel. Cheaper too, for the Yankovic wallet. He told his musicians to always help put the dishes away when eating at someone's house.

Yankovic knew how to lighten the mood when he wanted to. Bass player Pete Rogan was at the wheel once on a drive toward Milwaukee. They were stopped by a policeman who had noticed the car's trailer, which carried the instruments and was emblazoned, FRANK YANKOVIC, AMERICA'S POLKA KING. As the policeman approached, Yankovic told Rogan, "Just for the hell of it, tell him you're Frank Yankovic."

"Who's Yankovic?" the cop asked.

"I am," Rogan said.

The cop said, "Boy oh boy, I'm one of your fans. Give me your autograph." Rogan dutifully complied, signing a record and giving it to the grateful gendarme. The policeman then escorted the band to its job. Yankovic was huge in Milwaukee. At one time, he considered moving there permanently.

Another meeting with a policeman did not go as smoothly. Yankovic was relaxing by the pool at a Las Vegas hotel when a swimmer approached and introduced himself. "I'm a cop," he said. "I gave you a ticket in Chicago years ago but you talked me out of it. You promised me you would send me one of your records but you never did. How about one?" Yankovic had one of his men go to the car and give him one.

The travel continued to cause problems, but Yankovic was resourceful in a crisis. Once one of the band members fell asleep at 3 a.m. while driving. The car went into a field and crashed into a hill of snow. When they tried to drive out in the dark, they were stopped by a barbed-wire fence. Yankovic cut down the fence with pliers so the car could get through. He would replace flat tires and do work on the car. He was always very handy. "He treated us like he was our father," said Vadnal. "Until the day he died, there were two ways to do anything, Frank's way and the wrong way."

His driving never improved. He took too many chances. He was not above driving on the sidewalk if he had to get around traffic in a hurry. Once, when a heavy fog restricted visibility to one hundred feet, Yankovic drove at fifty miles an hour and went straight into a cornfield. After two and a half years, Sluga quit the band because Yankovic's driving scared him. He was so frightened the back of his neck started breaking out. Kenny Bass, a friend of both men, told Sluga, "You better quit this guy before you have a breakdown."

When Sluga made his last TV appearance with Yankovic, the King maliciously told the audience, "Ron is leaving because his wife is pregnant and he wants to spend more time with his family." Until then, the fans were not told Sluga had been married recently. It would have hurt his image with the young girls.

"The way he said it, you could tell he was mad," said Sluga. "I was disappointed. I gave him some good music." Yankovic was always angry when musicians quit him. Maybe he resented their freedom when he knew he was trapped on the road.

Yankovic and Sluga remained friends after they broke up. Yankovic often called on him when he needed a banjo player for a performance. When Sluga opened his music store in suburban

Cleveland years later, Yankovic arrived unasked and performed for nothing at the celebration. Sluga played on the record that won Yankovic his Grammy. "Whatever he did to us, we still loved the guy," Sluga recalled. "We had fun with him too. We laughed a lot and cried." Sluga clearly regarded Yankovic as his mentor. He has developed the same communication system as the King, sending letters to fans and media, keeping them informed of where he is playing and what he is doing. He and his wife, Patty, write songs together. He composes the music and she does the lyrics. She also has a radio show on WELW, interviewing women behind the scenes in the polka world.

A major change in the Yankovic band's travels occurred in 1957, when he bought a twenty-year-old bus in Red Lodge, Montana. He paid $775 for the vehicle, which had been used to carry sightseers at Yellowstone Park. Over the years, Yankovic put some $24,000 in improvements into the bus, including air-conditioning, new brakes, and an overhaul of the engine. Some of the seats were torn out and beds were installed across the width of the bus, allowing the musicians to sleep stretched out. The bus was good for publicity too, since Yankovic had his name and Polka King title painted on it. When the contraption rolled into a small town, the inhabitants stopped and stared. Yankovic used the bus for about eight years of hectic travel.

Musicians came and went. Accordionist Joe Sekardi played excellent counterpoint. Banjo man Eddie Teener, bassist Pete Rogan, and pianist Emmette Morelli were key sidemen. In the early 1960s, Yankovic made one of his most important talent discoveries in the person of a thirteen-year-old boy named Joey Miskulin, who was to become one of his best friends and finest musicians. Miskulin, who was of Slovenian-Croatian descent, lived in Chicago with his mother and grandmother. The grandmother had a big collection of Yankovic and Hoyer records. Miskulin became interested in polkas through her.

When Yankovic played in Chicago the mother and grandmother would bring the boy to the dances. Miskulin would sit by the bandstand and study Yankovic as he played. Yankovic took a liking to the boy. Miskulin reminded him of himself when he idolized Max Zelodec. He found out that Miskulin had learned to read music before he had learned to read English. One night he invited the boy to play with the band. He was a big hit.

Miskulin loved music so much that he wanted to quit school and join the band. This was impossible, since he was so young. But Yankovic, with the mother's permission, allowed him to travel and play with the Yanks during holidays and summer vacations. His first paying job was at Frankie Spetich's Easter Sunday dance in Barberton, Ohio, in 1962. When the summer was over, Miskulin reluctantly went back to school but continued to perform with Yankovic on weekends, flying back and forth between jobs and home. He constantly begged his mother and Yankovic to be allowed to play more often. He was absent about half of the time at J. Sterling Morton High School, but he still graduated with an A average.

The immensely talented Miskulin could play just about any instrument, but he was most valuable as Yankovic's second accordionist. He was also a fine singer. Their association lasted for the rest of Yankovic's life, in one way or another. According to Sluga, even Miskulin was not spared from Yankovic's temper. "He was really mean to Joey," Sluga said. "He put sugar in his gas tank once. He would abuse Joey's accordion."

Nevertheless, they remained close. They were in the bar business in Cleveland together for a time. In 1968, Miskulin left the band to go on a world tour with the Hawaii International Revue. He returned to Yankovic the next year and resumed travels with him. The two of them would fly to cities such as Seattle, New York, Portland, Oregon, or Boca Raton, Florida, and assemble musicians from the local union to perform with them. He would also play at Yankovic's Steak House in Cleveland in the 1960s. Miskulin left polkas in the 1980s to go into country music. But he would still answer the call to play on Yankovic's recordings. He did the heavy-duty box work, for instance, on Yankovic's Grammy-winning record in 1985. He composed one of the best modern polka songs, "I Wanna Call You Sweetheart." Looking back on his polka career, Miskulin says, "I'm most proud of the fact that I'm the only musician to have played on every major label that signed Frank: Columbia, RCA, MCA, Mercury, Smash, and Cleveland International." Miskulin moved to Nashville, capital of country music. For the last several years, he has been a touring member of the successful country group Riders in the Sky and is known as the Cow-polka King. Miskulin's reputation has continued to soar in Nashville. As a studio musician, he has performed with Andy Williams, Doc Severinsen, and Charlie Daniels, playing the piano, banjo, guitar, organ, accordion, and bass, along with doing some singing. He has worked on the recordings of Johnny Cash, U2, Paul McCartney, and Roy Rogers as a sound adviser.

Walter Ostanek, born on April 20, 1935, in the Canadian province of Quebec, was another accordionist who was close to Yankovic. Ostanek, of Slovenian descent, might be the closest to duplicating Yankovic's style and values. Like Yankovic, he has inexhaustible energy, speaks fluent Slovenian, and grew up in a household that took in boarders. One of them, John Jerman, taught him to play the button box, just as Zelodec had done for Yankovic when he was a boy. When the diamond mine where Ostanek's father worked closed up, the family moved to St. Catharine's, Ontario, about 235 miles from Cleveland. It was there, while the family was visiting friends, that Ostanek first heard a Yankovic record, "Andy's Jolly Hop," on the old 78 rpm disc.

"I instantly fell in love with it," Ostanek recalled. "It had a lot of zip. I started asking Mom and Dad for a record player." The first record Ostanek bought was Yankovic's "Blue Skirt Waltz," which he financed for ninety-eight cents by taking the money out of his mother's purse. He went on to buy every 45 and 78 record Yankovic ever made. He could not get enough of the music, listening to polka records from Cleveland's powerful WGAR Radio, many of which were Yankovic tunes. He would write him fan letters. He met his idol for the first time in 1950, at a dance in the Niagara Falls Arena. Ostanek, fifteen, watched him like a hawk. At the intermission, Yankovic came into the audience and talked to people. When he said hello to Ostanek's mother, she introduced him to her son and told Yankovic that Walter was crazy about his music. Yankovic replied politely, as he always did with fans. Ostanek was completely hooked. He formed his first polka band when he was seventeen. He wore the same kind of clothes Yankovic wore and bought the same kind of instrument, a Pancordion.

Their friendship really began when Yankovic starred on a weekly one-hour TV show in Buffalo, just across the Canadian border from St. Catharine's. The series ran for twenty-three shows. Ostanek was there for twenty-two of them. Basically, he served as a go-fer, anxious to help out in any way he could. He would go to a tavern across the street to buy a bottle of sparkling Burgundy wine, Yankovic's favorite drink. He would help set up Yankovic's solovox. After a while, Yankovic gave Ostanek and his band guest appearances on the program.

Later, when Ostanek had his own TV show for two years in Kitchener and Hamilton, Ontario, he would have Yankovic and Miskulin on every week. The station would fly them in from wherever they were performing. Once Ostanek was playing in a show with Yankovic in Niagara Falls. The place was absolutely jammed before they started to perform. Ostanek's wife, Irene, said, "Walter, what should I do? We can't get any more people in." Ostanek said, "Well, cut it off. Close the doors." Yankovic was aghast. "Whaddaya mean, cut it off?" he cried. "If people want to come in, let them in. They'll stand somewhere." He wasn't going to worry about a little thing like fire laws.

Ostanek, Canada's Polka King, travels about four months of the year, one-third of what Yankovic did. He is as much at home in Cleveland as he is in St. Catharine's. He is still amazed at how Yankovic was able to tame the road. "He didn't have four-lane highways in his early days," Ostanek said. "There were no turnpikes. He had to drive on two-lane roads. When he went to Canada it took him twice as long as it would today. He had to go through all those little towns and bus stops. They didn't even have gravel roads. They were mud roads. If it rained, you were lucky to get there. But the people were wall-to-wall. He was like a God. People loved him because he always had time for them. If somebody wanted an autograph or picture taken, he never snubbed them, no matter how tired or sick he might have been. He gave 100 percent of himself to the people. He sacrificed everything for his music."

In one way, Ostanek has surpassed Yankovic. He has won three Grammy Awards. Yankovic won only one, although he surely would have won many more in his heyday in the 1940s, 1950s, and 1960s before the polka Grammy existed. Ostanek is popular in polka circles throughout the U.S. and Canada, but he does not kid himself. He knows there was only one Yankovic. "I mention his name and play 'Just Because' and the 'Blue Skirt Waltz' at every job I play," he said "He's still my hero." Ostanek played second accordion when Yankovic appeared on the Johnny Carson show for the first time in 1964. He never cashed the $167 check he received for playing. He still has it pinned on his office wall, a valuable souvenir. He and Yankovic were fine friends for forty years, but they had their tiffs too. With Yankovic it was always that way.

Chapter Twelve

"Hitler's Home"

YANKOVIC'S OLDEST SON, FRANKIE Jr., loved his grandfather. When he was a child in Collinwood, he spent a lot of time with Andy, who died when he was only seven. He recalls those days fondly. "Grampa Andy was the greatest guy in the world," Frank Jr. said. "He'd put me in a stroller with a little shade over my head and we'd walk around the neighborhood. We'd stop at the Slovenian Home to watch the balinca [bocce] games and then he'd buy me a cherry soda. He always had a rolled-up newspaper in his hand. I didn't find out until years later that he always had a pipe inside the newspaper. He didn't want the Italians to come to the Slovenian side of the street."

An undeclared feud existed between the Slovenians and Italians in Collinwood, arising from the fact that in Europe, Italy was granted a piece of Slovenia after World War I. Italian soldiers occupied Slovenia in that time, causing violent disturbances between the two sides. The anger carried over to Collinwood. Neither the Slovenian nor Italian parents wanted their daughters or sons socializing with the children of the other nationality. As time went on and the old hostilities were forgotten by the younger generation, many Slovenian–Italian marriages took place.

When Frankie Jr. was about five years old, he watched his grandfather doing some painting around his house. The toddler asked if he could help with the painting. Andy refused, so Frankie Jr. took some paint and used it to decorate his grandfather's car. "He spanked me, but I loved him," he recalled. "We used to sleep together." The children called Yankovic's mother 'Banana Gramma' because she always gave them bananas to eat. June's mother was 'Chicken Gramma' because that was her favored food for the children.

That idyllic existence ended with the move to the big house in South Euclid, Andy's death, and Yankovic's flourishing career. The King's relationship with his family was as complex and frantic as his life on the road. It does not take a psychiatrist to explain the reason. It was simple: He was never home. During the peak of his career he was traveling 325 days a year. Sometimes he would be gone for half a year. He was on the road when seven of his eight children with June were born.

He and June had two daughters and six sons. She basically raised them by herself, with the help of Frank Spilar, Yankovic's cousin, who was a surrogate father to the children even though he was married and had his own family. Spilar helped June with the work around the house, from washing clothes to making repairs. Yankovic took care of the money while he was on the road. He was a generous provider, giving the children almost anything they wanted, sending them to the best private schools. He would send a five-hundred-collar check to June every Monday.

Linda, the oldest, was born on November 16, 1941. Frank Jr. came along on October 7, 1942, followed by Richard on August 19, 1946; Andrea on October 17, 1948; Jerry on February 14, 1951; Mark on October 17, 1952; Johnny on February 13, 1954; and Robert (Bobby) on June 5, 1955.

They were all good-looking, personable children, inheriting the traits of the parents. June had an effervescent personality. Yankovic could turn on the charm anytime he wanted. Besides that, the children had a lot of practice in perfecting people skills. There were always visitors in the house, especially when Yankovic was at home. "Sometimes there were so many you'd like to hit them," one of the youths said. The children felt they had to be on exhibit all the time.

"I know the kids, especially the boys, resented me for being on the road so much," Yankovic said many years later. "They felt I was never a real father and I can't blame them. I couldn't expect them to understand I was doing the best I could to make life comfortable for them." He meant that he was making big money for their benefit.

Frankie Jr., as the oldest son, probably had the most complex relationship with his father. There were times when the boy hated him, but he also admired him. He could not hold back his tears when a PBS television documentary on his father was shown in the Holmes Avenue Slovenian Hall to a large crowd in 1990. Only Frankie Jr. knows what memories went through his mind as the King frolicked and played on the screen.

"It was tough when I was a boy, but Frank Spilar pulled me through," Frankie Jr. said. "He was like my second father. We called him Uncle Spilar. He was rugged, but a gentleman. If it wasn't for him, I might have got into trouble too. He made sure we went to school. He'd take me to ball games and things like that. Then all of a sudden Dad would come home and I'd switch to having a second father. Dad had been playing, traveling hundreds of miles each day, sleeping in his car, and then somebody would tell him about something that had gone wrong at home. He didn't have time to sit down and one of his friends would be telling him about a broken window or a fender bender. He would explode."

"Hitler's home," June would say.

Aside from the normal pressures that come with being the sons of a famous man, Yankovic's overwhelming personality was especially tough for the boys to handle as they grew up. When he arrived home unannounced from a trip and found them sitting around, watching television, he would immediately get angry. He resented coming home to a cool welcome when he felt he was working so hard on the road. Remembering his days as a boy, when he had to roll the balinca court, serve drinks to the boarders, and help keep the house clean, Yankovic felt his sons should be doing something useful all the time. He would order them to rake leaves, cut the grass, and clean the swimming pool. If they did not do it quickly enough to suit him, he would grumble and angrily perform the duties himself. By his own admission, he was like an army sergeant, strict and unbending. He thought the boys were spoiled and that was what they needed. He would become angry if they slept past eight in the morning. He never struck them, but some of them were afraid of him. They all respected him.

"Dad would always help you if you were in trouble," Bobby said. "But when he'd come home he was crazy. He had a temper. He'd scream. He expected us to behave the way kids did when he stayed in their homes. That's not realistic. They were on their best behavior because he was there. He wanted us all to be perfect, like Beaver on that TV show."

Frankie Jr. took the brunt of Yankovic's anger because he was the oldest of the boys and was expected to control the others. "I feared him," the son said. "When he came home I hid from him as much as I could. Once he and Mom had a big fight and I tried to get between them. He swung and hit me but I never hit him back because he was my father. He was venting from all the road pressure and was taking it out on us. I had to be perfect. If one of my brothers got into trouble, he would come after me because I was the oldest. It was the old ethnic way of thinking. There were times I hated him." After an imagined or minor transgression, Yankovic would bellow, "I'm giving you one more chance." An undeclared war existed between the King and his oldest son. Yankovic felt the other sons were looking up to Frankie Jr. more than they were to him.

Yankovic was probably too tough on his boys. They worked harder than most kids. As teenagers they ran all sorts of businesses in the neighborhood, landscaping, cleaning gutters, painting houses, and plowing snow. When Yankovic bought his steakhouse in Cleveland in the mid-1960s they served as busboys and dishwashers. Frankie Jr. helped out with the bookkeeping. Nevertheless, they could not shake the impression that they were undisciplined. "My buddy resented me because I could do what I wanted," Bobby remembered. "I resented him because he had his parents."

The tireless Yankovic was always doing something when he was home. He could not sit still. He was not afraid to get into the grease and fix a pipe in the basement or repair a broken window. He was usually generous. When Frank Jr. graduated from Benedictine High School, Yankovic could not attend the ceremony because he was performing in Las Vegas. He bought the youth a brand-new F-85 Oldsmobile as a gift instead. "I would rather have had my father at the graduation," the son said. "It goes back to the old European tradition that a man shouldn't show his feelings. Parents never really showed love. Instead, he'd give me things."

Yankovic's generosity extended to all of his children. He bought Mark and Jerry new Chevrolet Camaros. One Christmas he gave each of his offspring a thousand dollars. The sons felt that was the only way he could show his love, by giving them things. They would have preferred having him just sit down and talk to them. They felt they did not really know him. Yankovic always had his mind on his job, thinking of the next trip, the next set of musicians, the next recordings. As singer Diana Ross once said of her idol, Barbra Streisand, "I know she's not happy. It's impossible to be that successful and be happy." In his own world, Yankovic was also that successful.

Yankovic felt he was doing the best he could for the children. Except for Frank Jr., all the boys went to Hawken School, a high-priced private school in suburban Cleveland. They even went to kindergarten there. It was more expensive than some colleges. Yankovic, who was never interested in reading books and had quit school at sixteen, did not think the pricey education was worth it. But June insisted on sending them there. "My mom didn't want us to be thinking about polkas all the time," Frankie Jr. said. "She wanted us to broaden our minds and learn about other people."

Johnny, who was extremely personable and handsome, had problems. When he was in the fourth grade, he was not doing well in school, so he was sent to a psychiatrist. The boy took it as a joke. He felt he did not need a psychiatrist. All he needed was his father. Yankovic sent the boy to Valley Forge Military Academy in Pennsylvania, hoping the discipline would get him on track. Johnny did well there but came home after a year. He felt homesick and confined at the academy. Back in Cleveland, he went to four high schools: St. Joseph, Cathedral Latin, Brush, and the Cleveland School of Friends. Once he was picked up for possession of marijuana. According to Frankie Jr., the younger boys all acquired the marijuana habit after he went into the army. "Everybody in the neighborhood was using it," Frankie Jr. said. "That was the big thing. They didn't do it around me."

Richard quit school in the tenth grade. He found it difficult to study but was a straight-A art student. He left home at seventeen and went to live in Chicago with Yankovic's close friends Carl and Ann Birsa. Yankovic paid the boy's way through hairdressing school and he became successful at the trade, becoming a top Chicago hair stylist. Years later, he moved back to Cleveland to live with Bobby. Richard had a unique view of his father. "He was a very lonesome man," he said. "So he converted his love into entertaining. That's why he was a great entertainer. He was very deep, very sensitive, an artist. Dad was his own best friend. An entertainer has to be. His head was always going. People like that are fantastic."

Bobby has the most resemblance to his father, physically and emotionally. He plays the guitar and banjo and became the only one of the Yankovic children to perform with him on a regular basis. (Linda, Andrea and Tricia, his daughters, sang with him for shorter periods.) Bobby also had a gift for skilled labor. Yankovic taught him to use a soldering iron, fix lights, and install sprinkler heads. Bobby suffered a traumatic experience when he was seventeen after taking Yankovic's Ford Bronco off the blocks in the garage without permission. He and seven neighborhood friends went for a ride. The Bronco rolled over on a steep hill in Gates Mills. Five of the boys, including Bobby and Claude Tanner, also seventeen, were injured. Bobby suffered a cut lip. Claude, the son of *Cleveland Press* executive editor Bill Tanner, died four days later in Hillcrest Hospital. Bobby and Claude were very close. Bobby took it hard. "I wanted to kill myself," he said. "I couldn't have made it without Mr. Tanner." The editor told him all the boys had to share the responsibility. For a while Bobby had nightmares and would leap up screaming in the middle of the night. Yankovic took him to a psychiatrist, who helped him.

When Jerry was eighteen months old, an explosion from a gas leak blew up his bedroom and he was badly burned. Linda, only eleven, saved him, wrapping him in a blanket and taking him out of the house. A truck driver stopped and rushed them to Huron Road Hospital. Yankovic was playing in Madison, Wisconsin, at the time and flew home immediately. When he saw Jerry he thought the baby would die. He had burns all over his face, legs, and arms. Fortunately, he survived. Jerry had eleven skin graft operations and came out of the ordeal in perfect condition. The East Ohio Gas Company gave Jerry $22,000 because of the accident, a fraction of the $300,000 the Yankovic family was asking. The money was held in trust for Jerry until he was twenty-one, when he received $14,000. The lawyers got the rest.

Jerry had more bad luck when he was twelve. He was playing neighborhood football when the ball hit him in the eye. He was taken to the hospital, where a doctor detected that he had eye cancer. The eye was removed. Looking for the bright side, the doctors said the accident was actually a lucky break for Jerry. Otherwise, the cancer would not have been detected and the boy might have died. Yankovic gave Johnny and Jerry four thousand dollars to start a landscaping business in Orlando, Florida, but it did not work out.

Jerry, now a salesman, lives in Alaska. He has six children.

Mark made the newspapers on December 27, 1971, at a Browns football game. Here is the way *The Plain Dealer* reported the story:

> Late in the game spectators and police had a minor melee. It started when George Gabuzda, 22, of 2077 Cornell Road, went on the playing field a few moments before the final gun. He was marched back to the box seat section by a policeman without incident, until a second policeman joined in. The vigor of the second policeman seemed to change the mood of things. Gabuzda reportedly spit on an officer's shoe. The nightsticks began to flail. Gabuzda was thrown between seat rows by three policemen, who battered him repeatedly. A friend of Gabuzda's, Mark Yankovic, 19, of South Euclid, ran up the steps after joining the initial encounter. He was caught by police. Gabuzda, Yankovic and two other men were charged with assault and battery on a policeman and with intoxication.

The newspaper also quoted a witness who said the police acted with unnecessary brutality. Mark was cleared. "I had to admire the kid for having the guts to help his pal when the police were beating him up," Yankovic said.

"We went on the field to scream for a touchdown, to get things moving," Mark recalled. "The police got rough with my friend. There were eight of them and two of us and I tried to stop them. I took a club away from one policeman. I could have hit him with it, but I didn't. I was standing there innocently when it started. I was in the wrong place at the wrong time."

Another time Yankovic was driving to a job in Dunkirk, New York, where he was to play for a Polish affair. An old friend, Eddie Grosel, was on the trip with him. When they arrived in Dunkirk, Yankovic received a call, telling him the boys had gotten into trouble at home and that the police were there. The boys had found the liquor he had in the swimming pool cabana. They had drunk too much and were yelling and running up and down the street. Yankovic sent Grosel back to South Euclid to investigate. Mark made a joking remark and Grosel slapped him. Mark just looked at him and said, "My father never did that," as though it was a revelation.

"I got everything as a kid, too much," Mark said. "I'd travel with Dad on the road once in while and we'd have good times. But then I'd have to go back to school. It messes up your mind a little after you've been on the road with him and then he comes home and disciplines you. Then he leaves again the next day." Mark later attended Kent State University and operated a used-car dealership in Cleveland.

There were nice moments. When they were infants, Yankovic would let the boys sit on his lap as he drove his car, pretending to let them steer. Sometimes, he took the kids trick-or-treating on Halloween. "Dad would put on a costume," said Frank Jr. "He would always try to be home for Christmas. We had some wonderful Christmases." Yankovic would take movies of the children as they came down the steps, rubbing the sleep out of their eyes. He would take the children on trips with him from time to time. They enjoyed being treated like visiting royalty when introduced as the King's children. Frankie Jr., Mark, and Johnny all took accordion lessons, but they did not keep at it. They could not progress at their own speed with people constantly checking on them and comparing them to their father.

When Linda was married in 1963, Yankovic threw a ten-thousand-dollar wedding reception for her at the La Vera Supper Club in Willoughby Hills, attended by a thousand people. That would cost at least fifty thousand in today's dollars. Linda, a graduate of the University of Detroit, was married to Henry Konrad, an electrician, for twelve years. They had five children and moved to Hawaii. It seemed to be a dream marriage, but they split amicably in 1975. Later Linda remarried and she now lives in California.

Andrea also left home after graduating from high school. She went to a business school in Chicago. A talented singer, she toyed with the idea of a show business career, but she gave that up because she felt marriage and family were more important. In 1971, she married Michael McKinnie, a college graduate who had a management job with the Ford Motor Company. They live in Avon Lake, Ohio, and are the parents of two grown sons.

Frank Jr. owns his own truck and makes deliveries and pick-ups within a five-hundred-mile radius of Cleveland. Ironically, he is constantly on the road, just as his famous father was. "I think we're all going to work all our lives, just like Dad," he said. However, he always passed up overtime on weekends so he could be home with his family. He married a woman who had three children with her first husband. They had two more sons together. Now divorced, Frank Jr. lives in Mayfield Heights.

Strangers still recognize his name. When he is introduced to someone, he is invariably called "the son of Frankie Yankovic." "That bothers me," he said. "They never use my name."

Chapter Thirteen

June Disappears

YANKOVIC'S LIFESTYLE HURT JUNE as much as it did the children, perhaps more. Only eighteen when they were married in 1940, she spent very little time with him in the next twenty-eight years. Yankovic had gone into the army only three years after they were wed. After he came back in 1945 he was almost always traveling. Sometimes he would take June on a short trip, but most of the time she was at home with the children. June and Yankovic saw each other maybe two months out of each year. She had spent the prime years of her life waiting for her husband. Very few women would be strong enough to live that way.

"I knew it was tough on my wife and kids," Yankovic said. "But I couldn't do anything halfway. Either I had to forget music and stay home or I had to keep going. I wanted to go all the way and see what life was like at the top of the mountain."

It is no wonder that when Yankovic came home he and June often argued. They did not try to cover up their bickering. They would shout at each other in front of other people, in front of the children, who would leave the room rather than listen. According to Frank Jr., June eventually deserted the family because of the verbal abuse she took from Yankovic and the pressure she felt from constant gossip. "She did the right thing leaving," Frank Jr. said. "If she hadn't left, she would have had an early grave."

Yankovic was disappointed in June's habits. "I wanted a Slovenian-type wife, somebody who would give the kids the kind of secure childhood I had," he said. "I wanted a wife whose whole life was wrapped around the children, keeping the house clean, making good meals, and getting the kids to school on time. June wasn't like that. She would stay up late watching TV and then sleep late in the morning. I kept hoping she would change, but she was spoiled by her mother."

Despite the arguments, everybody says Frank and June had a deep love for each other. That is what made their breakup such a tragedy. The circumstances of the life they had chosen were tearing them apart. It was good for the money and fame but not for much else. In the early days of their romance June had encouraged Yankovic to become a professional entertainer. When Columbia Records asked him to travel to promote his music, she gave him her blessing.

"My father wouldn't have been Frank Yankovic if it wasn't for my mother," Frank Jr. said. "She was the backbone of the family. She pushed him into performing on the road. He was afraid to do it, but she told him, 'Go do it. Don't sit home and cry.' If it wasn't for her, he might have been in Collinwood all his life. If he hadn't gone, I'd hate to see what he would have been like then." June never dreamed the travel would become an octopus that would threaten to choke them both. She never thought it would go as far as it had, to the point where her husband was almost a stranger.

"Frank's a good person, too good," she said years after their divorce. "But our ideas were different. If he hadn't been on the road so much, we'd still be together. Sometimes he'd be gone from home as long as six months. I begged him to stay home, especially in the late 1950s, when the boys were growing up, but he wouldn't listen. He said he couldn't afford to quit yet. Every year he would promise it would be his last year on the stage, but it never happened.

"He's done a tremendous job for his nationality and he's made people happy all over the country, but sometimes when you do that you hurt those who are closest to you. Big stars are usually that way. It's something in their makeup. They don't mean to hurt you, but they do. Frank was always determined to be a star and the ironic thing is I encouraged him."

Yankovic was making good money and provided generously for the family, but June was not money oriented. "It's not the most important thing," she said. "Having someone there when you need him is more important. Children can do only so much for you. They can't give you the emotional security you need, which a man can give you."

She tried everything to overcome her loneliness. She took classes at John Carroll University. She worked with retarded children. She involved herself in every aspect of the children's lives. It was not enough. She wanted to live like a married woman. She did not want a commuter marriage, which was pretty much what she had. June became convinced that her husband would be on the road forever. She felt he would die on the stage and that she would always be alone.

"I don't want to blame June for everything," Yankovic said. "I knew it was a tough life for her, but she still had the children. I felt the kids certainly should have given her all the love she needed. A lot of professional people are on the road as much as I was. Whenever possible, I would try to make things easier for her. I'd take her on trips to Las Vegas or New York. Once I sent her and a lady friend to Europe on a three-month vacation. I didn't believe in tying her down. If you can't trust somebody, it doesn't make sense to stay together anyway. I was no angel on the road, but I never ran around the way people said I did. A lot of people wanted to be seen with me, or to have their picture taken shaking my hand or giving me a kiss. I went along with it because it was part of my job, but it didn't mean anything."

Yankovic did not chase women. The polka groupies came after him because of his celebrity and charisma. It was a classic case of fame being the most potent aphrodisiac. When he was onstage in his younger days, he would sometimes invite women in the audience to meet him for sudden trysts, two of his musicians said. He would give a woman a prearranged signal, such as rubbing his nose or putting his nose on the microphone. The woman would excuse herself from her group and say she had to visit the washroom. Instead, she would head backstage. When she arrived Yankovic would leave the stage for a few minutes. He would embrace the woman in the privacy of the backstage area. In a few minutes he would return to playing and the woman would return to the dance floor.

One story of Yankovic's sexual escapades is humorous, scandalous, or frightening, depending on your point of view. According to longtime polka lore, a man found out his wife was having an affair with the Polka King. The enraged husband confronted Yankovic with a gun. Instead of running, or begging for mercy, or lying, Yankovic admitted the affair. "You can shoot me," he told the husband. "But first I want you to know it was not my fault." He said he had rejected the wife's advances several times, but that she finally seduced him.

The man believed him. They wound up having a drink together, both yelling angrily at the wife.

There is evidence that even Yankovic knew he had fallen into the trap of fame, money, and adulation. He told Frank Jr. several times that he wished he had never become a traveling musician, but that he could not stop because it was all he knew. He really meant there was no other way he could be so important. If he went home to stay, he would be just another bar owner playing polkas in Cleveland, which was already oversaturated with accordionists.

More than anything else, June was hurt by the rumors and phone calls. She heard Yankovic had girlfriends on the road. She would receive anonymous long-distance phone calls from women who said, "I was with your husband last night. He said he likes me more than he likes you." Other anonymous callers would tell her Yankovic had just been murdered or that he was in bed with somebody.

Sometimes, June would show up on the road where Yankovic was playing. Once she wore a blond wig and he did not recognize her. She wanted to see for herself if anything was going on. Nothing happened. Another time she came into the hall while he was onstage. "All of a sudden Frank put down his accordion and said, 'Take it,' and walked off," recalled Vadnal. "He sat down by June and put his head on the table, crying. June also started crying." It was typical of the emotionally charged nature of their marriage.

Yankovic said he was tortured by the same kind of rumors of marital infidelity about June. He did not know whether to believe them or not. He thought people might be making them up out of jealousy. Frank Jr. tells a story about talking to his mother at a restaurant, then kissing her when they parted. The next day somebody who had seen them planted a rumor that June had a young boyfriend, not realizing her companion was her son.

"Eventually both of us became vindictive," June said. "When somebody hurts me, I try to get back. I'd make him jealous or ignore him. A lot of things that were said about me weren't true, but I let him think they were. I liked to dance and a lot of people liked to dance with me. I had to try something. Unfortunately, it didn't work."

Both mothers-in-law were part of the problem in the marriage. "My mother was very domineering," June recalled. "She and Frank never got along. Frank's father was a generous, warm guy. A great guy. But his mother was different. Foreign women are that way. She would give you anything, but it was hard for her to show affection. Frank was the same way. He was generous, but he couldn't show you how he felt."

The final straw for her came on their twenty-fifth anniversary, when she was working at the steakhouse. She was sure Yankovic would somehow show up. She felt she had gone through so much for him. But Yankovic did not appear. A bartender gave her Yankovic's gift for their silver anniversary. "That was when I grew very cold," she said. "That was when I made up my mind to leave him when the time was right. I had tried to leave him before, but he always talked me into staying."

Yankovic had come to the same conclusion. In the 1960s he heard that June was having an affair with another Cleveland musician. When the musician became ill and had to be rushed to the hospital, June was with him. Yankovic said she got a doctor for him and took care of him. "I hit rock bottom," Yankovic said. "I remembered that when my back was broken in a car accident in 1963, I went home alone in a taxi after spending four months in the hospital." He, too, decided he would get a divorce at the right time. Or so he claimed. Their children never believed it. More likely, Yankovic was trying to save face, not wanting to look like a husband who had been abandoned by his wife.

In 1968 June went to Detroit for a Bonnie Prudden health course that was to last for ten days. She had been going there for several years to lose weight. Yankovic came off the road and went home on a Monday, the same day June was scheduled to return home. She was not there, so Yankovic got the children off to school. He figured she was a bit late. But she still did not come home that night, or the next night. Yankovic called the health club and was told that June had been there but had signed out to go home. She had driven out in Yankovic's Cadillac. Eight days went by without a word from her. Yankovic filed a missing persons report with the South Euclid police.

At the same time she disappeared, Yankovic was having the swimming pool installed in the backyard of his house. He would come home at 3 or 4 a.m. after playing a job and would check to see how the pool work was going. He noticed there were people watching him from behind trees. Later he learned they were South Euclid police. They suspected Yankovic had killed June and buried her under the pool.

While all this was going on, Yankovic's mother, Rose, died at age eighty-one. She had broken her hip and died in a nursing home. He was playing at Lake Tahoe when he got the news. In his mother's honor, he played "The Beautiful Rose Waltz," with his usual big smile. But tears were running down his face. Yankovic flew home for the funeral. While he was there Al Rodway, an old friend, gave him some jolting news. "Frank, I feel like a heel, but I promised I would never say anything," Rodway said. "I know that June is alive, but I can't tell you where she is. I swore to her I wouldn't. That's all I can say." June had been missing four months. She knew Rose had died but did not go to the funeral because she did not want to make a scene.

Three weeks earlier, June had called her son Richard while he was working at his hair salon. He had been lying awake nights trying to figure out what had happened to his mother. As soon as he heard her voice, Richard said, "Where the hell are you?" She made him promise to keep her whereabouts a secret so that Yankovic would not use his persuasive skills to talk her into coming home.

Yankovic hired a detective agency to find his truant wife. It took about three weeks but they finally tracked her down in Detroit. She was living with Dom Pacitti, who was divorced from his first wife, with whom he had four children. Pacitti was quiet and respectable. He was a successful illustrator with his own studio. He was an antique car buff and that was how he met June. She often went to car shows with Rodway and his wife. Rodway was an antique car collector and introduced June to Pacitti. Yankovic's Cadillac was parked in front of Pacitti's house. Yankovic had it towed away and brought back to Cleveland, then filed for divorce. June did not contest it.

"Frank was shook up," said Eddie Grosel. "He loved June like no other woman. If she said, 'I'm coming back,' he would have got on his knees and taken her. But he wouldn't beg her to come back. He was a stubborn Slovenian. They were both hotheads."

"Mom still cared for Dad very much," said Andrea. "It was just one of those things that happened."

Seven years later June said, "When I left him, I didn't take a penny because I loved him. I couldn't take him for money. After all, Frank is the father of my children. I love my present husband but I love Frank too. But I couldn't live with him. He is the type of person you can't reach."

The divorce shook the children badly. They could not understand it. Johnny, fourteen, and Bobby, thirteen, were so distraught they ran into the woods near their house, intending to spend the night there and then run away. The youngsters stayed in the forest for a few hours, then became frightened and came home.

Yankovic never spoke to June again. He probably felt humiliated because she walked out on him. He apologized to the children for being a poor father and told them they were all free to live with June and her new husband. They declined, but over the years they were all friendly with their mother, visiting her regularly. "I loved visiting them," said Bobby. "There was no pressure there. I thought of living with them all the time. Maybe I should have." When they came to Cleveland, June and Dom would stay with Frank Jr. and his wife. Once they visited the old house. The phone rang just as June walked into her former home. She picked it up. It was Yankovic. When he heard her voice, he immediately hung up.

He ignored her again at Andrea's wedding. "Aren't you at least going to say hello to me?" June said to Yankovic. He gave her the cold shoulder, saying, "Let's not make a scene." Some of the children felt he was still hoping she would come back.

June attended Johnny's wedding to a lovely young woman, Beth, at Diamond Jim's Restaurant in Cleveland's Flats in 1975. It was a bittersweet scenario. June sat with Frank Jr. and his wife, Janet, and danced frequently with her children and old friends. She was charming and articulate. The Yankovic children were all there, handsome people who knew how to laugh and have a good time. Dom did not attend, understandably wanting to avoid any confrontations. Yankovic, accompanied by Miskulin, played the songs that had made him famous. The first song he played was "Bye, Bye, My Baby," the number he had sung to June the night before he went into the army thirty-two years earlier. However, when he played the song, she had not yet arrived. When she did, he ignored her completely.

During the bridal dance, the King came to the floor and danced with the bride's mother. June danced with the bride's father. Yankovic made a point of refusing to look at June. The bride's father suggested Frank and June dance together. June was willing, but Yankovic immediately strode off the floor, frowning, and returned to the bandstand. June went back to the table and said, "You see how he is? I'm hurt. I've tried to be friendly with him, but it's no use. I don't understand why he is this way. Why make life harder? He has a new family now, so why not forget it?"

Yankovic had recently married his second wife, Pat. After they wed, June sent him a card congratulating him. She also tried to call him on the phone, but he refused to talk to her. "In a way, I feel sorry for Pat because she's going through the same things now that I went through," June said at Johnny's wedding. "I don't think Frank realizes he's doing the same thing."

Everybody in the family agreed Dominic and June had a good marriage. He was a kind, thoughtful man. They were active in antique car clubs and traveled to Hawaii, Europe, and Florida. "My mother was a very strong, beautiful person," said Andrea. "Dominic is a very nice man. He provided well for her. They lived very comfortably in Dearborn Heights. I know Dad still loved her, but that was in the past." Andrea's children often visited June and Dom, staying for days.

June died of lymph node cancer in August 2001, when she was almost eighty. "She looked like a girl when she died," said Frank Jr. "She never smoked or drank." Andrea recalled that June went to the hospital with what seemed to be a virus. "But her lungs filled up with water," she said. "She died in the hospital after twelve or thirteen days. I know Dad still loved her." The children bought her a gravestone in the Detroit cemetery. It reads, "Beloved Mother, Grandmother and Great-Grandmother, June E. Pacitti Yankovic, Aug. 23, 1921, Aug. 1, 2001, Always in Our Hearts, Linda, Frank

Jr., Richard, Andrea, Jerry, Mark, Johnny, Bobby." She was married to Pacitti for thirty-three years, five years longer than she was wed to Yankovic.

Chapter Fourteen

Cupid Strikes Again

AFTER JUNE LEFT HIM, Yankovic was a bachelor again. He did not lack for female companionship. He was only fifty-three, still near the top of his game physically and musically. Many a woman considered him a prize catch. He had money and was a celebrity. He received many propositions.

One lady who had been June's friend did some secretarial work for Yankovic. "She came after me real strong," Yankovic recalled. "She knew everything about me. I guess June told her all the stories. She was a very smart girl and religious too. But I never considered her as a possible wife. She wasn't my type. But she did a lot of typing for me."

As she got to know him better, the woman started telling Yankovic that June had given him a bad deal. "She told me she had always liked me and wanted to go out with me," Yankovic recalled. "She was trying to soft-soap me and I let her do it. But it wasn't getting her anywhere. I had no romantic interest in her whatsoever."

One day the secretary told Yankovic that the executives in the company she worked for were going to Boca Raton, Florida, for a convention. She told Yankovic she could get him a job playing at the convention. The pay was good. Yankovic accepted. He did not realize that the secretary would be part of the job. "When I got to airport she was waiting for me," Yankovic recalled. "She tackled me right there and wouldn't let go. She had made up her mind she was going to be in control. She laid out a schedule she had made up for me. I went to a few places with her, just out of courtesy, but then I had enough. She didn't show any signs of loosening her grip. Finally, I said to her, 'Wait a minute. I appreciate you getting me the job, but that doesn't mean I have to go everywhere with you.'"

The secretary said, "What do you think I brought you here for? I want to be seen with you. I'll look like a fool if you're not with me after all the trouble I went to." She probably had given the office staff the impression she and Yankovic were an item. She did not know the King. He dropped her right there.

It was in that same general period that Yankovic made his first retirement announcement. He said his doctor advised him to stop making strenuous tours. "Accordions have become so heavy they would tax the back of a Missouri Mule," he told *The Plain Dealer*. "I feel in A-1 shape, but I don't want to test my luck. Don Kotzman [one of his second accordionists] will take over the band and I will join him only for important dates and recordings." That was nonsense, of course. Yankovic could never stay away from the road for long.

At this point, most of his friends felt Yankovic would be an idiot to get married again. He had marred the lives of June and his children with his excessive traveling. Now the children were almost all grown. In a few years he would be completely free. Surely he would not get married again to hurt another wife, another family, and himself. But Yankovic liked marriage, no matter what it cost. He would be wed twice more.

Patricia Soltese, the young woman who became his second wife, was working as a combination bookkeeper-waitress in the steakhouse he had bought. She had been hired by Jimmy Jerele, Yankovic's partner in the restaurant, and had never seen Yankovic. One day he came home from a trip and went to the restaurant, where a friend was celebrating his birthday. Yankovic sang a couple of songs for his party. Pat said, "Who's that?" Another waitress said, "Don't let him hear you say that. He owns this place." By that time, Yankovic had cut down on his travel somewhat. He spent more time at the restaurant on weeknights, entertaining, working behind the bar and even doing some cooking. "I can cook nearly as well as a chef," he said.

Pat, twenty-three, was a pretty woman with a good figure. Yankovic was interested. "I'd watch her as she served the customers," he said. "I wanted to see if she played up to them. I can't stand phony people. I liked the way she handled herself. She was friendly but businesslike. I liked that."

Later he found out Pat was worried about the way he was studying her. "I was so intent on watching her, I guess I didn't realize I had a sourpuss look," he said years later. "She thought I was trying to catch her if she made any mistakes. She told me later she was afraid of me and that she wanted to avoid me. She liked the job and wanted to keep it."

As they got to know each other, he learned that she had been married briefly at age sixteen and had a son by that marriage. She had always lived in the Euclid area and had gone to Euclid High School, but had never heard of Yankovic and was not interested in polkas. He also noticed that a young man came to visit her nearly every afternoon in the restaurant. That bothered him.

After the bar closed one night, Yankovic asked her if she would like to join him with a party of his friends for a breakfast. She agreed and they had a nice time. He drove her home and became amorous. Pat got out of the car angrily. She said she had heard he was a Casanova. "I called her into my office and apologized the next day," Yankovic said. "After a while, I asked her if she would be interested in doing some extra work at my house. I was having it redecorated and the walls and floors needed scrubbing." He also needed somebody to cook and clean for the remaining children in his house while he was on the road on weekends.

Pat accepted the job, for it meant a raise in pay. She and her son, Greg, seven, moved into the caretaker's house on the grounds. The Yankovic children liked Pat. "I got along fine with Pat," said Andrea. "She was a lot of fun. She was like an older sister to me." She played softball with the boys. Bobby, thirteen, the youngest, was glad to see Greg. "My brothers were always picking on me because I was the youngest," Bobby said. "Now they picked on Greg. He was the youngest."

Yankovic phoned Pat nearly every day when he was on the road, checking to see if everything was all right. People were gossiping that he and Pat had a relationship by then, but he insisted that was not the case.

When he began a six-week engagement at Harvey's Wagon Wheel in Lake Tahoe, he suggested Pat bring the boys to Tahoe for a vacation. Pat agreed and drove Greg and Bobby, together with Johnny, fifteen, Mark, seventeen, and Jerry, eighteen, to Nevada. The trip took two and a half days. When they arrived, Yankovic scolded them for coming a day early and driving so fast.

A girlfriend was visiting him, another reason he was upset. This lady lived in Arizona. She was a sensible, middle-aged woman and very discreet. She had been married before and was not going with Yankovic just to be seen. In fact, she did not want anybody to know about them. Their affair seemed serious. She had visited him on many stops on the polka tour and often bought presents for his children. "I didn't want to spoil her vacation or do anything to embarrass her," Yankovic said. "That was why I yelled at Pat."

When Pat found out about the woman, she almost went back home herself. "That was when I realized Pat had some feelings for me," Yankovic said. "I already was thinking she was going to become more and more important in my life." That evening he took a party of about fifteen people to dinner, including Pat and the woman from Arizona. Yankovic sat with some of the other people, not the two women, trying not to offend anyone. As the night went on, with the drinks flowing, Yankovic and Pat started to act like a couple of teenagers. "I tossed some grapes across the table at Pat and I reached over and put some celery in her water, just like a kid," Yankovic said. "Then I went over and sat down next to her." That did it. When the Arizona woman saw the way

Yankovic and Pat behaved together, she left and went back home. She knew she was out of the running.

A few nights later Yankovic and Pat talked things out until four in the morning in the Wagon Wheel coffee shop. She told Yankovic she thought the world of him and wanted to know what she had to look forward to in the future.

"I told her I thought I would never get married again after June left," Yankovic said. "But I needed help with the kids. I couldn't keep going on the road and leaving them alone. I told her I liked her, but I was worried about our age difference." Yankovic was fifty-four and she was twenty-six. Nevertheless, they decided to get married right away. They made the six-hour drive to Las Vegas and were wed in an all-night chapel on the strip. The wedding, on June 28, 1969, cost about two hundred dollars. The chapel furnished an artificial corsage for fifty dollars, organ music for twenty dollars, and a small glass of champagne for twenty dollars. A best man and maid of honor were hired off the street for twenty dollars. The event might seem crass and meager, but the newlyweds thought it was funny.

Yankovic and Pat kept the marriage secret for a couple of days, not wanting to ruin anybody's vacation. Yankovic feared his children might resent it. But they accepted it without protest, except for Mark, who told Pat, "I think Dad married you to get revenge on my mother." One thing the boys refused to do was call Pat "Mom," as Yankovic asked them to do. They felt it would be treason against their mother. They were still holding out hope that someday their mother would come back. Yankovic banished his oldest son, Frank Jr., sending him to live with his married sister, Mary Kravos, in Willoughby Hills. "My father threw me out because my brothers still looked up to me more than they did him," said Frank Jr., who is one year older than Pat. "With me gone, he would be the father." Frank Jr. soon got married and had his own family.

The difference in age between Yankovic and Pat caused some

embarrassing moments. The King would take her to performances at times and well-meaning old friends would say they were glad he had brought his daughter along. Then he would introduce her as his wife. The couple had to endure whispers that Pat was a gold digger.

Pat had a few uncomfortable confrontations with June. One day she dropped in to visit Frank Jr. and his wife. June, who happened to be visiting from Detroit, glared at Pat. She said, "Frank Yankovic is the laziest son of a bitch that ever lived." Pat defended Yankovic and the two women argued heatedly. When June raised her arm as if to strike Pat, the younger woman walked out of the house. The next day June called Pat and yelled, "You'll see how hard it will be to live with him. His friends will destroy your marriage. None of them are any good." This was a reference to the fact Yankovic asked close friends to keep tabs on June and the children when he was on the road. They were quick to report any transgressions.

Another time Frank Jr. brought his mother to the house in South Euclid where she and Yankovic had lived for so long. June asked Pat if she could see the house for sentimental reasons. Pat gave her permission. June walked through the rooms and burst into tears.

Yankovic's sons and Pat continued to get along well. She understood them because she was only a few years older. But her son, Greg, had a hard time. He was always being harassed and taunted by the Yankovic boys. "That was our biggest problem," Yankovic said. "Greg is a nice fellow, but my sons just wouldn't accept him in the house. I guess they looked on him as an intruder. They were always picking on him. There were a lot of fights. Pat was caught in the middle. She had to try to discipline the boys, but at the same time she didn't want to show favoritism to her son. We didn't know what to do."

Greg was so miserable that after about three years he was sent to live with Pat's married sister, Gail Witlicki, in Henderson, Nevada, a suburb of Las Vegas. It was a hard thing for both Pat and the boy to do. They missed each other and talked on the phone every day.

For a while, the marriage worked. Yankovic liked Pat because she worked hard and was not a spendthrift. She was satisfied to buy dresses on sale for $9.95. With her shapely figure, she looked good in anything she wore. She was happy to stay home and take care of the house. They had two children, Teresa, who was born on June 19, 1970, and Tricia, who came along on April 23, 1975. Tricia, Yankovic's tenth and last child, was born when he was a few months short of age sixty. "I never enjoyed children like I do now," Yankovic said. "Teresa and Tricia jump on my lap and hug me when I come home. Pat gets upset when she hears people criticize me as a father. She says I couldn't be a better father."

Linda, Yankovic's oldest child, said, "I like Pat very much. I find it very easy to talk to her, almost easier than to talk to Dad. My children think it's great that I have two little sisters, Teresa and Tricia, who are younger than they are." Yankovic appreciated Pat so much he even put up with her smoking habit. He hated cigarettes. He had never smoked and forbade his children to do it, without success. Linda was the only one who never smoked. Pat promised she would try to cut down from her daily habit of a pack a day, but Yankovic knew it would probably never happen. For her part, Pat had to put up with Yankovic's snoring. He was a champion snorer, one who could make a room tremble. She had one unusual habit. Sometimes she simply refused to answer doorbells. A visitor could see her through the window, working in the kitchen, and think she did not hear the bell. The visitor would ring and ring, but Pat would simply not respond. This was probably because she was tired of having so many people visiting.

Yankovic tried to take one precaution because of Pat's age. According to Frank Jr., who had recently been married, the Polka King offered to trade houses with his oldest son, fearing that Pat would get the spacious South Euclid home in the event of a divorce. "He wanted protection," the son said. "He had a young wife." Frank Jr. refused and kept his smaller house.

In 1970, Yankovic's home was hit by a devastating fire. Yankovic was on the road when he got the news. He immediately drove home, arriving at 4 a.m. "I couldn't believe what I saw," he said. The blaze, started by a short circuit in the wires, caused extensive smoke damage. New ceilings had to be put into every room. All the frame work and woodwork had to be replaced. It was an eighty-thousand-dollar fire. The family lived in the Charter House Motel in Euclid for six months while repair work was done. "I had plenty of insurance," Yankovic said. "But they could never repay me for the things I lost, like my two gold records."

Yankovic's traveling continued. Pat eventually found it as hard to take as June had. Yankovic sympathized with her. "It's no life for a woman," he said. "I was never home. I don't think a traveling musician should ever get married." On August 24, 1978, the *Cleveland Press* reported that the Yankovics were going to sell their house in South Euclid and move to Las Vegas, where the king would go into semiretirement. Pat told the *Press* that Yankovic was in the best of health and that he wanted to spend more time with their children. Teresa was eight at the time and Tricia was three. Las Vegas seemed to be a logical place for them. Pat would be reunited with her son and married sister Gail, who had been living there for about ten years. Besides, much of Yankovic's work was in the West. He could get plenty of jobs within a reasonable distance of his new home. They moved into a nice ranch house that he had custom built in Henderson. The home contained a pool and steam room and was near a golf course.

By this time, all the Yankovic boys were out on their own. The youngest, Bobby, was already twenty-three. Things seemed to be going well, except that Yankovic was not really going into semiretirement. He was still playing about two hundred performances a year, a demanding task for a much younger man.

Pat's son, Greg, seemed to like his new environment. He was a nice-looking youth, thin, quiet, and about six feet tall. He enjoyed sports, playing football at Basic High School. He enjoyed riding dirt bikes. When he was nineteen, he moved to Pomona, California, to live with one of Pat's relatives. The story ended tragically. Greg was killed while climbing a cliff. According to Gail Witlicki, he fell and hit his head on a rock. Pat was heartbroken

A funeral service was held for Greg in Henderson. Many of his high school teammates and friends attended. Yankovic, who was off performing, did not come to the service. "Pat took it hard," said her sister.

"I needed him to be with me and he was not," recalled Pat. "I was all by myself, except for my sister. It took a long time to forgive him. I never let Frank down and when I needed him he was not there."

Soon after the tragedy Pat and Yankovic were divorced. She moved back to Ohio with her daughters and now lives in Middlefield, where she works as a water tester. Greg's ashes are in her home.

The years have cooled Pat's anger toward Yankovic. She now speaks highly of him. "Frank was very good to me," she said. "I loved him very much. He was always a good father to our girls and to all his kids. He bought a small house in the girls' name. I miss Frank. I wish we could go back. He was a wonderful husband and father. I can't say anything bad about him."

Tricia has great memories of Yankovic. "He was always there to help us," she recalled. "He'd visit us a couple of times a year after the divorce. He was my idol. I was closer to him than I was to my mom. He was the greatest, the best part of my life." Tricia sang on the road with Yankovic when she was eleven or twelve years old. She was a popular hit on songs such as "Little Sweetheart" and, of course, "Just Because." Yankovic bought Tricia her first car when she was sixteen. When she graduated from Pymatuning Valley High School, Yankovic bought her a ten-thousand-dollar trailer home because she was getting married. Yankovic came to the hospital when Tricia's daughter, Ashleigh, was born and attended the baptism ceremony. "I loved my dad," Tricia said. "I couldn't have asked for a better father." Yankovic helped her as much as possible when her first marriage ended in divorce. In 2004, Tricia married Jason Peters, a cabinet maker. They have an infant son, Jason Peters III, and are very happy. Tricia gave up her job as an office administrator to stay home and take care of the children.

After the breakup of his marriage to Pat, Yankovic soon moved back to Euclid. "I thought I would enjoy living in Vegas," he told *The Plain Dealer*. "But I was very disappointed in the people out there. They aren't very sociable. Their homes are all fenced in. So I'm back with my own people. I love it."

Chapter Fifteen

Holzheimer's Disease

THE MOST EMBARRASSING EPISODE of Yankovic's life occurred on July 25, 1983, when he was arrested for shoplifting $6.41 worth of meat from a Euclid grocery store, Holzheimer's Lake Shore Foods at 26588 Lake Shore Boulevard. According to police, a customer saw Yankovic put the meat in his pants pocket and told the store's assistant manager.

Yankovic paid for other groceries, but was stopped outside the store and arrested by police. He had a pound of bacon and a six-ounce sirloin strip steak in his pocket, *The Plain Dealer* reported. Yankovic, sixty-eight, of 251 East 262nd Street, pleaded innocent to the charge of misdemeanor petty theft before Euclid Municipal Court judge Robert F. Niccum, who warned that jail was a possible penalty. If convicted, Yankovic could face up to six months in jail and up to a thousand-dollar fine. He was released on a one-hundred-dollar bond.

Yankovic, who had nine hundred dollars in his wallet when arrested, said it was all a mistake, that he forgot he had put the meat in his pocket. When he was apprehended, the King took the nine hundred dollars out of his pocket and slapped it down on the counter, saying, "Why would I want to take anything when I have all this money?" He asked for a jury trial.

The Lake County *News-Herald* newspaper reported the incident. Numerous Yankovic fans called the *News-Herald*, angrily criticizing the paper for printing the story, and canceled their subscriptions. Miskulin came to the King's defense. "It has to be an oversight or something," he said. "Frank is well set financially."

Eventually, he pleaded no contest and was fined $250 and court costs, raising the price of the steak and bacon to $256.41.

Yankovic took the setback in stride. When he bumped into an old friend at a tavern, the man said, "Hello, Frank, I've been reading about you."

"Don't believe everything you read in the paper," Yankovic said, buying a round. He had the philosophy of many veteran entertainers, that publicity, even if it is unfavorable, is helpful to a career. "Good news or bad, it's still in the paper," he said.

Frank Gorshin, the Slovenian-American comic, heard about the incident. "I was out with Frank the other day," he joked in his Las Vegas comedy act. "We picked up a few things." He added, "Frank's got Holzheimer's Disease."

Numerous colleagues of Yankovic say he indulged in petty shoplifting throughout his life. Bobby said, "I think people looked the other way because they loved him that much."

"It was like a game to him," one of his musicians said. "He just wanted to see what he could get away with. He made us nervous when we went into a gas station. He'd take candy or potato chips and then he'd give it all away. He did it just to show he could do it." It is speculated he caught the habit from his mother, who would scoop up loose change from the boarders and at the bar. At one job, Yankovic was found with some bottles of lifted whiskey in his accordion case. When the manager asked about them, Yankovic feigned innocence and speculated that one of his musicians had put the liquor there. "I'll fire him," Yankovic said. He didn't, of course.

According to polka legend, Yankovic's most spectacular case of kleptomania occurred when he tried to steal a grandfather clock from a hotel because he felt management had cheated him. Nobody, however, has proof that it happened.

Chapter Sixteen

"The Best Persuader I Ever Saw"

ONE SUMMER SUNDAY AFTERNOON I was at Enon Valley, Pennsylvania, home of the national SNPJ campground. (SNPJ stands for Slovensko Narodna Podporna Jednote. Translated, it means Slovenian National Benefit Society, a fraternal organization.) It is a place of about five hundred acres located midway between Cleveland and Pittsburgh. Americans of Slovenian descent go there from all over the country to enjoy music and socialize. There are usually three or four bands playing at once at different venues. I was there with my family and friends and noticed that Yankovic was scheduled to perform in the back pavilion at 6 p.m. I had not seen him play for a while, so I left my group and hiked about a half mile to see his show.

It was 5:45 p.m. but about four hundred people were already there, standing in the pavilion in anticipation of seeing Yankovic, who was about sixty-five then. He finally arrived, carrying his own accordion and case. He wore Bermuda shorts and a tank top shirt, a more informal costume than usual. He looked grumpy, as though he had a bad trip. Or maybe he was upset about something that happened at home. He did not greet, or even look at, the crowd. He turned his back to the audience and began setting up the band's sound system on the stage. He was always very careful with how the speakers and wires were arranged. The crowd watched in total quiet and respect as he and his band members went about the mundane chore. Finally, one intrepid fan near the stage blurted out, "Hey, Yonkee, have a beer." Yankovic turned around, took a gulp of the beer without a word, and handed it back to his benefactor, then went back to his homely duty.

Finally, he was ready to play. He had accordionist Miskulin, son Bobby on banjo, and drummer Bobby (Kolka) Chick with him. Nobody paid attention to the sidemen. Even the brilliant Miskulin was ignored. Everybody stared at Yankovic. Suddenly, he was smiling, back in his element. Whatever had been bothering him was gone. He was where he wanted to be and doing what he lived for. He was ready to take the audience for a ride it would never forget. The band went into action, with Yankovic playing the accordion and singing. He went into a nonstop medley that lasted for about an hour, singing every polka song he could think of, including the following standards: "The Cleveland Polka," "We Left Our Wives at Home," "I Wish I Was Single Again," "The Rendezvous Waltz," "You Are My Sunshine," "Hoop Dee Doo," "Everywhere You Go," "When I Was a Painter," "Two-Timing You," "The Beer Barrel Polka," "Over Three Hills," "I Stopped for a Beer," "Smile, Sweetheart, Smile," "You'll Be Sorry," "Three to the Left, Three to the Right," "I Wanna Call you Sweetheart," "Just Because," and the "Blue Skirt Waltz."

He sang some of them twice, shouting to the band, "One more time." He did "E-I-E-I-E-I-O" at least three times. He did "Hey, Ba Ba Re Ba." It was an amazing performance, full of vitality and spontaneity. The band members had to be on their toes, ready for any kind of song. The crowd loved it, giving him an ovation when he finally finished. This wasn't just another polka band smoothly going through its repertoire. This was an experience. I have seen Frank Sinatra, Tony Bennett, Vic Damone, Abbe Lane, Lena Horne, Peggy Lee, Ann-Margret, Barbra Streisand, Tony Bennett, Waylon Jennings, and Paul Anka perform. They were all great. So was Yankovic.

Plain Dealer writer Anastasia Pantsios, who normally covers contemporary music, saw Yankovic play at the Front Row Theater in Mayfield when he was seventy-two. She gave the following objective review about a person she had never seen perform before:

1. The Polka King at age three. He was already flashing a smile. *(NCSPHF)*

2. Boarders, relatives and friends gather in the Yankovic yard, about 1925. Yankovic's sister, Rose, is second from left, standing next to Mary Chaperlo Ujcich. The accordion player is Joe Dolgan, father of the author. Rose Yankovic, Frank's mother, stands behind the car. Frank is in the center, with uncle Joe Yankovic (with mustache) and Herman Kravos, Frank's brother-in-law, to his right. Yankovic's father, Andy, with hands on knees, sits on the running board, next to Antonia Chaperlo, Frank's cousin. Frank's sister, Josephine, is second from right. Others are unidentified. *(Author's collection)*

3. Yankovic sings with banjo player Ron Sluga. They weren't always this happy with each other, but their friendship lasted. On the left are accordionist Joe Sekardi and bassist Al Leslie. *(Courtesy of Ron Sluga)*

4. Cleveland polka greats in a jam session at Yankovic's bar after World War II, in 1945 or 1946. From left, Mickey Kling, Pete Sokach, Kenny Bass, Eddie Habat, Yankovic, John "Hokey" Hokavar, Jim Kozel, and Johnny Pecon. Jitterbugging was not allowed because it interfered with flow of polka dancers circling floor. *(NCSPHF)*

POSITIVELY NO JITTERBUGGING

5. Yankovic with his first wife, June, when they were young and in love. They were married for 28 years and had eight children. She left him because he was almost always on the road. *(Courtesy of Andrea McKinnie)*

6. The great lineup that made the million-selling records "Just Because" and "Blue Skirt Waltz." Front row, from left: Georgie Cook, banjo; Yankovic; pianist Al (Naglitch) Nagle. Rear, from left: bassist Adolph "Church" Srnick; accordionist Johnny Pecon. Bassist Stan Slejko took Srnick's place on "Blue Skirt Waltz." *(NCSPHF)*

7. Yankovic surrounded by fans in a personal appearance at Piasecki's Radio Shop, Milwaukee, Oct. 25, 1947. Behind his right shoulder you can see pianist Al (Naglitch) Nagle. Over his left shoulder are banjo player Georgie Cook and drummer Whitey Lovsin (the taller man with blond hair). *(NCSPHF)*

8. All-time Cleveland polka stars, from left, Georgie Cook, Eddie Habat, Johnny Pecon, and John "Hokey" Hokavar, when life was good. Man in rear is unidentified. *(NCSPHF)*

9. Yankovic and Joey Miskulin, the brilliant accordionist who started playing in his band when he was 13 and performed with him longer than any other musician. *(NCSPHF)*

10. Eddie Luzar, left, and his wife, Mary Luzar, owners of a popular polka bar, were friends of Yankovic. She wrote the words to "Rendezvous Waltz," his first vocal recording. This photo was taken when he was making his million-sellers. He was a bit plump and wore an expensive peasant costume. *(NCSPHF)*

11. The public always loved Yankovic. Here he wears a delighted smile as three women in Denver, Colorado, present him with a cake and other goodies in honor of his 45th birthday in 1960. The accordionist is Joe Prunk. *(NCSPHF)*

12. Yankovic and his children get together for a sing-along in Pennsylvania. From left: Mark, Bobby, Jerry, Yankovic, Andrea, Frank Jr., Johnny. *(Courtesy of Andrea McKinnie)*

13. Yankovic, with second wife Pat and daughter Tricia, 1975. *(Courtesy of Tricia Yankovic Peters)*

14. A handsome family in good times. From left: Bobby Yankovic; Laurie, his wife; Frank Yankovic; Beth, Johnny Yankovic's wife; Johnny Yankovic; Mark Yankovic. Bobby would go to prison for five years. Johnny would die of a self-inflicted knife wound. *(Courtesy of Beth Yankovic Ianni)*

15. Yankovic after winning the first Polka Grammy award, which rejuvenated his career. That's the Grammy in his right hand. *(NCSPHF)*

16. Yankovic with his third wife, Ida, who was with him to the end. *(William Lopinski)*

17. Walter Ostanek, Canada's Polka King, idolized Yankovic and grew up listening to his music. In later years they had a close relationship, musically and personally. *(Joseph Valencic)*

18. Ron Sluga became one of the most popular sidemen in Yankovic's band. Yankovic resented his popularity. Sluga was nominated for a Grammy in 2006 *(Courtesy of Ron Sluga)*

19. Weird Al Yankovic clowns it up with the King in 1986. Weird Al, a West Coast comedian, plays the accordion and listened to Frank's music while growing up. The two are not related. *(NCSPHF)*

20. Tony Petkovsek, the Polka Ambassador, emceeing at one of his giant Thanksgiving dances. He is the most influential polka disc jockey in America. *(Glenn Kiesel)*

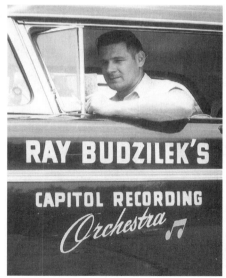

21. Ray Budzilek, a Cleveland musician who was wounded in the Korean War, drives his car with specially-equipped controls. *(Courtesy of Helenrae Budzilek)*

22. Lynn Marie Rink, "the sexiest accordionist," plays a new kind of polka music aimed at a younger generation. *(Kisa Kavass, courtesy of Lynn Marie Rink)*

23. Yankovic has no comments for newsmen as he leaves Euclid Municipal Court after being charged with shoplifting a steak while he had $900 in his wallet. *(Marvin M. Greene, courtesy of the* Plain Dealer*)*

24. Accordionists play at Yankovic's gravesite on the day of his funeral. From left: Bob Kravos, Yankovic's great-nephew; Fred Ziwich; Walter Ostanek; Jerry Robotka. *(William Lopinski)*

Yankovic has the conviviality and charm of a favorite uncle. He played his one-hour set as if he was at a party or wedding, greeting friends by name, mentioning wedding anniversaries, introducing band members by telling anecdotes about their fathers. Yankovic is not a great singer but he is extremely sincere and that quality worked in a song like 'I Wish I Was Eighteen Again.' It was an emotional direct hit with the audience. What's interesting about Yankovic is the variety. He also did a George M. Cohan medley featuring banjoist Ron Sluga.

Myron Floren, the splendid accordionist from *The Lawrence Welk Show*, was also in the show. "He didn't chat or show off like Yankovic," Pantsios wrote. Yankovic dominated the show, getting all the ink and most of the applause. It was understandable. Floren played the accordion better than Yankovic, but Yankovic was a show business genius.

"Frank is not the greatest player, but he has power," said Joe Trolli. "Some guys can play strong for an hour or so and then they peter out. Yankovic can go with a lot of steam longer than anybody."

"He's the hardest worker I've ever known," said Ann Birsa. "He performed many times when he had a 104 fever. Some people say he gets mean if one of his musicians says he's sick. That's not true. He just can't understand why a man can't keep going if he can. He thrives on pressure. If he didn't have it, he'd fall apart."

Yankovic impressed Ken Novak, a professional accordionist who is a graduate of the Cleveland Institute of Music. "I follow his philosophy and play for the people, not to impress other musicians," said Novak, of Tucson. "Once I worked in a tavern and I asked the owner if he liked my music. He said, 'I'll let you know when I count the money at the end of the night.' That's why they liked Yankovic. Who else could fill up a place on a Wednesday night in Cleveland?" Jeff Winard, Yankovic's frequent partner on the accordion, said, "Nobody ever lost money when they hired Yankovic."

Bill Savatski, a Wisconsin accordionist, was once performing with Yankovic before an uncharacteristically small audience. "I was tired and I guess I wasn't trying too hard," Savatski recalled. "Yankovic gave me hell. He said, 'We give 'em the best we have. If there's one person here or one thousand.'"

"A lot of guys can play Yankovic into the ground, but they can't entertain anybody," said Clevelander Joe White, one of his banjo players. "Once a woman in the audience got so excited she ran on the stage and grabbed Frank out of happiness. We had played a song that meant a lot to her. Then she fainted. One day a priest asked me what it was like to be in Yankovic's band. I told him, 'We both work for perfectionists. You work for God and I work for Yankovic.'"

"He played at the most unique dance I ever saw," said Johnny Sandison, a disc jockey in Regina, Saskatchewan. "Several patients from a hospital danced in their wheelchairs. He had tears of happiness in his eyes."

Yankovic's old friend, tavern owner John Rebernisek of Milwaukee, saw him play for retarded children. "He'd call them up on stage and hold their hands so they could play the electric organ," Rebernisek recalled.

Ray Smolik, a Cleveland pianist, spent six years traveling with Yankovic. "As a musician he was average," Smolik said. "But if I wanted to sell anything to anybody at any time, I would hire him. He was the best showman and persuader I ever saw."

Bill Bykowski, who operated a Milwaukee nightclub, recalled that Yankovic wanted to play there. "I refused, because we only featured pop music," Bykowski said. "But he kept asking. So I let him play for a private party on a Monday night. When the people in the street heard him, they started coming in. We couldn't squeeze in another person. Our stage held three musicians. Yankovic had eight up there."

Yankovic was unpredictable onstage. One of his banjo players, Roger DiBenedict, had promised to bring his daughter a Collie puppy dog. Yankovic arranged to get him one from a friend in Chicago. But the friend backed out when his daughter cried and said she didn't want to give up the dog. Yankovic settled the matter onstage at the Club Irene. He yelled to the crowd, "Attention, please. This is a matter of life and death. I need a dog. Does anybody here have a dog?" A man in the audience owned a pet store and DiBenedict got his puppy.

The King was a master at quickly establishing a rapport with audiences. He would shout, "Good evening, everybody. We're gonna have a good time tonight. But first I want you to shake hands with the person behind you." The people would do it, blushing a bit as they greeted strangers. If people were timid and not dancing the polka, he would play a slow tune to get them out of their chairs and onto the floor. Then, before they had a chance to sit down, he would play a polka and they had to dance, their inhibitions overcome. "The more they dance, the better I like it," he said.

A woman who saw one of his performances remembered Yankovic well. "He put on a great show," she said. "He was a ladies' man, a flirt."

He intrigued celebrities. Acerbic comic Don Rickles often watched him perform at the Sahara in Las Vegas. They got to know each other pretty well. Liberace and Jerry Colonna were in attendance almost every night when Yankovic played at the Wagon Wheel. Yankovic would always introduce the performers to the audience. They would stand up and be cheered.

Yankovic was on the same bill with an obscure jazz group in Elko, Nevada. "They looked down on us," he recalled. "They thought we were square." One night, the Yanks played the same number the jazz group did and did it better, with Miskulin displaying his virtuoso skill. Afterward the jazzmen wanted to know why they didn't play more songs of that style. "We know where the money is," DiBenedict said.

"Yankovic would have been a success at anything," said Kenny Bass. "The man was brilliant. He was raised to be a businessman, to entertain and to be competitive. It was unheard of for a major record label to put out polka records. But when he broke through on Columbia it opened the doors for all of us. It was like going from the minor leagues to the majors."

Tony Granata, former president of the Cleveland Musicians Union, knew firsthand of Yankovic's national reputation. "When President Ford came to town during his election campaign, the White House guys phoned me to arrange for a photo of Yankovic with Ford," he said. "When Vice President Walter Mondale came here, the first thing he asked was, "Where's Frankie Yankovic?" Ford was from Michigan and Mondale from Minnesota, states that Yankovic had conquered many times.

Chick recalled a performance in Chicago's Aragon Ballroom. "The place was supposed to hold five thousand people, but there were seven thousand there," Chick recalled. "Caesar Petrillo, president of the musicians' union, heard about it and said we had to have ten musicians with a crowd like that. We only had five men, so Frank hired five more musicians, paid them union wages, and told them to go to the bar and drink. We didn't need five more players."

Chapter Seventeen

Sudden Tragedy

JOHNNY YANKOVIC AND HIS wife, Beth, had a happy life. They had been married for almost nine years and had two children, Colleen and John Jr. "I loved my marriage," Beth recalled. "Johnny was the most honest, warmhearted person. We had a lot of fun raising our kids and there were always a lot of people around, nieces and nephews. John had a lot of true, true friends. All of his brothers had great personalities. They were always having good times."

The young couple was living in Cleveland, where Johnny was a self-employed electrician. Yankovic helped him land some big accounts and he had plenty of other work. Johnny was thirty. He and Beth were not getting rich, but they were doing fine. There was no hint of the tragedy that was about to take place.

On Friday, March 31, 1984, Johnny went out on the town with some of his brothers. He felt he deserved some fun after a long week of hard work. It was an era in which many young people used cocaine recreationally. Johnny was not an addict, but he did occasionally get high on coke, as did so many others. In the 1940s and 1950s, people drank beer and whiskey to unwind. In the 1970s and 1980s, they used drugs. Beth did not go out with Johnny and the brothers. They were going to pick her up later and then all were going to a party at a friend's house.

When the young men came back to pick up Beth, she saw that Johnny was not his usual happy self. He was making some weird remarks as they arrived at the party. Beth was worried. She calmed him down enough to get him home, with the help of his brother, Mark. "How did he get so high?" Beth asked. Nobody had a good answer.

To her horror, Johnny went into the kitchen and grabbed a knife. "He was standing by the stove, holding it," Beth recalled. "I screamed for Mark. We wrestled him all over the kitchen." Johnny could not be controlled. He stabbed himself in the abdomen.

Beth screamed, "Oh my God!" and pulled the knife out of his body. She threw it into the bathroom. When she returned to the kitchen, Johnny had plunged a larger knife into his stomach. It was sticking out of his body when she walked in. The terrified young woman again pulled out the blade.

She and Mark made phone calls to 911 and to family members, including June in Detroit. The police arrived and took Johnny to Hillcrest Hospital. June arrived while her son was still alive. When she saw him, she fainted at his bedside. Yankovic, who was performing out of state, came home immediately. He was completely shattered. Surgery was performed on Johnny in the emergency room. "He never came to," Beth said. He died six hours later in the hospital. The police questioned Beth and Mark separately, wanting to know if their stories matched. They did.

"I felt totally numb," Beth said. "I didn't tell my kids until the next day." When she told Colleen her father had died, the seven-year-old girl thought it was a joke. "April Fool, April Fool," she shouted. When assured it was true, Colleen cried and said, "I want to die so I can be with Daddy."

The family felt the most extreme pain in the loss of this blond young man, the most charismatic of all the lively Yankovic offspring. Beth was heartbroken. "There were times in the next few months when I wanted to die," she said. "It would have been easier."

The circumstances of the death were never announced in the newspapers. The family put a standard funeral notice in *The Plain Dealer* on April 2, 1984, with nothing to suggest the circumstances of his death. Visitors to Zele's Funeral Home were told Johnny died of a brain aneurysm, but the truth leaked out over the years.

It was a huge funeral. Johnny looked like a sleeping choirboy in the casket. A gigantic line of cars accompanied him to All Souls Cemetery in Chardon. Yankovic had wanted his son to be buried in the family plot at Calvary Cemetery in Cleveland, but Beth preferred All Souls. "I like it there, it's quiet," she said. "I visit there a lot. So do the kids."

Beth never got over her love for Johnny. Today she drives a school bus and likes the job. Colleen graduated from Arizona State University and is teaching in a high school in that state. John is an assistant chef at a party center in a Cleveland suburb. "Everybody thinks we had an easy life because Frank Yankovic had money," Beth said. "But my kids never got anything from him. They always worked for everything."

She regrets that the Yankovic children have drifted away from her. They never see each other anymore. But everybody will always remember the handsome, charming Johnny, who knew how to have fun. "I'll kick his ass when I get up there," Bobby said, looking up to the sky.

Chapter Eighteen

The First Polka Grammy

By 1985, when Yankovic was seventy, some critics were saying that time had passed him by, that he was in rut, grinding it out. He was not making major recordings anymore. Columbia had dropped him back in 1968, after twenty-two years. However, Yankovic never really had a slump in his performing career. He was in constant demand, traveling and playing all over the country. The gigs might not have been as lucrative as they once were, but he was still making good money. He produced at least one record every year for small independent companies. The CDs were not even close to selling like his big hits of old, but they served to keep his name in front of the polka public. That all changed after he won the first polka Grammy. It rejuvenated his career. "He was reborn," said Walter Ostanek.

The trail toward this triumph began one day in suburban Cleveland, when Yankovic stopped in at a Bob Evans restaurant. He found an old acquaintance there, Steve Popovich, who had become a major player in the record business, promoting the singer Meat Loaf, who had sold millions of recordings.

Popovich, born in a small coal-mining town in Pennsylvania in 1943, had sprung from the same sort of ethnic culture as Yankovic. His mother was Slovenian-Croatian and his father Serbian. Music was just as important in the Popovich household as it had been with the Yankovics. Popovich played the tamburitza, a string instrument similar to a mandolin, and started his first band when he was eight. Yankovic was one of his musical idols, along with Fats Domino and Hank Williams. In high school Popovich had a band that combined polka and rock music. The group called itself "The Hunkies" and played in taverns for fifteen dollars a night. That was great money for youngsters in the 1950s. When Popovich's father died in 1960, the family moved to Cleveland.

One day in 1963 Popovich read that Yankovic had been in a car crash and was confined to a Cleveland hospital. He also read that Columbia Records was opening a warehouse in Cleveland. Popovich had hopes of making some kind of living in music, so he decided to call Yankovic at the hospital, even though he had never met him. He told Yankovic that his own band had always played the King's music, and he asked if Yankovic could help him get an interview for a job in the Columbia warehouse. Yankovic did so. Popovich got the job, making thirty dollars a week, while working eighty hours. The clever youngster had his eyes set on something bigger. By 1968 he had talked himself into a job in sales and promotion for Columbia. Cleveland was a hotbed of recording then, and Popovich made a lot of connections. The next year Columbia brought him to New York as the assistant to the head of promotion. He was only twenty-six. He was very successful, working with popular music icons such as Tom Jones and Michael Jackson. He remained with Columbia until 1977. By that time, his role was being diminished.

"They always want somebody younger," Popovich said. "I saw what corporations can do to people. So I quit. I got them before they got me." He started his own company, Cleveland International Records, which was partially funded by Columbia. His centerpiece singer was Meat Loaf, who had been passed up by everybody in the business. Popovich had faith in him. His judgment was correct. In 1982, Meat Loaf's *Bat Out of Hell* was the biggest-selling album in the world. When it hit platinum (one million albums in sales) Popovich threw a "platinum party" before eighteen thousand fans at Blossom Music Center. Yankovic attended and posed with Meat Loaf in a memorable photo. *Bat Out of Hell* is still selling and has now passed the 30-million mark. By 1985, however, Popovich's association with Columbia had come to an end. He felt the company was not giving him his fair share of the record profits. His personal life was not at its best either. He was going through a divorce and drinking too much. That was his state of mind when he met Yankovic in the restaurant.

"He wasn't making records and I wasn't doing anything," Popovich recalled. "I asked him, 'Why don't we do some records?'" Yankovic agreed. Popovich also wanted to get Joey Miskulin involved. The great accordionist had already fled the polka world and was making a good living in Nashville as a country musician. Popovich had the highest respect for his ability. "He is the greatest there has ever been in polka music," Popovich said of Miskulin. "Joey can play every instrument there is on a world-class level." Miskulin was happy to come in and help out on the projected CD.

Popovich, Miskulin, Sluga, and drummer Dave Wolnik drove to Youngstown in a blinding snowstorm to make the album at a favorite studio for polka musicians, Peppermint Records. Popovich's mother came along on the two-hour ride, bringing sausages, pork, and sauerkraut she had cooked. The musicians ate in the studio as they recorded. Peppermint is an informal, friendly place. Nevertheless, it has every recording convenience, with all of the necessary modern technology. "Joey played the accordion, solo-vox, bass, and piano," Sluga remembered. "He knew all of Frank's keys. I did the banjo work. Frank came in later and sang."

The record was called *Seventy Years of Hits*, featuring the best Yankovic songs. The CD sold about five thousand copies, which is huge for a polka effort in these days. The timing was perfect. The National Academy of Recording Artists (NARA) had decided to honor polka music for the first time at its Grammy Awards show in 1986. Yankovic had a good record out. He appeared in a TV show with Weird Al Yankovic (no relation) on the West Coast. Weird Al grew up listening to Yankovic records and featured him on a segment called "Frankie Goes to Hollywood," which might have served to acquaint some of the eighteen thousand NARA voters with his music and long trek through polka history.

Whatever the reason, Yankovic was deservedly voted the winner of the first polka Grammy, beating out two Polish polka legends, Eddie Blazonczyk and Walter "Li'l Wally" Jagiello.

Jeff Winard of Milwaukee, one of the dozens of accordionists who accompanied Yankovic over the years, was working with the King in Mesa, Arizona, when he received the news of the honor. "I don't think Frank understood how big this was at first," Winard recalled. "With all the things he had done, it took a lot to impress him. I don't think it hit him until we went to the Grammys."

Yankovic went to Los Angeles for the festivities on February 25, 1986, accompanied by Popovich, Winard, Steve Brunton, a musician from Racine, Wisconsin, and Ann Birsa, his old friend from Chicago. Everybody wore tuxedos at a pre-Grammy party. Musical legends such as Benny Goodman, Linda Ronstadt, Sting, and Buddy Rich were there, along with all the notables of the recording industry. White-gloved waiters served food and champagne. "Drink up," Yankovic joked. "The drinks are on me." An ice sculpture stretched from the floor to the ceiling of the huge room. "I don't think I ever seen anything like this," said Yankovic, with his usual inattention to grammar. When he was introduced to Sting, the rock star, Yankovic said, "Stink? What kind of a name is that?"

Rich, the great but obnoxious drummer, said to Yankovic, "All accordionists belong in hell." Yankovic countered, "Do you know who I am?"

"Yes, I know who you are," Rich said.

"Well, I don't know you," said Yankovic, walking away. Actually, they were old acquaintances.

Everybody had a good time. Yankovic sang "Blue Eyes Crying in the Rain," one of his hits, to Goodman as they sat at the same table. The press was everywhere. "I was tickled pink when I was nominated," Yankovic told reporters. "Win or lose, I'm honored.

And polka music is honored. Polka is the happiest music this side of heaven."

The awards were bestowed in the Shrine Auditorium the next day. Most of the celebrities came in limousines, but Yankovic and his six-person entourage arrived in a modest rented sedan. "In fact, he sat on my daughter's lap," Popovich said. Winard and Brunton did not have tickets to the black-tie event, but Yankovic told them not to worry about getting into the auditorium. He let them in the side door, opening it himself. "Only Yankovic could do that," laughed Brunton. "There was security all over the place." As the program wore on, Yankovic became extremely nervous. He did not know what to expect. When master of ceremonies Kenny Rogers finally called out his name as the winner of the polka Grammy, Yankovic let out a yell, shook hands, and hugged his entourage, and he fairly ran to the stage. Smiling widely, he spoke briefly, saying it was a great honor and thanking the musicians who had worked with him through the years. The rocky relationships were forgotten in this moment of triumph.

Yankovic went backstage, where he was interviewed by a crowd of reporters. Camera lights were popping. He was getting so many phone calls of congratulations he had a phone to each ear. "He never expected to win," Brunton said. "He didn't really want to go to the show because he thought one of the Polish bands would win," recalled Ostanek. "There are so many more Polish than Slovenians."

The smile never left Yankovic's seventy-year-old face as he dashed from party to party, including a stop at Hollywood's famed Chasen's restaurant. "He was on cloud nine," Brunton said. "He looked twenty years younger." Petkovsek called from Cleveland as soon as he heard the news, putting Yankovic on the air for a live interview on WELW. "He was so excited," the veteran radio host recalled. "It was really a highlight in his life. It came at a time when he thought maybe this polka thing isn't as great as it was, or he wasn't as great as he used to be. It was a tremendous shot in

the arm for him and for the whole polka business." It was vindi-
cation for Popovich too. He had recorded Yankovic when nobody
else wanted to do polkas.

Glasses were being raised in Yankovic's honor in polka bars
all over Cleveland and the country. A Los Angeles newspaper
gave Yankovic top billing alongside Bruce Springsteen, the folk
and rock singer. The headline read "Springsteen Still The Boss;
Yankovic Still The Polka King." It was quite a tribute, consider-
ing the fame of so many of the award winners. *The Plain Dealer*
headlined the story and carried a photo of a euphoric Yankovic
holding the Grammy high. When Yankovic returned to Cleveland
a month later, a hero's welcome was held for him at Tony's Polka
Village, Petkovsek's record store on East 185th Street. More shin-
digs took place at other polka spots in town, such as Simcic's in
Euclid.

Yankovic was suddenly in demand again. TV talk show hosts
Phil Donahue and David Frost had him on their programs.
Johnny Carson, the king of late-night television, wanted him to
appear on his show. Yankovic had spent his show business life on
the fringes of the big time, every once in a while getting a chance
to appear with people like Bob Hope, Patti Page, and Doris Day.
He knew he had to be at his best for the Carson program. His
intensity never burned higher. He took Miskulin, Bobby, and
Wolnik with him to New York.

"Joey and my father, mainly my father, were so nervous they
were driving me and Dave Wolnik nuts," Bobby recalled. "They
wanted everything to be perfect and were telling us to smile
and not to be a bump on a log. I got nervous because they were
nervous."

"They argued all night," Wolnik recalled.

Carson could not have been nicer. Chatting with Yankovic and
his band before the show, he remembered the days when the
King played in his hometown of Norfolk, Nebraska. "That was
always the biggest event of the year in Norfolk," Carson said. He

recalled that he used to play Yankovic records all the time when he was a young disc jockey starting out in Nebraska. Yankovic reminded Carson he had been on his TV show twenty-two years earlier. "They got along real well," Bobby recalls. "Carson was very professional. He respected my dad because he was serious about his work."

Yankovic held on to his integrity when it was time to perform. He was not going to change his style just because he was going on a highly rated network TV show. The only concession he made was in his shirt. Instead of the blue peasant shirt he usually wore, he came out with a white silk peasant outfit, befitting a special occasion.

Where another bandleader might have played something generic for fear of being ridiculed before a non-polka audience, Yankovic started out his medley by singing a Slovenian song, "The Silk Umbrella," that was his first recording forty-seven years earlier. He sang it in Slovenian, defiantly showing pride in his ethnicity. Then he launched into "Hey, Little Sweetheart," "Just Because," and "Blue Skirt Waltz." He played the accordion and sang each number, inviting the audience to sing along on "Beer Barrel Polka." As always, he proved he could rise to the occasion. It was a good show. He received generous applause and Carson invited Yankovic to join him on the couch near his desk.

"I felt like I was back in Omaha, doing *Polka Parade* at 6 a.m.," Carson said. "I used to play a lot of your songs. Are polkas having a revival?"

"I've been on the road fifty-five years," Yankovic said, exaggerating slightly. "Polkas will go on forever."

"It's happy music," Carson said. Yankovic fired back with his familiar refrain about polkas being the happiest music this side of heaven.

"How many one-nighters do you do?" Carson asked.

"We do about 175 to 200 a year," said Yankovic. "We used to do more. It keeps me young. But it's not like we're staying in hotels all the time. We stay with people we know. It's almost like going to a wedding."

Helping Carson along with the interview, Yankovic told the story of how his Slovenian-born mother bought him his first accordion and how his first teacher had almost dropped him.

"Where is Slovenia?" Carson inquired.

After Yankovic gave a geography lesson on network TV, Carson asked, "Do you speak Slovenian?"

"Oh, yes, I speak it fluently," said Yankovic, brimming with self-importance. This was true to an extent, but it was a running gag among Clevelanders that Yankovic butchered the Slovenian language. Carson, of course, had no way of knowing that.

"Did you meet a lot of ladies in your travels?" Carson asked.

"Now you're getting to the nitty-gritty," Yankovic replied, and they both laughed. "I like young girls. I married a girl thirty years younger than me. The younger they were the more I liked it. I had eight children with my first wife and two more with my second wife."

"Ten kids," Carson exclaimed. "You weren't on the road every night, were you?" That drew a good laugh from Yankovic and the audience. "Do another number for us, Frank," Carson said. Yankovic went back to his band and they banged out "Cleveland the Polka Town" and "I Wanna Call You Sweetheart," with the King playing and singing. When it ended Carson stood up, applauding heartily. "Thank you, Frank," he exclaimed.

It was an unqualified success for Yankovic. Most other polka bandleaders would have felt intimidated. That was not the case for the uninhibited Yankovic. He was the King and he knew it.

Chapter Nineteen

"Is There a Chance for Me?"

YANKOVIC WAS ON A hot streak. The year after he won the Grammy, he also got married for the third time. This marriage, to the former Ida Smodic, would last for the rest of his life. Numerous people who knew the couple well say she was a big help to Yankovic in the final years of his reign as the Polka King. "She was a classy lady," said Petkovsek. "She was perfect for his later years and was quite a representative of his image." Yankovic often told friends she was the best thing that ever happened to him.

Ida was born in Herminie, Pennsylvania, outside of Pittsburgh, and was also of Slovenian heritage. She had met him when she was married to her first husband. They often attended dances at which Yankovic and his band performed. Yankovic, as was his congenial habit, often said hello to the couple, in the same way he did to everybody.

They got to know him better when he played for three nights at a club owned by Smodic's uncle. Yankovic chatted with them at their table. Her husband, with Ida's permission, invited Yankovic and the band to their house for dinner. Yankovic was happy to come. Ida cooked soup, noodles, klobase (sausage), and strukle (boiled dumplings with cheese and walnuts). The dinner was a success. From then on Yankovic put the Smodics on his mailing list, letting them know when he would be playing in the area. He and the band came to the Smodic house several more times. Yankovic loved Ida's boiled dumplings. "Don't touch these," he would say to the musicians. "These are for me." One time Yankovic played the accordion at a surprise birthday party for Ida in her house. This was around the time Yankovic was courting Pat. In fact, he told the Smodics he was going to marry Pat.

Several years went by. Ida's marriage was troublesome, but lasting. She was a homebody who loved cooking and baking and taking care of their three children, but her husband left her several times. She always took him back. After the seventh departure, she had had enough. She began divorce proceedings after thirty-three years of marriage. Ida said she had a nervous breakdown over the split. Slowly, with the help of her family and friends, she overcame her depression. She decided to attend Yankovic's seventieth birthday party at Cleveland's ornate Slovenian National Home. She and her mother went to Cleveland on a chartered bus filled with Pittsburgh-area fans and friends of Yankovic.

Ida saw Yankovic in the Slovenian Home bar. He was wearing a blue tuxedo and was surrounded by people. As he left the bar for the stage, Ida tugged his coattail and said, "I came all the way from Pennsylvania to wish you a happy birthday."

Yankovic, who had not seen her for about fifteen years, said, "That's nice. Who are you?"

Ida was embarrassed. She had always heard that Yankovic remembered everybody. "My name is Ida Smodic," she said. "You came to a surprise birthday party in my honor."

Yankovic either did not hear her or did not catch the name. "Oh, yeah," he responded vaguely, heading for the stage. Ida walked back to the table where her mother was sitting and watched the birthday program along with about eight hundred others. After the festivities were over, Yankovic was talking to Marty (King) Kukovich, an old Pittsburgh friend and musician who had organized the bus trip. "Do you know that Ida Smodic's here?" Kukovich asked. "Is she?" Yankovic exclaimed, the lightbulb finally going on. "Tell her to come over and talk to me."

They chatted and Ida recalled that Yankovic's two youngest sons, Johnny and Bobby, used to play with her boys years before on trips to Pittsburgh. All of the Yankovic children were at his birthday party, except for Johnny. She asked where he was and Yankovic told her he had died. "I don't want to talk about it," he said. "Let's dance." Ida was worried she would not know how to dance in the Cleveland style. She was more used to the old-fashioned Herminie style. But it was an easy waltz and they did all right, until two people cut in. Another woman was suddenly dancing with Yankovic and Ida was dancing with another man. Somebody else in the big crowd cut in and presently Ida and Yankovic were partners again.

"Is your husband here?" Yankovic asked.

"No, I'm on the verge of a divorce," Ida said. "My husband thought the grass was greener on the other side."

"Is there a chance for me?" Yankovic asked.

"You've got to be kidding, Frankie," she said. "No, I've had enough of this for a while. I just want to wait." They continued to chat and Yankovic said he would stay in touch.

Several months later, Yankovic was scheduled to play at a wedding reception for a doctor in Churchill, Pennsylvania, and he invited Ida to meet him there. Ida wasn't sure if she should go. She called her daughter, Sonya, and asked for her advice. "Oh, Mom, put on your prettiest dress and go," Sonya said. Ida went to the reception but Yankovic was not yet there. She thought to herself, "If he doesn't show up or recognize me I'm going home. No big deal."

When Yankovic arrived, he had a woman on each arm. One of the women was his niece, Dorothy Hock, and the other was the wife of an old friend. But Ida did not know that then. Yankovic smiled and said hello to Ida but walked right past her. He had not recognized her again. Ida was ready to go home, but suddenly he came back, grabbed her hand, and said excitedly, "You did come. You're going to sit down with me. We're going to eat."

Prime rib was served but Ida had trouble eating because Yankovic kept holding her hand. She told him to eat because he was going to have to play. "I'm not worried about that," he said.

It was just another job. He had done thousands of them. Ida sat with Dorothy, who was selling Yankovic's tapes, while the band performed. During an intermission, Yankovic invited Ida to come to the SNPJ Farm in Enon Valley, Pennsylvania, the next day. He was to be the grand marshal at the Slovenefest there, with thousands of people coming from all over the country.

Ida agreed to go. Yankovic picked her up the next day and they drove to Enon Valley. As always, Yankovic was the center of attention. Ida did not mind. A good mixer, she said, "I know a lot of people here. You do your thing. Don't worry about me."

Later, Yankovic was being interviewed by a radio disc jockey. Yankovic motioned for Ida, telling her to come by. "Who's this?" said the disc jockey on the air.

"I'd like to introduce you to Ida, the lady I hope will be my wife," Yankovic said, astonishing her.

The disc jockey, alertly picking up his cue, put the microphone to Ida's lips. "What's it going to be, Ida?" he said.

"I looked at Frankie's big blue eyes," Ida recalled. "My heart melted and I said yes. He hadn't even kissed me yet." Yankovic turned to the DJ and said, smilingly, "We're going to wait a while."

Ida was having none of that. "Oh, no," she told the world on the air. "You're going to marry me before you change your mind or I change my mind." They were married December 27, 1986. Yankovic was seventy-one and Ida fifty-two. The ceremony was held in Yankovic's house on East 262nd Street in Euclid. His old friend Common Pleas judge Norman Fuerst performed the nuptials. Miskulin was the best man and Sonya was the matron of honor. Yankovic's daughter Tricia, eleven, was a flower girl, along with Ida's granddaughters, Lindsay and Stephanie. Yankovic cried when he said his vows before about a dozen people. A small reception was held at Sterle's Slovenian Country House in Cleveland, one of Yankovic's favorite restaurants. The couple went on a cruise for their honeymoon.

They had a second wedding about five years later, after both had their previous marriages annulled by the Roman Catholic Church. They were remarried at Our Lady Queen of Peace Church in Milwaukee, where he was playing. Yankovic's close Milwaukee friends, John and Ann Rebernisek, were the best man and matron of honor. Yankovic had tried to keep the ceremony secret. "Don't go telling everybody I'm getting remarried," he told his Milwaukee accordionist, Jeff Winard. He gave Ida the same order. Nevertheless, word got around. The church was packed for the nuptials, to Yankovic's complete surprise.

Unlike his two previous wives, Ida married Yankovic on the condition she would travel with him. He was still playing about two hundred dates a year. Ida quickly learned what it was like to be on road with the King. "I did the driving until he wanted to drive," she said. "That's when the rosaries came out." Like everybody who ever traveled with Yankovic, she had some harrowing experiences and would try to tell him to be cautious. "Shut up, I'm driving," said the stubborn Yankovic. They had their contentious moments and disagreements, but they aired them out.

She was amazed at the number of friends he had all over the country. "These were men he knew for twenty or thirty years," she said. "They were like his brothers. Everybody loved Frank wherever he went." Once, while on a job in the West, Yankovic and Ida went to the dance hall in a horse and carriage. The horse was brought right into the ballroom as everyone applauded. When Frank and Ida stepped down from the carriage, the crowd insisted they do a solo waltz together. "All the people got in a circle around us and applauded," she recalled. "The tears flowed. He had a charisma that was just beautiful."

She saw firsthand the tyranny of the road, which made her wonder how Yankovic had ever been able to endure it for all those years. While they were driving in Ohio, a tire in their station wagon exploded at 3 a.m., starting a fire under the vehicle. Ida woke up Yankovic, who was sleeping in the backseat, and they left the flaming wagon. He lost three sets of performing shirts, all of the tapes and records he had brought to sell, and his false teeth.

The indomitable Yankovic stood on the highway, hailing passing cars in an attempt to get help. That was long before cell phones had arrived to make communication easier. Finally, a car stopped and drove him to a truck stop. Ida and a couple of the musicians stayed with the burning car. After an hour or so, a van approached them and the driver said, "Are you Ida? Your husband told us to pick you up." When they arrived at the truck stop, Yankovic was quietly eating a meal, as if nothing unusual had happened.

"I lost it," Ida recalled. "I cried. There was just so much I could take. I guess he had so many things happen in his life that I wasn't accustomed to." The troupe went to a small hotel for the night. It was in such disrepair that Ida felt she had rags that looked better than the furnishings. Yankovic took the setback in stride, renting a car to drive to Cypress Gardens, Florida, where he had a playing engagement in a few days. He could not go on the stage without his teeth, however. Yankovic told Ida to look in the Yellow Pages and find a dentist who could make teeth for him within twenty-four hours. Yankovic wound up paying more than a thousand dollars for a new set of choppers. The next day he played at Cypress Gardens and was as successful as ever.

"Why don't you give this life a rest?" Ida asked him as he approached eighty. He promised to retire. In fact, he retired more times than Sarah Bernhardt, the famed actress who made a career out of it. "He didn't really mean it," said Ida. "It was just another excuse to have a party."

On November 27, 1988, Yankovic was in the first class of inductees into the Cleveland-Style Polka Hall of Fame, along with Pecon, Hoyer, Vadnal, and Ostanek. "This is one of my greatest honors," Yankovic said at the elaborate ceremony, which resembled an Academy Awards show. He played "Just Because" and the "Blue Skirt Waltz," delighting the crowd of more than a thousand at the Euclid Shore Cultural Center.

Chapter Twenty

Jimmy Sturr, Grammy Champ

WHEN HE WAS IN his seventies, Yankovic became a good friend of Jimmy Sturr, the current polka wizard. Sturr has won fifteen polka Grammy awards, far more than anybody else. Strangely, he is not of Slavic descent, as are most polka bandleaders. Sturr is Irish. He grew up listening to Polish polka music in his home-town of Florida, New York, a village of eighteen hundred where numerous Polish and other East European immigrants lived and worked. Frank Wojnarowski and Gene Wisniewski, famous in Polish polka circles throughout the East, led the two most popular bands on the town's airwaves. "The music was everywhere," Sturr told the *Polka Times*. "All the weddings had polka bands. I just thought polkas were the biggest thing going." Sometimes a Yankovic record would be played, showing that Yankovic was one of the few musicians who could bridge the gap between Polish and Slovenian music. "The Polish people kept Frank in business his last few years," Jimmy Maupin, Milwaukee accordionist, said. "If it wasn't for them he would have been finished years before."

Sturr, whose father is a banker, started out as a baseball player. The five-foot, ten-inch left-hander went to Scranton University on a baseball scholarship. He was a .400 hitter with no power, he admits. In Babe Ruth baseball, he pitched a couple of no-hitters. After graduation, he went to work in a hometown bank in which his father was president. A lifelong bachelor, he still lives with his parents in the house in which he was born. "Nobody's asked me to get married," he joked. He said he was born in 1951, but *Polka Times* listed him as sixty-four years old in 2006.

An Americanized Polish sound remains at the core of Sturr's

music today, but he has also branched out to include country and popular music He won his fifteenth Grammy in 2006 with an album called *Shake, Rattle and Polka,* a collection of rock and roll oldies reworked with a polka twist. His band includes three saxophones, three clarinets, three trumpets, an accordion, drums, piano, and bass. In addition to singing, Sturr plays the clarinet, sax, and drums. Genna Rose Slattery, a comely alto, also stars as a singer. Sturr was the lead clarinet player until a Nashville music guru told him, "You've got a great band, but you'll never get anywhere unless you get out in front."

Sturr took the advice and took over the master of ceremonies role, much like Lawrence Welk or André Rieu, the internationally known Dutch violinist and conductor. Sturr's move to the front was a departure from the usual humble ethnic behavior, which disdains conceit and pretense. The outstanding Polish drummer Walter Solek, for example, had one of the most successful polka bands, but he always stayed in the back of his band.

With Sturr displaying his showmanship in the key central role, his band's popularity took off. He has made more than one hundred albums and has been the subject of feature stories in the *Wall Street Journal* and *U.S. News and World Report.* He has made TV appearances on CNN, ABC, NBC, and CBS. When Charles Osgood of CBS had him on his show, he mistakenly played a Slovenian polka with his introduction, not realizing Sturr excels at the Polish sound. Osgood probably does not know the difference between the two.

Sturr has been on *Saturday Night Live* several times. He performed in Carnegie Hall seven times to sold-out audiences and has sung and played with people such as Willie Nelson, the Oak Ridge Boys, Charlie Daniels, Mel Tillis, Boots Randolph, Brenda Lee, and Arlo Guthrie. Sturr's group was the first polka band to appear at the venerable Grand Ole Opry.

Sturr does not travel as much as Yankovic. Nobody ever has. But he is on the road for about 165 dates a year, covering about

180 days. The band travels in two plush buses. This is not a mom-and-pop operation. Sturr has an office staff in Florida, New York, conducting business and handling public relations. He performs on polka cruises booked through his travel agency. For major events, he can call on as many as seventy musicians, singers, and technicians to put on a show. As this was being written, Sturr was under contract to appear on a nationally televised TV series to be seen on satellite TV (Dish Network, channel 9409) and DirecTV (channel 379), with a potential audience of 30 million. Sturr says that 70 percent of the people who attend his shows are age forty and younger. They are attracted by the band's fast, exciting style.

There is a big difference between Polish and Slovenian polka music. Horns dominate the Polish music, with the accordion in the background. It is just the opposite with the Slovenians. The Polish music has a vigorous, choppy beat, while the Slovenian sound is smoother, related more to the swing mode. The Polish dance style requires a bouncier step, fun for youngsters but hard to do for older people.

Yankovic met Sturr for the first time in the late 1980s, when their bands played at the same concert in Minnesota. In the 1990s, Yankovic sang as a solo performer in several of Sturr's Polkapalooza shows, performing for a concert crowd of thirty thousand in San Antonio. Yankovic, in his eighties, would sing a set of three songs, then leave the stage. After a rest, he would come back and sing three more with the full power of the Sturr band behind him.

"He was really unique," Sturr recalled. "The years were taking their toll, but the people loved him. I looked up to Frank. He was the best." Sturr always appreciated the Cleveland-style polka. He also featured Jeff Pecon and his band at a show at Mountaineer Park, West Virginia. "I'm a big fan of Jeff's," Sturr said. Another time, he performed with Habat, Ostanek, and Yankovic.

The friendship between Yankovic and Sturr ripened when both lived in the state of Florida. Sturr has a winter condo on Singer

Island, near West Palm Beach. He would often have phone conversations with Yankovic, who was living in New Port Richey. "He and Ida came to my condo," Sturr recalled.

Sturr often visited Cleveland in the days when baseball pitcher Phil Niekro was with the Cleveland Indians. The Hall of Fame hurler was one of Sturr's biggest fans and would play his music on a tape cassette in his locker at the ballpark. Niekro loved to dance and would show up at Sturr's performances whenever possible. Niekro would get him tickets to games and bring him into the baseball team's clubhouse to meet the major league players. Indians catcher Ron Hassey was another Sturr fan.

Sturr unexpectedly showed up at the SNPJ farm in Kirtland in 1998, a few months before the King's death. A crowd of about twelve hundred attended the weekday afternoon bash, a tribute to Yankovic, who had led the revelry when the farm opened in 1939. Sturr spoke words of praise for Yankovic from the stage and thoroughly enjoyed himself. He stayed for the whole day. "I'd never been at a Slovenian festival before," he recalled. "It was a lot of fun. Frank thanked me for coming. He was a great man, a nice man."

Despite his enormous success, Sturr still has a cause. "Polka has taken a bad rap," he said. He threatened not to attend future Grammy Awards ceremonies because the polka awards are presented in the daytime, rather than on the live TV broadcast at night. "Look, I know where my place is," he said to the *Polka Times*. "I know the whole thing has to do with ratings. I know they're after young people, and that's all well and good. But there's always the old people out there."

Chapter Twenty-One

Ray Budzilek, Cleveland Hero

THE LATE RAY BUDZILEK was one of the most prominent Cleveland Polish polka musicians, along with the late Chester Budny and Henry Broze. Budzilek and his twelve-piece band appeared many times on *Polka Varieties*, the WEWS Channel 5 TV show. Budzilek recorded for Capitol records. His biggest hit was "Ice Cubes and Beer," which sold about seventy-five thousand discs in the 1950s.

But that is only part of the tragic Budzilek story. In 1952, he was hit in the spinal cord by shrapnel while serving in the army during the Korean War. Two other U.S. soldiers were killed in the same grenade attack. As Budzilek fell a vision of his new bride, Helen, wearing her wedding dress, flashed through his mind. They had only been married a few months. He was paralyzed and never walked again.

"At first, Dad was paralyzed from the neck down," said his daughter, Helenrae. "He got the feeling back in his arms when he was taken back to Japan. He had at least ten operations but he didn't feel sorry for himself. He felt lucky he came home."

Born in 1929, Budzilek grew up in the East 71st Street and Harvard Avenue neighborhood of Cleveland. The six-footer attended Cleveland Trade School and was an excellent athlete, roller skating and playing baseball. "He received an offer to play professional baseball, but turned it down because his mother did not want him to go," Helenrae said.

He formed a polka band in his teens, playing the piano accordion. His war wounds prevented him from playing the accordion in his wheelchair, so he switched to the clarinet, saxophone, and organ. Budzilek was a natural musician who did not read notes.

Budzilek and his wife, Helen, had three children, two girls and a boy. He lived in constant pain because some of the shrapnel settled near his heart and could not be removed. He constantly used Tylenol for relief, but music was his chief remedy. "When I'm playing I have no pain," he said. It was the only thing that could make him forget what had happened in Korea. He hated the yearly July Fourth fireworks because they reminded him of the war, in which fifty thousand Americans were killed.

Budzilek refused to surrender to the paralysis and never felt sorry for himself. "He stayed active," said Helenrae. "He did more than most men who are in perfect health. He changed tires and liked to work with wood. He bowled and played tennis in his wheelchair. He was such a good swimmer us kids couldn't keep up with him. He had powerful arms and would lift us over his head."

In those days, there were no automatic wheelchairs, so Budzilek had to push himself everywhere. He moved around so much he wore out two sets of wheels every year. He drove a car with hand controls and also put hand controls on his riding lawnmower so he could cut the grass.

Budzilek and his band members played Polish gigs on weekends, traveling through surrounding states and Canada. During a performance in New York State, a young man kept asking Budzilek if he could come onstage and play with his band. Budzilek had never seen him before. Finally, Budzilek allowed him to come up and play his clarinet. The young man was Jimmy Sturr, who was unknown at the time and had not yet formed his first band.

That began a friendship that lasted for the rest of Budzilek's life. "Ray Budzilek was my inspiration," Sturr said. When Sturr made his first record, it was with Budzilek. Both of their pictures were on the cover. Budzilek's songs filled one side of the record and Sturr's were on the other side. Title of the album was *Ray*

Budzilek Meets Jimmy Sturr. Even today, Sturr writes letters to Helenrae and her mother, Helen. He sends her and the family his new records before they are released.

Budzilek, like Sturr, played in the fast style of the Polish polka, developed by Wojnarowski, Wisniewski, and Solek. Only the most agile dancers can keep up with the pace. "People still joke that if Dad was still around we'd all be thin," said Helenrae. The Chicago style, featured by bands such as those of Marion Lush, L'il Wally, and Eddie Blazonczyk, is slower. Lenny Gomulka of Chicago favors the new Push Style, which is somewhere in between in speed.

Cleveland polka disc jockey Paul Nakel, who was heard on WJMO Radio daily during the 1950s polka craze, helped Budzilek get a recording contract. Nakel arranged to have a Capitol Records representative hear Budzilek and his band play at a dance in the Polish Women's Hall on Cleveland's South Side. The Capitol man was impressed and phoned Budzilek, offering him a contract. "Dad thought somebody was playing a joke on him and hung up," said Helenrae. He hung up again when the call was repeated. Finally, he was convinced the call was for real. Budzilek made four records for Capitol.

His band consisted of twelve pieces: three trumpets, three clarinets, two drums, a saxophone, piano, bass, and accordion. Trumpeters Lenny Daniels, Jackie Stulak, and Ed Bednar, accordionists John Uhrin and Ernie Kudra, and drummer Harry "Pete" Pietrzak were among his musicians.

He left Capitol because the company wanted him to move to California and play modern popular music, as Lawrence Welk had done years before. Budzilek refused, saying, "I got popular playing Polish polkas and that's what I want to do." Yankovic and Kenny Bass then arranged to have him record with Epic Records. Budzilek was a friend of Yankovic and Bass because they were all members of the Polkats, a social club of mostly Cleveland Slovenian musicians.

Budzilek was inducted into the International Polka Association Hall of Fame in 1973. Yankovic, Pecon, and Trebar have also been honored by that predominantly Polish group. Budzilek died on June 21, 1982, at the age of fifty-three from bone cancer. He had been scheduled to play in New York City the week he died.

Helenrae is active in the polka world. The Slovene style dominates Cleveland polkas, but the Polish sound is on display every year at the Quality Inn in Middleburg Heights, when the U.S. Polka Association holds its annual weekend convention. "We attract a much younger crowd than the Slovenians do," said Helen. "We get about twenty-five hundred people there for the weekend. Jeff Pecon was there and couldn't believe the number of young people we had."

Helenrae also likes Slovenian music. She has always hoped the Slovene and Polish factions would unite into one group, but it has not happened. The two styles are distinctly different and the sides are not interested in merging. "Maybe it will happen when the two worlds get so small they'll have to get together to survive," Helenrae said.

Chapter Twenty-Two

Eddie Blazonczyk:
From Rock to Polka

EDDIE BLAZONCZYK, THE CHICAGO Polish polka institution, was another friend and colleague of Yankovic. They shared the stage many times, harmonizing on "Just Because," with both men singing and banging out the second parts in the Slovenian and Polish rhythms. (Yankovic sang "Just Because" in Slovenian, Polish, Italian, and just about any other language, never worrying if the pronunciation was not exactly right.) Blazonczyk, who played bass guitar and was the lead singer in his band, won the second polka Grammy with an album called "Another Polka Celebration," one of sixty albums in his résumé. He has spent his whole life in the music business. "My mother owned a ballroom in Chicago and I worked in the coatroom from the time I was a boy," he recalled. Unlike most polka musicians, who have regular daytime jobs, he earned his living as a musician, recording, playing dances, teaching music, publishing songbooks, and promoting events.

Born on July 12, 1941, he originally played in a rock band. In 1963, he started his polka band, The Versatones, featuring Chet Kowalkowski and Lenny Gomulka on the lead trumpets. Along with Marion Lush and Walter (L'il Wally) Jagiello, he was Chicago's leading interpreter of the Polish polka, working about 165 dates a year.

Blazonczyk suffered a stroke in 2000 and is now semiretired. His son, Eddie Blazonczyk Jr., a graduate of Lewis University, has taken over leadership of the band and continues in his father's style. The son plays the concertina and fiddle as the band performs eighty to eighty-five dates a year at major festivals all over the nation. During the week of July Fourth a couple of years ago, they played for six days at the Seven Springs (Pennsylvania) resort, drawing two thousand to three thousand dancers and listeners every day. Eddie Jr., thirty-eight, a married father of two children whose full-time occupation is in sales and training for a computer company, joined his father's six-piece band in 1989. He has combined to play with Sturr many times.

Eddie Jr. has a clear-eyed view of the polka world. "It's great music," he said. "Young people would enjoy it. But I don't know if we can bring them in. The polka could have a spurt. All it takes is for somebody to get lucky with a record." He told *Polka Times* that the word *polka* gives the music its stigma. "Today's polka is alternative dance music, related to zydeco and Cajun and Tex-Mex and so many vibrant and exciting kinds of music," he said.

The two Blazonczyks agree on the importance of Yankovic in the polka genre. "Yankovic was monumental," said Eddie Jr. "I don't know if the polka would exist if it wasn't for him. He paved the way for all of us. I don't know if any of us could have done it without him being there first. He was getting the air play all over the country."

Blazonczyk Jr. saw the public television documentary made about Yankovic in the 1980s. The documentary carried a lot of footage of one of his old bands, the one that featured Tops Cardone, Carl Paradiso, Buddy Griebel, and Al Leslie. "I would travel a mile to see that band," said Blazonczyk Jr., who was not yet born when it was flourishing. "He was playing true-blue American polka music. It wasn't Slovenian or Polish. It was American. I love his early stuff."

"Polka music is getting into the mainstream," claimed the elder Blazonczyk. "People are getting tired of that heavy metal bullshit."

His son contends that Polish people accept the Slovenian sound more readily than Slovenes accept the Polish style. However, more and more Slovenians dance with the Polish step-and-hop to Slovene music. Yankovic would have appreciated the unification of the two styles. "I always wanted to create a sound that all people, no matter what their nationality was, would like," he used to say.

Ed Ostry, born in 1931, is a classic example of the Polish Clevelander who enjoyed the Slovenian records of Yankovic, Pecon, Vadnal, Bass, Habat, and all the others. "When one of them came out with a polka record, I made sure I got it," he said. An accordionist, he always played Cleveland-style at Polish dances and weddings, using the Polish beat. As a youth, he played at his parents' bar off Fleet Avenue every Thursday, when the factory workers came in to get their checks cashed. "I played 'Just Because' all night," he recalled. "They loved it."

Ostry hosts a polka show that plays both Slovenian and Polish music on WELW Radio. An avid dancer, he attends functions of both nationalities. On one recent Saturday, he went to Enon Valley for a Slovene polka festival. The next day he was in Summit, Pennsylvania, to hear a Polish band.

Chapter Twenty-Three

Lynn Marie Rink,
Sexy Accordionist

THE MOST UNIQUE AND controversial musician on the modern polka scene is Lynn Marie Rink, a Cleveland native who now lives in Nashville. Rink is trying to move the music a step forward, just as William Lausche did when he began the Cleveland-style polka sound in the 1920s. A button box player, her music is a combination of polka, country, and rock. She has a dynamic performing style in which she makes use of her well-shaped body in leather outfits. Her songs often have daring words and she wears clothes that some in the older generation might call "provocative," with boots and short pants.

"I dress to feel comfortable," she said. "If the shirt's a little low, and I'm comfortable with it, I'll wear it. When I get dressed I always ask, 'What would Mother say if she saw me in these clothes?' I want young people who are watching me to see my outfit and say, 'That's cool.'" Music critic Austin O'Connor said she is "undoubtedly the sexiest player ever to strap on an accordion."

Rink identifies with Yankovic. "He was criticized for going Hollywood and not sticking with the true Slovenian music," she said. "I hear the same thing. They say I'm selling out, that I don't really care about the music, and that I'm in it for the glitz and glamour. But I'm only trying to help. If you don't let music evolve, it will die. I love the traditional Slovenian music but you have to package it right or the kids aren't going to listen. I'm trying to bring the polka to the masses, like Frankie Yankovic did. He was an innovator for his time. He's my inspiration." Rink's sidemen play the electric guitar, bass, and drums. She often plays and sings popular music, but always with a polka beat.

Rink is the daughter of Ludwig Hrovat, who owned a tavern in Maple Heights, a Cleveland suburb, for many years. Hrovat was an excellent entertainer in his own right, playing the piano accordion and singing. There is little question he could have succeeded with a band, but he was making good money in his bar, without traveling, and had a family. When Rink watched him perform in the bar she knew she wanted a career in music.

Rink, who graduated from Lake Catholic High School in 1983, writes her own music and lyrics. She tells stories in her songs, feeling that most polka lyrics lack substance. She plays about forty-five dates a year with her band, Lynn Marie and the Box Hounds, and has appeared with Yankovic and Sturr. She has performed at the Grand Ole Opry. The International Polka Association named her the Female Vocalist of the Year in 2001 and 2002.

Rink has been nominated for three polka Grammys and is the first woman to be cited for the honor. She knew Yankovic well, for the King and her father were friends. "Frankie always told me to keep smiling," she said. Rink has recorded several albums. Her biggest seller was *Squeezebox*, in which the cover showed her sitting on the floor with her legs around an accordion. She felt she had made records that were just as good, or better, but this one sold the most because the cover caught people's attention. After the album came out, she was invited to perform on Jay Leno's NBC television show. He called her "The Dixie Chick of Polkas."

One of Rink's biggest thrills came when she shared the stage with Chet Atkins, the legendary country guitarist. One of his musicians had seen her play in Nashville and recommended her for the appearance. She and Atkins played duets on "Just Because" and the "Beer Barrel Polka." The crowd loved it. Afterward, Atkins asked her, "Why aren't you doing this for a living?" The comment confirmed Rink's belief that there was a place for the polka outside of ethnic audiences. Rink and her husband of nineteen years both work as TV producers in Nashville. She tours with the band from June to November, then takes time off to write new songs and set up a schedule for the next season. One of her best compositions is "That's What I Like About the North."

In the spring of 2005, Rink scored a hit in Slovenia, a nation that loves American rock but can still respond to the polka. She received tumultuous cheers from a youthful Slovene crowd that was dominated by people under twenty-one. Some say the show was a success because of the revealing costumes worn by Rink and a couple of other Slovene women accordionists. Sex sells everywhere.

Chapter Twenty-Four

Walter Ostanek,
Canada's Polka King

THREE-TIME GRAMMY WINNER OSTANEK had a long, complex relationship with Yankovic. He saw the King at his most churlish and most likable extremes. Through all their triumphs and conflicts, Ostanek still considers Yankovic his mentor and all-time polka icon. "There will never be another like him," Ostanek said. "He was so unique. You could love him one minute and hate him the next."

Ostanek has an autographed collection of every record and album Yankovic ever made and the last trailer the King used to carry his instruments. He was present the day Yankovic moved out of his South Euclid house, when he and his second wife, Pat, moved to Las Vegas. Ostanek asked him what he was going to do with the wooden address sign he had hammered into a tree, reading YANKOVIC 1544 BELVOIR.

"I don't know, throw it in the garbage I guess," Yankovic replied. "Why? Do you want it?" Ostanek still has the sign as part of his memorabilia, along with the uncashed checks from their appearances on network TV.

Ostanek, who has his own fine group, was never a steady member of Yankovic's band. He is not sure he could have lived with him day to day for extended periods. "He was tough all the way around," Ostanek remembered. "Tough on his family, tough on musicians, and for no reason. He'd have a little bit of a bad day and he'd make sure you weren't happy either." Nevertheless, Ostanek always accepted when the King called on him to play for special occasions, such as the Johnny Carson show, the Phil Donahue show, or on trips to Europe or Hawaii.

He was amazed by Yankovic's daring. On the last day of a Hawaiian cruise on which they were performing, the King casually asked Ostanek, "Walter, how would you like to play with me in New York tomorrow night?" The conscientious Ostanek would never consider such a booking for his own band because of the six-hour time difference. There were too many things that could go wrong. The flight to New York would take about twelve hours, leaving little time to get to the job. The plane could be held up by weather or mechanical trouble on the six-thousand-mile trip. But Yankovic had no trouble taking a chance such as that when the money was right. Ostanek, playing as a sideman and under no responsibility if the plane was late, wound up in New York with Yankovic, in time to perform.

Once they were driving near Buffalo and stopped in a restaurant at 2 a.m. When they walked in, they realized they were the only white men there. The place was filled with black men. Ostanek was apprehensive, fearing Yankovic might say something to ignite a controversy. It was just the opposite. Within two minutes, Yankovic was introducing himself to the patrons, saying, "How do you do? My name is Frank Yankovic." One of the patrons replied, "You mean that polka guy?" They had seen him on TV. They talked like old friends. Yankovic always had a good rapport with blacks. A black youth was a good friend of his at Collinwood High. "I knew his whole family," Yankovic said, "You couldn't find a better guy." Another black fellow hung out with the Collinwood Slovenians so much that he could sing in the old-country language and peck out tunes on the button box. Tony Petkovsek, who was a bartender in his father's bar before becoming a disc jockey, recalled that whenever a Yankovic tune was played on the jukebox in the tavern, the black customers were quick to say, "That sounds like Frankie Yankovic."

The competitive testosterone always burned in Yankovic's soul and body. When he learned that Ostanek was making an album, *Walter and Friends*, he employed one of his favorite phrases to ask a question. "Walter, how's come you're recording this album, *Walter and Friends*? What do you expect to get out of it?"

"Why did you make *Yankovic and Friends*?" Ostanek retorted. "What did you expect to get out of that?" Yankovic probably resented the imitation of the title, along with thinking Ostanek was potentially cutting into his record's sales in the shrinking polka market.

Ostanek asked him to play on a video an old friend was producing in Eastlake, Ohio. Yankovic was not anxious to do it, for he was having his own video made. He agreed to play, then backed out a couple of times, causing rescheduling and extra expenses for Ostanek's friend. Finally, Yankovic arrived for the recording session, after flying in first class, with the ticket being paid for by the producer. "That just triggered me off," Ostanek recalled. "He never flew first class. He was doing anything he could to goof things up. He was grumpy, complaining about everything. He made that day miserable for everybody."

Ostanek had had enough. He told friends, "When this is over, I'm never going to do anything professionally with Yankovic again. We're still friends, but I'm wiping my slate with him. I just had enough." Yankovic and Ostanek's eyes shot daggers at each other through the recording, but nobody in the audience could tell. Their smiles and music covered up the hostility.

The anger did not last, of course. A few days later Yankovic played at Ostanek's anniversary party in St. Catharine's, and then joined Ostanek and Eddie Habat in a concert with Jimmy Sturr and Myron Floren that drew four thousand people. Afterward Yankovic said to Ostanek, "You know, Walter, I got a whole week off. If you have some time, maybe we can reminisce." Ostanek understood. Yankovic did not want to apologize but was making up for his previous surly behavior. Knowing how Yankovic's mind worked, Ostanek called the recording studio to see if it had some open time. When the answer was affirmative, Ostanek asked Yankovic, "How would you like to record some tunes with me?"

"I think that's a goddam good idea," Yankovic said in his expansive way. The recording was made, Yankovic's favor to Ostanek.

Once Ostanek asked Yankovic to guest star at a dance in Regina, Saskatchewan, where the performance would be put on video. Yankovic was a day late because of a Minnesota snowstorm. Ostanek and the band spent a day at the airport waiting for him. The next day they were there again, when Yankovic finally arrived. As a greeting, they played "Just Because."

Yankovic did not even say hello in appreciation of the welcome. His first words were, "Walter, you're a lucky guy. You can fall into a pile of shit and come out smelling like roses. I was stuck in the snow." He did not consider the inconveniences Ostanek and his band had gone through. He just wanted to make them feel indebted to him.

At the dance, Yankovic was caught up in the spirit of the occasion. The band played for four hours and he was having a great time with all of the applause and tributes. Suddenly, Yankovic yelled to the musicians in the middle of a medley, "Okay, B-flat, 'The Last Time I Saw Henry.'" It was an obscure old polka tune.

"That was a song I hadn't heard for ten years," recalled Ostanek. "He gave us no clue. We were all looking at each other, trying to figure out where to go. He'd throw that monkey wrench at you. He wanted to throw you off. Things were going too good."

As he did with Sluga and Cook, Yankovic could still resent and fear contenders for his throne. He dominated the stage at Tony Petkovsek's annual Thanksgiving dance in Cleveland. He wouldn't get off because he knew Ostanek was scheduled to perform next. Finally, at 11:45 p.m., when people were leaving, he called him up. It was as though he was telling the fast-rising Ostanek that he was still the King and that he would not get a chance to play until His Majesty was good and ready.

At other times Yankovic could be unbelievably softhearted. He and Ostanek went to a Roman Catholic mass in a church in the Catskills. During the service, he turned to Ostanek and said, "You know, Walter, I think the world of you." Ostanek started crying and so did Yankovic.

Ostanek admired Yankovic's appearance and demeanor. "He wasn't a super-looking guy, but he had personality and a great smile," Ostanek recalled. "He had those bulging eyes. I've had many women tell me those eyes made them melt in their younger days, know what I mean?"

When Yankovic was eighty, he and Ostanek, sixty, celebrated their birthdays by leading a tour of about a hundred polka fans to Slovenia. Ida and Ostanek's wife, Irene, were also on the trip. On one of the stops, Yankovic and Ostanek were to entertain at a thirty-fifth-anniversary party for a local celebrity. It turned out they were one of fifteen bands there, before a large crowd in an auditorium. "If I'd known this, I never would have come," Yankovic grumbled as they waited to perform. He had cut short his dessert after dinner to attend the affair. As the night went on and on, Yankovic said, "When are we playing, today or tomorrow?"

Ostanek told him he was being delayed so the crowd would stay to hear him. Yankovic was the featured attraction. Finally, just before midnight, they performed, with Yankovic singing and Ostanek playing to robust applause.

Yankovic received wonderful treatment in Slovenia, where he was a celebrity. His 78 rpm records had been played on Slovenian radio when Slavko Avsenik was still a boy. Avsenik, the great Slovene polka composer and accordionist who had played before crowds of seventy thousand in Germany, threw a sumptuous party for Yankovic in his restaurant. Two bands played. The food was magnificent. There was a big cake and presents for Yankovic and Ida. The next day they drank champagne with Milan Kucan, the president of Slovenia, in the parliament. "He talked to us for an hour," Yankovic recalled in wonder in later years. "I thought he was going to give us ten or fifteen minutes."

Ostanek adds, "Nobody, not me or Jimmy Sturr, has done what Frank did. No question he deserved winning the first Grammy. He promoted polkas across the country, bringing them to non-polka people. There's only one polka guy everybody knows. That's Frankie Yankovic. Go on the street and ask people to name some polka bandleaders. They heard of Yankovic and nobody else."

Ostanek, like many others, complimented Ida. "I really like her," he said. "If it wasn't for her he'd have died years earlier. She looked after him. He was so tough. But she stuck it out. I think she really cared for him."

On several occasions, Yankovic told Ostanek he regretted not being with his family more. But Ostanek can understand what drove him. "You do this all your life and if you try to retire you can't," the Canadian said. "People ask me when I'm going to retire. My answer is 'Never.' I'll be playing somewhere, at old age homes or for charity, but I'll never retire." In 2004 Ostanek, sixty-nine, had heart surgery. After a rest of a few weeks, he was playing again, as entertaining as ever.

Chapter Twenty-Five

"Yankovic Liked Hoods"

YANKOVIC WAS FIVE FEET, eight inches tall and weighed about 160 pounds in his heyday. He had the quick moves of a street-wise baseball shortstop. Something was always going on in his face. You knew he was planning something, working on some idea. He could not sit still. He once brought Ostanek to his home in South Euclid and told him to relax by the swimming pool. They were there about five minutes when Yankovic had Ostanek working, asking him to help cover the pool. "One day you'll have your own pool and you'll have to know how to do this," Yankovic explained.

After a round of golf at Berkshire Country Club, he invited his partners to his restaurant on Euclid Avenue in Cleveland, say-ing, "We'll have some steaks and drinks." The golfers were glad to accept the offer of a free meal. They ate filet mignon and por-terhouse steak and drank Manhattans. After they were finished eating and drinking, he presented them with the bill.

Yankovic never ate much, but he ate often, four or five times a day. He liked eggs and soup, but ate meat sparingly. He loved the kidney stew at Sterle's restaurant. Eddie Grosel called him the Pepper King because he put pepper on everything. Yankovic was intelligent, but was a dese-dem-dose guy in his speech, primarily because he quit school and because of his Slovenian upbringing. (There is no "th" sound in the Slovenian language.) He often was hired to sing the "Hawaiian Wedding Song" at nuptials and the opening line was a favorite of his imitators: "Dis is da moment," he would croon, and very effectively too.

Yankovic's distinctive style of speech, a mix of Slovenian and Cleveland dialect and slang, is mimicked perfectly by Ostanek and many others. Yankovic grew up speaking Slovene but was careless about it, making many grammatical errors, both in speech and records. He did not worry about it. "Leave the clinkers in," he would say about minor errors in recordings. "The people like it better that way." He knew his audience. Once a Cleveland newspaper writer quoted him as saying, "The therapy of music alleviates people's ills and problems." That was obviously an invention of the writer. Yankovic did not even know what "therapy" or "alleviate" meant. If he did, he would never use the words.

His speech was dotted with familiar phrases, some original, some ungrammatical, such as "How's come?" or "Let's go see what's what." He frequently answered yes-or-no questions by saying, "Without a doubt," a working-class cliché. "It does my heart a lot of good," was another of his favorites. When he mentioned his musicians in interviews, he would refer to them as "the boys in the band." His great-nephew, accordionist Bob Kravos of Chardon, honors Yankovic's memory by calling his band, "Bob Kravos and the Boys in the Band." In earlier days, Yankovic referred to his band as "me and all the Yanks."

He knew he was a blue-collar type and never tried to behave as though he was somebody important. He wanted to be appreciated, however, and was extremely competitive. When Ann and Carl Birsa of Chicago, two of his closest friends, displayed an autographed picture of singer Wayne Newton in their home, Yankovic angrily turned it to the wall. Ann mischievously gave Yankovic a Wayne Newton pin for Christmas. "Only you would do that," Yankovic said. He wore it in his suit lapel, showing a rare bit of humor.

Rather than being upset that so many accordionists imitated his style, he was proud of it. "They play better than I do," he said. He loved gangster movies and was an enthusiastic gambler at the dice tables in Las Vegas and in casinos on cruises. He hated to buy photos on cruises, feeling they were a waste of money, but had no trouble dropping $2,000 while shooting dice. He did not like to stay at the table a long time. He made fast, large bets. "He won about $5,000 one day at Caesar's Palace," Grosel recalled. "He gave me $3,500 and blew the rest. It was the first time he came out ahead in Las Vegas." He was not as lucky on other occasions. He went into a crap-shooting session in Lake Tahoe $4,000 ahead. By the time he was finished, he had lost that, plus another $7,000.

Accordionist Richie Vadnal was with him once when he stopped his car at a Cleveland police station. "Wait here," Yankovic said. "I want to see a friend. He's in jail. He's a good guy."

"Yankovic liked hoods," Vadnal said. "He was like Sinatra." His attraction to high-riding adventurers cost him a lot of money. During the divorce proceedings from June he worried that she was going to demand huge amounts of money. He could not get the fear out of his mind, so he gave a friend, who owned a company, all of his money and stocks to protect in the event of a legal battle. "I figured if the court said June deserved half of the estate, I could say I lost it at the racetrack," he said. The friend's business collapsed and Yankovic never got the money or stocks back. He did not prosecute. "What good would it do to put him in jail?" reasoned Yankovic. "I was hoping he could get back on his feet and make the money back, so he could pay me." It never happened.

He was victimized again by silver-tongued Fred Staup in the late 1940s. Staup was a tall, handsome man, about forty, beautifully dressed. He loved playing the horses and had a gorgeous wife who was an entertainer. He shot golf in the 70s and always seemed to have a lot of money. Yankovic was a perfect foil for the flashy operator. When Staup offered Yankovic a chance to invest in his finance company, the King quickly accepted, giving him $40,000. "For a while everything was beautiful," Yankovic recalled. "Staup was paying me 8 percent regularly. I showed a check to my father and said, 'Look how easy it is.' I told my father he ought to invest with Staup."

Andy might have been a peasant from Slovenia, but he read Staup like a book. He said, "You could wipe your ass with any receipts you get from him."

Andy was right. It wasn't long before Staup disappeared. "He had taken a lot of suckers like me and and left," Yankovic said. *The Plain Dealer* said he absconded with an estimated $100,000. That was equal to about $1 million today. It was a big story in the Cleveland papers. The fact that Yankovic was one of the people who was fleeced added to the sensational news. A nation-wide manhunt was launched. Eventually, Staup was arrested at a Chicago racetrack and brought back to Cleveland. All the money was gone. Staup had $250 in his pocket. Yankovic claimed he was owed $32,500, but a court cut that to $10,000. Staup was found guilty of embezzling and sentenced to one to ten years in prison on March 9, 1951. Yankovic interceded in his behalf, asking the court to grant him probation so he could get a job and make restitution. Yankovic offered to make him his publicist, since he had such a gift of gab. The court refused and Staup went to prison. He was released about eighteen months later. Yankovic never saw him or the money again.

Yankovic dropped another $10,000 when he invested in a casino in Cleveland. All he got for this illegal activity was two free meals. A show business friend stuck him for $45,000 in loans. He gave away another $10,000 to another embezzler who disappeared.

Despite his weakness for slippery characters, Vadnal emphasized that Yankovic liked older, gentler people too. "He always told us, 'Be nice to them. Someday you'll be old yourself,'" Vadnal said. He was loyal to old friends. When old friend Ulrich Lube's daughter was married, he drove nine hundred miles to play for free at the wedding reception. "People don't realize how often he gave up his time and played for nothing," said Cleveland disc jockey and musician Eddie Bucar. "Many a time I've seen him come into a Slovenian or Croatian club and somebody will hand him a button box. He'll play for forty-five minutes. That's just the kind of guy he is."

He was physically courageous, getting into fisticuffs several times. He once punched a piano player who had been on the job with him only a couple of weeks and wanted to quit. The pianist apologized and stayed on until Yankovic got another man. Vadnal also heard a story that he punched a fan at a dance who was riding him about his smile.

Yankovic loved the sun and heat. "He would lay on the beach and just cook," Ostanek recalled. "I was with him in a steam bath and he wanted the heat turned up. I had to get out of there. It was just too hot. But he stayed in another twenty minutes."

The only son in a family of four children, Yankovic was his parents' prize possession. The youngest of the brood, he was doted on by his three sisters and his mother. He wore beautiful suits as a young musician and later changed to long-sleeved, solid-colored peasant-style shirts for travel convenience. Many other polka bands, including Ostanek's, copied the style.

He seldom swore in English, favoring a choice bit of Yugoslav profanity, *Je bemti boga*. He had doubtless learned it from his father and the boarders who were his role models as a boy. He loved sounding and acting like an old Slovenian. He was extremely emotional. His many birthday parties were usually drenched in tears, with old friends hugging him and giving speeches.

His memory for names and faces was remarkable, but on the occasions when he did forget somebody, he covered up cannily. He would say, "Look who's here," in greeting. Then he would ask questions of the person until he figured out the name. He had a true nomad's style. You would not hear from him in two years and one day you would pick up the phone and he would quietly say, "Yankovic" in greeting, as though you talked to him every day.

Nearly every polka musician in Cleveland played with Yankovic at one time or other. He kept a roster of their names and phone numbers. He would casually meet a musician and ask if he was available for a date eight months away. If the musician said he was, Yankovic would tell him to mark it down so he would not forget. He might not see the man for months, but two weeks before the date, he would call him and say, "You still got that date marked down?"

He always seemed to need a musician to pick on, but if one fought back he quickly backed down. Frankie Mullec, the accordionist and bandleader who wrote and recorded "Tell Me a Story," a big polka hit, performed at the organ for a few years at Yankovic's restaurant. For some unknown reason, Yankovic began making detrimental remarks about Mullec on the stage microphone. Mullec, a proud man, told Yankovic, "I'm giving you two weeks' notice. I'm not putting up with that." Yankovic gave him a fifty-dollar raise. He apologized, blaming his remarks on drinking. It happened twice. Mullec got a raise each time.

Yankovic used to criticize one of his best drummers over his weight. "Look how fat that son of a bitch is," he would say. "What the hell's wrong with you?" He did it in a way that made everybody laugh, including the drummer.

Lawrence Welk brought his TV band to the Yankovic steakhouse a couple of times. Yankovic had performed with him several times on TV. Welk went up on the bandstand to play his accordion with Mullec. "I was shocked that Welk played so lousy," Mullec recalls. "But he had the smile. He and Yankovic were like twins." Welk arrived at 9 p.m. and planned to stay only one hour, feeling he needed rest at his age. But he had so much fun he stayed until the place closed at 2 a.m.

Yankovic's bad driving was legendary. His worst escapade came on July 29, 1963, when he was returning to Cleveland from a job in Wisconsin at 4:30 a.m. He was driving a Volkswagen with his son, Bobby, eight, and accordionist Don Kotzman as passengers and tried to pass a police paddy wagon at the corner of Kipling and Ivanhoe Avenues in Collinwood. The wagon made a left turn as he passed and ran into Yankovic's car, nearly killing him. The car flipped over and Yankovic was thrown out, landing on his back. Bobby and Kotzman were unhurt, but Yankovic was taken to Huron Road Hospital with a broken back. A cast was put over his entire body and he stayed in the hospital for three months, with Kotzman taking over the band.

Yankovic set hospital records for sympathy. He was receiving one hundred cards and phone calls every day. People sent him cheese and strawberry blintzes from Lindy's restaurant in New York and steaks from Kansas City. He hired a secretary and dictated replies to all the people who sent him messages. Except for his fingers, he could not move at all, a horrible penalty for a man of his enormous energy. The clavietta kept him from going stir crazy. The clavietta is a wind instrument with keys like an accordion. Yankovic was able to play on it and keep his fingers nimble. He entertained visitors with it. There were a lot of champagne parties in the room. But champagne was not Yankovic's drink. He stayed with his favorite, sparkling burgundy.

The broken back healed, but it still bothered him in later years, especially when the weather was bad. Nevertheless, he amazed fellow musicians with his stamina in handling his twenty-five-pound accordion as he grew older. He continued to play for more than three straight hours a night into his late seventies.

His health was generally good, but on August 27, 1983, when he was sixty-eight, he had an emergency heart bypass at Huron Road Hospital. The problem was discovered during a routine checkup. After recuperating in the hospital, Yankovic was anxious to leave. "They tell me I had a heart attack," he told a friend.

"How long will you be in the hospital?" the friend asked.

"I don't know," Yankovic replied, "but they can't keep me in past Saturday. I have to play that night."

He begged his doctor to let him out so he could fulfill an engagement in Brecksville, the North Coast Oktoberfest. The doctor

advised against it, saying that would be the worst possible thing
he could do for his health. Yankovic disagreed. "For me, it's the
best thing," he said. The doctor shrugged and discharged him. He
performed shortly after. He could not play, but he sang. The audience gave him a standing ovation. Immediately after, he went to
Cedar Point for another performance.

"He played for us in a Bohemian hall right after his big accident," said Lud Leskovar, Chicago disc jockey. "People said he
couldn't play anymore but there he was. What a thrill. He was in
some kind of contraption and he didn't play much, but his presence was enough."

The applause is what drove Yankovic. No matter what kind of
personal problem he had, no matter how much trouble there was
at home, he could always escape in the arms of his best friend—
the stage. Life might have been unceasingly solemn and chaotic,
but before those crowds there was no reason to stop to evaluate
his existence and where he was going.

Many people say he should have quit years earlier, for he was
no longer the performer he had been. He often said he was going to retire, but in a rare moment of honesty, he said, "I'd rather
die."

Chapter Twenty-Six

Traveling the Back Roads

CLEVELAND DRUMMER DAVE WOLNIK was one of the King's stalwarts during his later years. Wolnik, who is of Polish descent and is married to Yankovic's great-niece Karen, was a sideman for eighty-nine bands in his long career, but his time with Yankovic was the most memorable. A tall, blond man with a good sense of humor, he had the kind of low-maintenance personality that Yankovic respected. Wolnik didn't need much more than good music, a good crowd, and a good time. He tells countless yarns about Yankovic.

His choice as the funniest took place as the band pulled into Louisville, Kentucky, after an all-night drive from Pennsylvania. Yankovic had slept all night in the backseat as the younger men drove. He woke up just as they pulled into Louisville and said, "Let's look for a place to get some coffee." They drove into a McDonald's restaurant and Ida asked him, "What do you want?"

"Hot milk," Yankovic said. "As hot as you can make it." The younger musicians, feeling tired, went into the men's room to wash up. They were still groggy as they came out of the washroom, just in time to see Yankovic walking in. He was bare-chested, a towel around his neck, wearing pajama bottoms and flip-flop slippers and carrying a shaving bag, whistling merrily. The seasoned traveler knew how to make himself at home no matter where he was. The crowd in the packed restaurant stared at him.

Ida, who was standing in line, exclaimed, "Did you see that? I hope he doesn't do anything to embarrass us." A few minutes later, Yankovic emerged from the washroom, beautifully shaved, hair combed perfectly, still bare-chested and in his pajamas. "Ida," he called out. "Get me one of those bacon and egg McDougald sandwiches." The restaurant crowd roared with laughter. Wolnik is not sure whether they knew who he was or not.

Whenever possible, Yankovic avoided eating in restaurants as an economic measure. He always had lunchmeat and bread in the car. If one of the musicians protested there was mold on an old piece of bread, Yankovic would tell him to cut it off and eat the rest. On their way to an engagement at Boys Town, Father Flanagan's institution for youngsters in Nebraska, they ran out of sandwiches and existed on chocolate cookies.

Yankovic had a major problem with his false teeth and hearing aids. "He lost so many he could have bought a Cadillac for what it cost to replace them," Wolnik said. On one occasion, Yankovic was swearing and cursing, trying to find his teeth. He had taken them out and put them in his pocket the previous night. He was blaming everybody but himself as he searched the car they were driving. Finally, he slammed the car door shut and there was a loud crack. They had found the teeth. They were in the car's doorwell.

When the band played at a Florida country club, the local radio station threw a beautiful lunch for the musicians. A pretty female reporter sat next to Yankovic, interviewing him. The teeth felt uncomfortable, so he took them out and put them in a napkin. When the lunch and interview were over, the musicians got into their car to drive to their hotel. Yankovic suddenly remembered. "Go back, go back," he yelled. "I left my teeth on the table." Wolnik came to the rescue. "I've got your teeth," he said. "I picked up the napkin." Yankovic was grateful. "You saved me," he said.

Another time, Yankovic removed the bottom plate of the teeth before playing the last set of a job. He put them on the music stand. When they packed up to leave, Yankovic said, "Ida, give me my teeth."

"I don't have your teeth," she said. She often carried a spare set, but not this time. A cleaning lady heard the discussion and said,

"I saw the teeth and threw them away into that ashcan. I didn't know they were yours." Yankovic did not hesitate. He reached into that fifty-gallon drum, filled with rubbish, mustard, and gravy, and plunged his arms deep into the mess, searching frantically. He found them and came up grinning. "That saved me some money," he said, triumphantly.

Yankovic was always ready and willing to give young talent a chance. It was a way to popularize himself and keep the genre going. Accordionist Grant Kozera of Milwaukee was only twelve years old when he performed with Yankovic at the Wisconsin State Fair. Yankovic did not have a second accordionist at the time, so he allowed the youngster to fill in, playing the melody while Yankovic harmonized. After a few days, the local musicians' union protested, saying Kozera was not in the union. The union threatened Yankovic with a five-hundred-dollar fine if he continued to allow Kozera to perform with him. When Kozera arrived for another gig, Yankovic told him, "You'll have to get off the stage." The boy was crestfallen. Then Yankovic went on the microphone and shouted to the big crowd, "Whoever turned in this little boy, I hope you die." The crowd applauded loudly.

Yankovic's performances often resembled grand reunions. Fans would come to the bandstand and recall songs he played for them the night they became engaged, or talk about the great time they had as he played on a New Year's Eve. "Polka fans have more fun than sophisticated people," he said, truly believing it. He was a best man and godfather so many times he lost count.

To the end, he was as mercurial and unpredictable as ever, especially behind the wheel. The elements all came together in a memorable incident of road rage. One night he told his musicians they would be leaving Joliet, Illinois, at eight the next morning. They showed up ten minutes early to find a furious Yankovic. He was cursing. "You don't pay attention to anything I tell you," he said. "You're late."

"You said eight o'clock," Wolnik said.

"Don't tell me what I said," Yankovic yelled. "I said seven o'clock." Steve Kucenski, a young accordionist, was with the group. Yankovic wanted to know where he was. One of the men went to get Kucenski, who was taking a shower. "We gotta leave," Yankovic shouted. "I don't care if he's naked. Get him."

The youth came running down the stairs, wearing a towel, shorts, and no shoes. "I'm going to fire everybody, you too Ida," the angry Yankovic yelled, taking the wheel. For an hour and a half, he did nothing but scream, swear, and yell at the musicians. He finally quieted down when they reached the Ohio Turnpike. Now he wouldn't say a word. He grimly passed a semi tractor-trailer, going close to the truck. He was doing about seventy miles an hour. Then he cut off the truck and slowed down to sixty, forcing the truck to pass him. The scene was repeated four times, with Yankovic and the truck taking turns passing each other. "The last time he got so close I was saying a Hail Mary," Wolnik recalls. "I was in the death seat. The truck driver got mad and he cut us off real close. Frank wouldn't even look at him. My knuckles were white. I said, 'Frank, let's get out of here.'"

Yankovic replied tersely, "I'm okay. Don't worry." He tried to pass the truck again, but this time the driver pulled out and actually tried to run Yankovic's car off the road. Wolnik could not take it anymore. "Stop this car," he yelled. "I'm getting out. I'll get a ride back to Cleveland." Yankovic did not say a word. He just kept driving. Thirty miles later, he stopped the car and said, "Dave, you take over." It was the closest Wolnik ever came to getting killed with Yankovic.

The King was a stickler when it came to saving a few pennies on gasoline. In his long tour of the polka circuit he had learned exactly which stations offered the best deals. Musician Eric Noltkamper was once driving the car in Wyoming as Yankovic slept in the back. The tank was getting low, so Ida told Noltkamper to stop for gas. They did so, filled the tank, and drove on. Five miles down the road they saw a station where the gas was five cents cheaper. "Don't let him see that or we'll have trouble," Ida thought. Yankovic suddenly woke and asked where they had stopped for gas. When they told him, he lectured them for the next ten miles over their choice of gas stations.

Grosel said the King was on the road so much he knew how fast the car was going even if he was asleep. "Once we were driving to New York and I was doing eighty," Grosel said. "Frank had his eyes closed, but he poked me with his elbow and said, 'Slow down.' The fastest I ever saw Frank drive was when we were taking Father Perkovich from Cleveland to Valparaiso, Indiana, where he was having a Polka Mass. We had a flat tire. Frank got out and fixed it and it was ninety miles an hour the rest of the way."

Cleveland accordionist Anthony "Corky" Godec was with him when they drove from Presque Isle, Maine, to a job in Wisconsin the next night, a distance of about a thousand miles. "He drove one hundred miles an hour for the last hour," recalled Godec. "We got there an hour late, but the people didn't care. They loved him. Once I was driving from Milwaukee to Cleveland. I got sleepy about five in the morning and told Frank I couldn't drive anymore and pulled over. He said what he always did, 'Damn kids today can't do nothing.' So he took the wheel and I fell asleep. It wasn't long before he was sleeping too. He crashed right through a tollbooth, going about seventy miles an hour. The police came and he talked his way out of it, said that his brakes failed."

Sometimes Yankovic conducted mystery bus trips out of Cleveland, filling the vehicle with fifty polka lovers. They did not know where they were headed but were confident Yankovic would show them a good time. Once they went to Ann Arbor, Michigan, where Yankovic was performing. Everybody enjoyed the festivities. Afterward, a retired Ford Motor Company executive who was present invited the entire busload to his mansion. "What a sight," recalled the late Cleveland realtor Ray Strumbly. "The bus rolled into this exclusive neighborhood at 2 a.m. The executive's wife looked like Sophia Loren, the movie star. We had a ball. The next day Frank flew to Canada and we went back to his house, where Pat had an all-day pool party."

Yankovic was used to people with money. Once a friend gave him a two-thousand-dollar tip for playing at a party.

Everyone was amazed at Yankovic's continuing energy. "I don't know how he can keep going the way he does," said bass player Marty (King) Kukovich. "Maybe it's the homemade soup that keeps him so tough. He loves it. No matter what part of the U.S. we're in, the ladies always have some good chicken or beef soup waiting for him." He thought nothing of working late into the night in Cleveland one time, then setting out alone for Chicago. About 4 a.m. he became tired and pulled into a gas station. He slept in the car for a few hours, woke up refreshed, and finished the ride. He was about sixty at the time.

Denny Bucar, who hosted a polka show on WELW Radio and was also a bass player, performed with Yankovic many times. His favorite memory is of a show in Marion, Ohio, during a popcorn festival. "Thousands of people came to see this man," Bucar said. "The theater was packed. They had a rock band on the next block and they shut down in five minutes because everybody was watching Yankovic. It was amazing."

Jeff Winard, the Milwaukee accordionist, also acted as an agent for Yankovic. Once he booked a job for him in California. Yankovic agreed to play, but then he heard that Winard would be making just as much money for the gig as he was. He began griping. He told the sponsor of the event that he wanted more money. It didn't have to be much, but he wanted more than what Winard was being paid. It was a matter of pride. He got the money. Yet Yankovic could be completely humble. Winard owned a tavern and Yankovic often slept in the apartment upstairs. When Yankovic woke up, he would go downstairs and sweep out the tavern floor as though he was a cleaning man. He was never ashamed to work.

Jimmy Maupin of Milwaukee, who played second accordion

with Yankovic for many years, knew both sides of the King. After a monthlong jaunt through Canada, Yankovic tried to pay his band members in Canadian money. Maupin objected. He was getting thirty-five dollars a night in American money. Thirty-five dollars in Canadian would be worth only twenty-five in the U.S. Maupin complained and Yankovic paid him in American cash.

Maupin was popular in Milwaukee, but he was not a nationwide polka celebrity like Yankovic. He was on the cover of only one album, sharing space with the King. Yankovic produced the album, which cost about five thousand dollars. He took 60 percent of the sales and gave Maupin 40 percent. That happened after Maupin's daughter was born retarded. "Why are you doing this?" Maupin asked Yankovic. "Never mind, I got my reasons," Yankovic said. Maupin suspects Yankovic made the gesture out of sympathy for his daughter. The record sold well.

As close as they were, the two got into a bar fight in Milwaukee. "He hit me in the nose," recalled Maupin. "I tried to fight back but I couldn't do anything. They were holding me back. He had a lot of friends wherever we went. Later he claimed he got mad because I didn't give him two weeks' notice that I was quitting."

"We had a lot of arguments on the road," said Ray Smolik, a Yankovic pianist. "They were nothing important. You're traveling and you argue. It's almost like passing time. He wasn't the easiest guy to work for, but he treated me well enough. He always picked on the new guys.

"Once he tried to drive the bus through four feet of snow and it wouldn't move. So he just laughed and said, 'The hell with it.' We stayed there and had a good time on the bus."

Musically, Yankovic tried to stay current. He incorporated comparatively modern songs such as "Proud Mary" and "Somewhere My Love" and "Please Release Me" into his repertoire. In Nashville, he played before a crowd of ten thousand with Johnny Cash, Jerry Lee Lewis, and the Everly Brothers and held his own. Popovich understood the King's singing talent. "If he would have concentrated on the blues or country music, instead of polkas, he would have been on the cover of *Rolling Stone* magazine," Popovich said. "He always gave the people their money's worth."

Yankovic branched out to do a wider variety of music than other polka leaders, recording novelty songs such as "Who Stole the Kishka," a Polish number, and "I Wish I Was 18 Again," a country tune. He incorporated country, Western, and pop songs into his repertoire on the road to attract a broader audience that crossed all ethnic lines.

Cleveland accordionist Art Perko recalled a long trip on which Yankovic brought some tents for sleeping. Two of the musicians refused to sleep on the ground and went to a hotel instead. When they went back to find Yankovic the next morning, he was gone. They had to get to the next job by bus.

His hearing gave him more and more trouble as he aged. At a wedding in Iowa, he sang a solo that received much applause. Near the bandstand a woman yelled for him to sing "Spanish Eyes," one of his favorite numbers. Bathing in the applause, he could not hear her. "Thank you, thank you," he said to her. He thought she was screaming in delight over the previous number.

Bobby, his son, remembered Yankovic's driving habits. "He always took the back roads because he figured he could get away with more there. I miss him. If I ever wrote a book about him the title would be *Traveling the Back Roads*."

Chapter Twenty-Seven

Bobby Goes to Jail

YANKOVIC LIVED A LIFE that was full of highs and lows. The nadir of his old age came when his youngest son, Bobby, was convicted of robbery and sent to prison. "Frankie's health started failing when Bobby was put in prison," Ida recalled. "That actually killed my husband and I'm not afraid to say that. He was very proud of having Bobby in his band, even though they fought like cats and dogs. They were both stubborn. But Bobby must have been his favorite. When it happened, he said, 'Look what Bobby did. I have nothing to live for now. Why don't I just die.'"

Bobby resembled Yankovic more than any of his other sons did, except that he was born with a slight upward paralysis on the right side of his mouth. He was self-conscious about it. "People said it looked cute but it bothered me all my life," he said. "I had a crooked smile and I didn't like myself. I don't think Dad realized how much it hurt me. He kept telling me to smile onstage. Joey Miskulin told me if it worried me that much I should see a doctor." Bobby underwent plastic surgery.

He has the same kind of extroverted personality as his father, with more humor. At his brother Johnny's wedding reception, Bobby jumped on the stage, played the banjo, and sang. Everybody loved it. Yankovic encouraged him to take banjo lessons so he could go on the road with him.

"I took three crash lessons from Ron Sluga and Dad thought that was enough," Bobby said. "I started practicing. Next thing I knew I was on tour with Dad. The banjo was expendable onstage. He and Joey were the important ones, but I played and also sold his CDs. He tried to practice with me on the banjo in the motor home, showing me how to change keys. That was a nightmare. He was always yelling at me. I loved Dad, but there were times I wanted to hit him over the head with the banjo, especially when he yelled at me onstage." Bobby would answer back angrily.

Yankovic, in turn, was hurt. "My own son, my own son," he bellowed. "Nobody ever talked back to me, but my own son yelled at me."

Even the great Miskulin was not safe from Yankovic's darts. "If he didn't play the song the way he wanted it, Dad would make him go back and play it again and again," Bobby remembered. "He forced him to learn and look where he is now." Yankovic never complimented his musicians for playing well. If he did not say anything about their work they knew he was pleased. But he would climb all over them if they made too many mistakes.

Secretly, Yankovic was highly pleased with Bobby's showmanship and flair. He bragged to a friend, "My son is a son of a bitch onstage," meaning that he could command attention with his singing and playing. Bobby had no problem adjusting to the rough-and-tumble existence of the road. Sometimes four musicians would sleep in two beds in a hotel. "Boy, did Dad snore," Bobby recalled.

He picked up a lot of show business savvy from Yankovic, the consummate professional onstage. When the band played before a rare small crowd of about a hundred in a North Dakota barn, he told his musicians, "We've got to work twice as hard because there's less people." They would finish playing one job, then drive to another town and get up at 5 or 6 a.m. to do a radio interview. Yankovic might have been tough on musicians, but he could also be extremely kind. "He would play in nursing homes for nothing, just to see certain people he used to know," Bobby said. He was a regular visitor to his sister, Mary, who was in a nursing home for several years before her death.

His years on the road with his father are among the highlights of Bobby's life. "I had the opportunity of a lifetime," he said. "At the time I didn't always think it was fun, but when I look back it was a great experience." The apex came when he played on the Johnny Carson show after Yankovic won his Grammy.

He remains steadfastly loyal to his father. "I've heard people knock him as a musician, especially in Cleveland," Bobby said. "But he had charisma. There was just something about him. I don't think there's another polka musician who could do what he did. I don't care how many Grammys they win, how many shows they do, there's only one Frank Yankovic, just like there was only one Elvis Presley. As Joey once told me, there could be a hundred musicians better than you, but if you've got the feel for it, people can tell."

Bobby played with the Yanks on weekends and whenever he was on vacation, for about a decade. At the same time, he was working as a heating and cooling inspector for the City of Cleveland and taking courses at Cuyahoga Community College. His life began to crash when he suffered a splitting headache while sitting in his office in January 1994. He lost consciousness and was rushed to a hospital. He had suffered a brain aneurysm. He underwent two brain surgeries and spent three months in the hospital. Bobby recovered completely and expected to resume playing with the Yankovic band. However, he was told he could not rejoin the band for medical reasons.

"That ripped me apart," Bobby recalled. "I asked myself, 'Why is this happening to me?'" Another blow came when Bobby and his girlfriend split up. He was depressed and turned to liquor and drugs. He committed holdups in small stores on Cleveland's West Side, wearing a bandana over his face and using a starter's pistol, not something that could shoot bullets. "He did it to get money to buy more drugs," a family member said. "He got in with the wrong people. He wasn't thinking straight." Bobby was caught after holding up a cleaning establishment. Police told *The Plain Dealer* he was suspected of netting about twenty-six hundred dollars from robberies at gas stations, a drugstore, a restaurant, and a grocery store. He was convicted on two counts of aggravated robbery and sentenced to seven to twenty-five years on each count, the sentences to run concurrently.

"I could not believe what I did," Bobby recalled. "The son of Frank Yankovic doing robberies. It embarrassed the family. It hurt my dad. I did something stupid, but the support he gave me was unbelievable. I served my time. It saved my life."

Bobby was first sent to Lima Correctional Institution, then to Grafton Correctional Institution. Yankovic visited him numerous times. "He didn't yell or cry when he came to see me," said Bobby. "He just shook his head and gave me that look. It killed him. It killed me."

"I don't understand," Yankovic would say sadly. "You know I would give you anything." Bobby would hug and kiss him and tell him he loved him. Yankovic would constantly write letters to his son, to such an extent that Bobby felt agitated he had to write back so much. Yankovic would tell him he had a natural feel for music and that he was proud of him, trying to encourage him. He wrote to the warden, telling him Bobby was a good son, and he told his friends to write to Bobby. "I would get letters from people I didn't even know," Bobby said. June, with whom he was very close, also visited him in the minimum-security prison.

"My biggest supporters were my sister, Andrea, and my brother, Frank," Bobby said. "Andrea would put food boxes together and send me canned meats, canned goods, candy, clothes, and tennis shoes." Bobby tried to show his family he was handling the situation well. He was going to school and playing in four or five bands in prison. In Grafton, his fellow inmates wanted him to start a polka band. Bobby would entertain them by singing "Just Because" and "E-I-E-I-E-I-O," just like his father, and they would sing along with him. Everybody in Grafton, just outside Cleveland, knew who his father was. They would tease Bobby, calling him "Big Money." Bobby would reply, "And don't you forget it." The other convicts could not understand how Bobby could be imprisoned. They felt that anybody with the kind of money his father must have had should be able to beat a rap.

Bobby did not resent his incarceration. "I did the crime and did my time," he said. "I told Dad, 'I'm doing OK here. I'm studying and learning about myself.' There are tough penitentiaries for certain crimes, but where I was the old-timers called it 'the camp.' There were programs. If you wanted to better yourself, you could do it."

Yankovic told many people he would gladly trade places with Bobby and go to prison if his son could be released. "He's too young to be in there," Yankovic said. Bobby was still doing time when age and illness began to grip Yankovic. He could not visit him as often as he wanted. But he still kept up the encouragement. "When you get out, we'll go on the road again," he wrote in a letter. They often talked on the phone. "Bobby, I feel like I'm giving up," he said in one conversation.

"When he told me that I knew he was going to die," Bobby said. "I never heard my father talk like that. He was a working machine. He wanted to keep going so he wouldn't think about things. He helped so many people. A lot of people used him."

After serving five years, Bobby was released from prison. He was grateful that he was freed before his mother died in August 2001. He was able to see her while she was still alive.

Bobby now lives in a house he owns in Lakewood. He is as personable and friendly as ever. He and his girlfriend, Tamara, have a beautiful blond daughter, Kristalynn, three, and are planning to get married. Tamara also has a daughter, Stephanie, six. Bobby wants to finish college. He needs one more course credit to graduate from Tri-C. Then he would like to go to Cleveland State University. "I'm doing good," he said. Thoughts of getting back into music are never far away.

Chapter Twenty-Eight

The Final Act

IN 1989, WHEN HE was seventy-four, Yankovic told Ida he was ready to cut back on his workload and move to a warm climate. He gave her three options and told her to pick one locale for their old age: Las Vegas, Arizona, or Florida. She chose Florida on the grounds it would be easier for their children to visit them from Cleveland and Pittsburgh. They talked about building a new home but finally decided to move into a retirement village in New Port Richey, where the ownership took care of the gardening and cut the grass.

The sun-loving Yankovic went to the pool or ocean every day, but he soon grew weary of the idleness. In Florida he was just another old-timer counting the days. He was no longer the King. Few people there knew who he was. He had no hobbies. He liked golf, but when walking the course was too much and he had to ride a cart, he saw no point in playing. He needed more action. He wrote letters to Bobby, saying, "I don't know what to do with myself. These people are too old."

"He felt selling the house in Euclid was a mistake," Bobby recalled. "He wanted to keep going. He enjoyed the travel. I wish he had died onstage, doing what he wanted."

Up north, Yankovic was still remembered. When he turned seventy-five in 1990, *The Plain Dealer* took note on the editorial page, calling him the Aladdin of the Accordion. "Congratulations to Frankie Yankovic on his 75th birthday," the newspaper said. "Like Detroit's love for Motown, like New Orleans' affection for jazz, Cleveland has had a decades-old romance with the polka.

The polka harkens to a sliver of Cleveland history when Slovenes came home from factories to dance and play away their day's toil on accordions. Forgotten for a few hours were the hardships of being immigrants, their drudgery replaced by polka revelry. Thanks, Frankie, and the happiest of birthdays."

He was constantly being offered jobs and he took as many as his aging body would allow. Ida continued to accompany him much of the time, but not always. They would stay in Bobby's home while performing around Cleveland. Often they stayed for a week at a time. He liked to watch Bobby's team play softball. Bobby told him he didn't have to come, but he said, "I want to." He was trying to make up for all the things he had missed as an absentee father.

Andrea, his daughter, has nice memories of his visits to her home in Avon Lake. Her son, Patrick, played hockey and Yankovic was very interested in that, questioning the youth about the game. He went to the team's practice and enjoyed it. Andrea's son, Mark, played the piano for Yankovic. "That was really a great moment," Andrea recalled. "Just to have my father sit there and listen and be a grandfather. That meant more to me than anything he ever did onstage. He would stay three or four days with us."

Andrea was the central figure in another heartwarming Yankovic performance. He was being honored at a Pennsylvania ceremony and was singing and playing when she suddenly joined him onstage, an unplanned surprise. She sang "Smile, Sweetheart, Smile," one of his old hits. Yankovic was delighted and joined her in the duet. For Frank Jr., who was also present, it is his favorite memory of his father. "That was the time he showed the most love," he said.

By this time, Yankovic was treated as an icon in Cleveland. Many of the musicians who had scorned his playing in the old days were gone, or their views had mellowed. When he attended concerts at Slovenian halls he was the object of much love and wonder from the newer fans. Sitting quietly in his chair, he was, as always, pleasant to all who approached him to say hello, get his autograph, or shake his hand. When he stood, he was bent. His height shrank to about five feet, five inches.

As he approached eighty, he acknowledged his declining appearance. "I know I don't look good on the bandstand," he said. "It don't look right. I see the pictures people take of me. These kids [his fellow musicians] are next to me, jumping around, and I look like an old grandfather. I have to sit down to play. If I was smart, I'd quit, but it's hard to do. I'm not looking for work, but if somebody calls me I'll make a guest appearance."

He feared retirement. "What am I gonna do with myself after all these years of being active?" he exclaimed. "That's the tough question. It's not going to be easy. I'll have a lot of time to hold hands with Ida. I'm lucky I have her. She takes good care of me. I don't think I'd be playing the last year or two if it wasn't for her. She came into my life at the right time, when I needed somebody."

He insisted he was virtually retired, but his itinerary showed that in July, August, and September of 1995, when he was eighty, he had performed in Louisville for an Eagles Convention and in Cross Creek, Pennsylvania, Janesville, Wisconsin, and Sheridan, Wyoming; at the Pittsburgh Italian Fest and the 185th Street Festival in Cleveland; and in Columbus and Punxatawney, Pennsylvania. "The mayor gave me the key to the city in Punxatawney," he said. "They picked me up in a big limo."

Yankovic often visited his daughter-in-law, Beth, widow of Johnny. He pitched a whiffle ball to Beth's son, John Jr., when he was little. When John, a tight end and defensive end, played football for Brush High School in Lyndhurst, Yankovic attended some games. He watched Brush games on tape. "He was really into what his grandchildren were doing," Beth recalled. "I liked him very much. He had to have his hot milk every night before bed, and it had to be pretty darn hot. And he loved soup. He would live off it if he could. He loved ice cream too. The big thing for him was to take the kids for ice cream. He loved animals and kids. He was always bringing us dogs."

Yankovic's bad hearing became a joke with the family because he would never admit he had a problem. He always told Beth she talked too quietly. "Beth, you gotta talk louder," he would say. He was not interested in wearing his hearing aid, which always seemed to be getting lost. He never played the accordion or talked about polkas while relaxing at Beth's house.

Yankovic was on many prescriptions for ailments such as heart trouble, back pain, deafness, and dementia. He carried all the pills in a container, different ones for each illness. Once he spilled the whole case and Beth had to call Ida in Florida to get them lined up correctly. Many of the pills were generic, with no name on them. It took the women a couple of hours on the phone to get them in order, so Yankovic would know which ones to take and the hour he should take them.

Beth praised Ida too. "She was very nice and worked hard for him as manager and wife," she recalled. "She lifted a load off him. He never thought he was going to be old. He didn't think that way. He had energy almost until the end. He was bionic. He was happy in his profession and happy with each of his marriages, and at times happy with his children. Life can change in a minute."

Another of his stopping-off places when he came north was at the Youngstown home of Dorothy Kravos Hock, his niece. He would sit in a big leather chair in Dorothy's living room, his feet propped up, sleeping. On occasion, she thought he was taking his last breath. A couple of months before his death, Dorothy said, "Uncle Frank, you're not just going to sit around and mope today. I'm taking you to Enon Valley." He jumped up and said that was a good idea. Yankovic, the ultimate extrovert, loved to be with people. It was a weekday in the fall and the campground was not crowded. Yankovic went to the SNPJ Heritage Room at Enon and spent three hours looking at photos of musicians, leaders of the labor movement, and old friends, reading everything. "I knew him," he would say, pointing at a photo. It is a memory that Dorothy cherishes. She still gets tears in her eyes when she hears a polka band playing the "Blue Skirt Waltz."

Rose Keba, who lives in a Cleveland suburb, was another favorite niece. She would make barley soup and kidney stew for Yankovic, the kinds of ethnic foods he loved. Like the others, Rose always had hot milk ready for him before he went to bed, but she recalled that he liked tea spiked with whiskey, too.

One of the saddest experiences of the era came when Yankovic was eighty. He was nominated for a Grammy for the fourth time. Yankovic, using a walker, was accompanied to the ceremony by Ida, Miskulin, Petkovsek, and Popovich. It was a fine album. There were high hopes that the King would win the award again. However, it went to Sturr. Ida, who was at the Grammy ceremony for the first time, took the defeat harder than anybody. "When Jimmy Sturr's name was announced I fell apart," she recalled. "I cried. It wasn't fair. It was such a good album and Jimmy had already won so many before. I thought surely they were going to give this one to Frankie, being up in age. Frankie was okay. He took it in stride." She did not go to the Grammy party that night, giving her ticket to a friend. Ten years after the disappointment, Ida still cried when she talked about it.

"He felt depressed after that one," Ostanek recalled. "I think he knew it was his last hurrah."

But he kept going. In 1995, Brian Sklar, leader of the Western Senators band, wanted him to perform again in Edmonton, Canada, but he was hesitant about asking Yankovic because of the King's frail health. He thought he should postpone the trip until the spring because of the fierce Canadian winter. "Do it now," Ostanek advised. "He might not last that long." Yankovic joined Ostanek to perform for Sklar on a tour of Saskatchewan. He and Ida arrived in a snowstorm. Yankovic was prepared for the tough weather, wearing a new coat with a fur collar. Sklar was not sorry he extended the invitation. Yankovic was a big hit. "When Yankovic walked into a dance hall there was a spontaneous outpouring of affection," recalled Sklar, a media specialist for the Edmonton legislature. "I was blown away. You had to get a hook to get him off the stage. He was a man after my own heart."

Yankovic had one more reunion with Miskulin. They performed at Ironworld in Chisholm, Minnesota, and in Calgary, Alberta, Canada. Yankovic visited Miskulin in his studio in Nashville, where they recorded, most appropriately, a song called "For Old Times' Sake." "It was the end of a thirty-six-year journey," Miskulin said. "Good times and bad, I wouldn't trade the experiences and knowledge I gained from him for anything."

Yankovic had another disappointment in the 1990s, when he and the band were to play at the Kennedy Performing Arts Center in Washington, D.C. He had to back out because of ill health, but accordionist Frank Moravcik fulfilled the engagement, along with Ron Sluga, Eric Noltkamper, and accordionist Dan Peters. The show was a big success. The band played for an hour and a half to the acclaim of the crowd. Moravcik told the audience about Yankovic's long career. Many listeners told stories of their own about the King. It is the only time a polka band ever appeared in the arts center. Moravcik said Yankovic was his inspiration. He often joined him in gigs around Ohio and surrounding states in the 1990s.

In that same period, Yankovic had another bad accident while driving to Florida. His car hit a truck and slammed into a guardrail. The truck driver did not realize his vehicle had been hit and just kept going. Yankovic was found wandering around a field in a daze. "He probably had a concussion and didn't know it," Ostanek said. "He didn't drive much after that."

Grant Kozera, the Milwaukee accordionist who was a longtime Yankovic sideman, said it was painful to see him deteriorate. "We tried to preserve him," Kozera said. "He always wanted to be the workhorse, but we'd do more of the playing and driving." Yankovic's hands began shaking one night on the stage. He was staring with a blank look on his face. Kozera called paramedics and they took him to a hospital.

He was discharged shortly after, but Kozera wrote him a long letter, urging him to stop performing. It was a difficult thing for

Kozera to do. Yankovic was his idol. Still is. The heartfelt letter made Yankovic and Ida cry. They knew Kozera wanted only the best for him, and they knew their young friend was right.

A happier moment came in 1996, when the King attended a Cleveland Indians baseball game at Jacobs Field on his eighty-first birthday. He was surprised and delighted to see a message on the huge electronic scoreboard: WELCOME FRANKIE YANKOVIC, AMERICA'S POLKA KING. He received a big hand from the patrons and signed autographs in the ballpark the rest of the night.

His hearing was getting worse and worse. Once, he called Ida frantically, yelling, "I lost my hearing aid. Help me find it. I can't hear anything." They spent fifteen frantic minutes looking for it. "Oh, never mind, I just found it," Yankovic said. "It's in my ear." Ida laughed so hard she almost fell on the floor.

Once he fainted while playing at a Veterans of Foreign Wars event in Florida. He was taken outside for some fresh air. After fifteen minutes he went back to the stage, against the advice of friends, and finished the job. Another time, he was practicing his accordion when Ida said she had to leave their house for a routine visit to a doctor. She warned him not to do anything foolish. He promised he wouldn't. When Ida came home, a neighbor told her Yankovic was in the hospital. He had fallen off a stepladder in the garage. There was blood all over the garage floor. Ida was so upset she was shaking. She hurried to the hospital emergency room and found Yankovic had suffered a concussion. Seventeen stitches were put in his head. He said he had been trying to reach some albums that he had stacked high in the garage. "Don't you feel sorry for me, Ida?" he said plaintively.

"No," said Ida, who was relieved he was not hurt even worse. "I told you to behave yourself." Yankovic had hurt his back so badly he had to sleep on his stomach in one position for several weeks, increasing his discomfort.

Ostanek visited him frequently in Florida. One day they were sitting in the family room, staring at the television. There was no conversation. Suddenly Yankovic said, "Want a beer?" Ostanek refused. A few minutes later, Yankovic repeated the question and again Ostanek refused. "Well, I'm going to have one," Yankovic said. "Well, then, I'll have one too," said Ostanek. Yankovic went into the kitchen and brought out two beers.

"You know, Walter," he said, referring to his feebleness. "I never thought this would happen to me."

Ostanek felt the same. "In my heart, I thought he would never die," he said. "I thought he'd be here forever. When he was in the coffin, I expected him to raise a finger and say, 'One more time.'"

Yankovic suffered from congestive heart failure. "His heart was getting weaker and weaker," Ida recalled. "But he wouldn't give up the music. We could see him slipping, hitting sour notes on stage." He had the best of medical care in Florida and was in and out of the hospital several times. Yankovic wanted surgery to have a pacemaker installed. He and Ida flew to Rochester, Minnesota, for the operation.

The day after the surgery he and Ida had a long talk. He told her he had never been able to talk to his two previous wives the way he talked to her. She asked him why he had eight children in his first marriage when he was on the road so much, and then two more in his second marriage. "I always thought it was up to the women to decide how many kids we were going to have," Yankovic said. All of his children came to Florida to visit him near the end.

He sincerely regretted he had been away from them for so long as they were growing up. "I never played baseball with them, or swam with them, or was chummy with them," he said. "But I did what I thought was best. I tried to make a good living for them."

One of Yankovic's last major performances came four months before his death, on June 3, 1998, when a crowd of twelve hundred came to the SNPJ Farm in Kirtland on a weekday afternoon. It was a combined good-bye to Yankovic and a fund-raiser for the Cleveland-Style Polka Hall of Fame. Yankovic did not play much, but he sang. Norman Fuerst, the judge who had married the King and Ida, attended. He had known Yankovic since he was in the navy during World War II. Fuerst, then a young bachelor, would visit Yankovic's bar for the music and fun while he was home on leave. Now they were both old men. Yankovic hugged him and cried.

The next month, Ida had a surprise party for Yankovic at their house. He told her to put his accordion on his lap so he could play for the guests. He could not play anymore without fumbling. "Ida, take this accordion and burn it," he said. "I can't do it no more."

"We knew he would never retire unless he just couldn't pick up his accordion anymore," Andrea said. "That's what happened. It broke his heart."

Nevertheless, Yankovic performed almost to the end. About three weeks before he died, he had a singing engagement in Pennsylvania. When he was young, his voice had been light and strong. Now it was deep and full of character on songs such as "That Silver-Haired Daddy of Mine" and "I Wish I Was 18 Again." Wolnik was with him. "He was ill, old," Wolnik recalled. "I wondered how he was going to sing, but when the bell rang he went out there. He couldn't hear well and he forgot the words. But the people went nuts. They had tears in their eyes. When he finished he signed autographs. I'll remember it forever. Every job was a total adventure, traveling with the King. I miss the guy dearly." His last performance was at the Cuyahoga County Fair in Berea, again to audience acclaim.

In New Port Richey, Ida would come into the family room and see tears flowing from his eyes as he sat in the recliner watching TV. He missed his children. He missed the old action. He missed Cleveland. He had nursing care around the clock. A month before he died, they sold the house in New Port Richey and planned to move back to his hometown. Before the sale was finalized, he was gone. The night before his death, he sat up in his bed and took Ida's hand. "I love you more than anything in the world," he said.

"I love you too, Frankie," she said. He lay back, his pulse getting weaker and weaker. Death came quietly and peacefully.

After the massive funeral, Ida sent ten thousand dollars to each of Yankovic's children. Several felt they were shortchanged in the will and blamed it on Ida. "They thought Frankie had a lot of money," she said. "He didn't. I was accused of instigating him not to leave them more money. But he had told me what he wanted to leave each of the children. I did as he requested."

"I'm disappointed," one of the children said. "Even in death we were left on the outside."

The value of his estate is unknown. Ostanek, who knew him as well as anybody, said he was a millionaire at one time, but not at the end. A family member guessed he had about two hundred thousand dollars in cash.

Ida moved back to Pennsylvania to live with her daughter. After a year or so, she wanted to be independent and moved into a double mobile home. She lives there today. She is a caregiver for the aged mother-in-law of Marty (King) Kukovich, one of Yankovic's old bass players. The lady had been released from a nursing home, where Ida had visited her. Her daughter told Ida they were looking for somebody to stay with her. Ida quickly accepted. It would get her mind off the depression she felt with Yankovic's death.

Ida was determined to keep Yankovic's memory alive. She continues to sell his tapes and records, advertising in various polka and Slovenian newspapers. One thing bothers Wolnik. "There isn't one street in Cleveland named for him," he said. "He deserves it. Nobody put Cleveland on the map for as long as he did."

Chapter Twenty-Nine

Yankovic's Legacy

IN 1963 TONY PETKOVSEK, who had recently started his Cleveland polka radio program, decided to throw a dance. The twenty-three-year-old's motives were twofold. He would be promoting polka music and creating attention for his show. Petkovsek knew exactly where he wanted to have the dance. It would be at the legendary Slovenian National Home on East 64th Street and St. Clair Avenue, where so many concerts, weddings, and dances had been held since 1924.

It was not as easy to pick a date. At first, he thought of holding it on a Saturday or Sunday night. But that was too mundane. He wanted a special kind of night, something that would add meaning to the event. Someone suggested the night of Thanksgiving Day. Petkovsek was not certain about that. Most people stayed home and ate turkey on the holiday, or watched the Detroit Lions play the Green Bay Packers on television. But he finally decided to take the chance, renting the hall and advertising the dance on his program. There was an unforeseen worry. President Kennedy was assassinated the week before and many people were still mourning, disdaining social activities. Nevertheless, the dance was an immediate hit. More than seven hundred people jammed into the hall for the first big Cleveland polka dance since the rock-and-roll revolution.

Yankovic and his Yanks were the most prized guests among the roster of bands. They had driven hundreds of miles to be there. Yankovic refused to take any payment for his performance. He recognized a kindred spirit in Petkovsek, someone who was anxious to perpetuate polkas. Anybody who did that was Yankovic's friend. "I'll come here for every dance you hold," he told Petkovsek. "And I'll play for free." At the time, Yankovic was forty-eight years old, still as dynamic as ever. His presence legitimized the show. Yankovic was true to his word. For the next thirty-five years, until his death, he always played at the dance, once flying in from the West Coast at the last minute. He missed only once, when he was hospitalized.

Petkovsek is a quiet, canny promoter. He has been on radio daily since 1961. For the last twenty-five years, he has been performing out of WELW in Willoughby, reaching listeners in Cleveland, Euclid, and points east. The program is simulcast worldwide on the Internet at 247polkaheaven.com. Petkovsek owns almost half of WELW. Ray Somich, the majority owner, gives the polkas full support. Petkovsek's Thanksgiving dances have become an institution, expanded to an entire weekend. People come from all over the country and Canada to attend the polka party.

After nineteen years at the St. Clair Slovenian Home, Petkovsek moved the dances to the even larger hall at St. Joseph High School for eight years. The event was transferred to the downtown Cleveland Stouffer's Hotel (now the Renaissance) in 1990. Since 1992 the festivities have been at the nearby Marriott Hotel. The Marriott offers the polka lovers free parking and special room rates negotiated by Petkovsek. People begin arriving on Wednesday night and stay through Sunday, partying and dancing. It is a veritable polka convention, although there are no meetings or speeches. It is all about having fun. *Plain Dealer* publisher Alex Machaskee and his Serbian tamburitza band, The Continental Strings, have played at the event. Machaskee, who retired from *The Plain Dealer* in 2006, has been a major supporter of the polka fete for decades, running free advertisements in the newspaper. In gratitude, the Polka Hall of Fame gave him its trustees' award.

The action starts on Thanksgiving Eve, when accordionists and other musicians jam and drink at various polka hotbeds. These sessions are an outgrowth of the Thanksgiving dance. Before the St. Clair neighborhood deteriorated, the first Thanksgiving Eve jamborees were held at Mihcic's Tavern on East 72nd Street and St. Clair. The saloon would be crammed with a cross-section of people. You might see a Cleveland Browns player or two, swells from Chagrin Falls or Hunting Valley, lawyers, sportswriters, and policemen.

Brothers Zeke and Charlie Vrtovsnik led the house band. Zeke, an Ohio Bell telephone company executive whose real name was Edward, played the cheesebox. Charley, a repairman for the East Ohio Gas Company, strummed the banjo and sang. Their fiery music was aided and abetted by accordionists Steve Valencic, Tony Spendal, Frank Zitko, Frank Zitko Jr., and Marty Sintic, bass players Don Slapnik and Marion Belle, and drummers Wolnik and John Gerl. Zeke, the Slovenian Don Rickles, threw hilarious insults at certain patrons while playing the best second parts in Cleveland-style polka music. The drinking would be heavy and the dancing exuberant.

Zeke, seventy-one, died in 2004 and Charley retired after a stroke. But their spirit carried over into other polka havens. Fritz's Tavern, on East 185th Street, would also be packed wall to wall with polka people on Thanksgiving Eve. Today most of the action has shifted to the St. Clair Slovenian Home annex, which has a sixty-foot bar and has room for about 250 patrons. Various bands rotate on the stage as the listeners dance, drink, and eat roast beef and sausage sandwiches. The same scene can be found in the Slovenian Society Home clubroom in Euclid.

The centerpiece of the week is still the Thanksgiving Day dance in the Marriott ballroom. About two thousand people attended in 2004. Polka buses delivered fans from Canada, Michigan, Wisconsin, and New York. The Marriott registered guests from New Jersey, Illinois, Texas, Florida, Colorado, Arizona, Maryland, California, New Mexico, Tennessee, Pennsylvania, Minnesota, and Connecticut.

A dozen people came from the Netherlands, where the Cleveland-style polka is enjoying a spurt of popularity. Several politicians, including U.S. senator George Voinovich, were on hand. (Petkovsek has become one of Voinovich's most important aides, often serving as master of ceremonies at his fund-raising dinners at places such as the Landerhaven Party Center.) Weatherman Dick Goddard, Cleveland TV's most popular personality, showed up to sing "April Showers." Ten bands, including Ostanek's, provided dance music from 4 p.m. to past midnight. "Just Because" and the "Blue Skirt Waltz" were played several times. Ida was there. Yankovic's memory was never far away.

On Friday, the next night, the revelry continued. A polka dance contest was held. The winners were Milan "Potsy" Jenovic and his partner, Nancy Glass, and Frank Vidmar and partner Cheryl Pittard. Both couples performed the seldom-seen full pivot in a manner that would have done credit to Fred Astaire, whirling around the floor with continuous grace. To many, this was the highlight of the entire week. If the polka is ever to come back into the mainstream, it is the full pivot that may lead it. The athleticism and style necessary to perform this difficult step would appeal to the younger crowd. The Polka Movement, as Petkovsek calls it, is awaiting a change in societal attitudes and a hit song to catapult the music back into the front ranks, at least for a while, as Yankovic did with his million-sellers.

On Saturday afternoon, the Cleveland-Style Polka Hall of Fame handed out its awards at the Euclid High School auditorium, with Somich as the capable and humorous master of ceremonies. A full house of about fifteen hundred saw the Grammy-style show, which cost about thirty thousand dollars to stage. Many winners and performers wore tuxedos. Bob Kravos, Yankovic's great-nephew, was a triple winner. He was chosen Musician of the Year, his band was voted the year's best, and he and Ostanek shared the award for the recording of the year, "Just for You." Christine Hibbs, a pretty mother of two who lives in Chesterland, was named the top vocalist. Ron Likovic was chosen best button box player. Top sidemen were Sluga, Gerl, and Eric Noltkamper; veteran singers Eddie Kenik and Paul Yanchar brought nostalgic tears to many eyes with their rendition of "O, Ja Waltz," named one of the all-time top songs.

Accordionist George Staiduhar was honored for lifetime achievement. Staiduhar, a court reporter, is one of the most precise and exhilarating players in Cleveland polka history. Polka legend Eddie Platt, a saxophonist and singer with the old Johnny Pecon band, received a trustees' honor roll award. Bill Randle, the broadcasting friend of the polka, received a posthumous honor. Then it was back to the Marriott for a "Meet the Winners" dance that night. The week concluded with a Polka Mass at the Marriott before Saturday night's dance. Rev. Edward Pevec, auxiliary bishop of the Cleveland Roman Catholic diocese, officiated, assisted by the Polka Priest, Father Frank Perkovich of Minnesota.

The Hall of Fame show hit another grand slam in 2005, when Joey Miskulin returned with the other members of Riders in the Sky. Dressed in Western outfits, the globe-trotting group delighted another huge audience with its effortlessly entertaining numbers. Jeff Pecon and Miskulin sang a duet of "Cleveland the Polka Town." Hibbs won the best singer award again and Yankovic's old sideman, banjo-playing Ron Sluga, now seventy, won the lifetime achievement award. Ostanek joined Canadian Brian Sklar and the Western Senators in a musical tribute to Yankovic. "Let's Have a Party" was named to the list of greatest all-time polka songs. The Hall of Fame All Star band, including Ostanek, Pecon, Miskulin, and Yanchar, completed the rousing finale.

Polkas may be sagging a bit in the midriff, but the beat continues to percolate, especially in the Cleveland-Youngstown-Pittsburgh belt. Continuing to perform are bands headed by the Pecons, Ed and Chuck Sumrada, Bob Kravos, Fred Ziwich, Eddie Rodick, Joe Novak, Ray Polantz, Don Wojtila, Wayne Tomsic, Joey Tomsick, Don Slogar, Hank Haller, and Frank Moravcik, all

Clevelanders. Frank Culkar, a seventy-three-year-old master of the chromatic accordion, and his son, Anthony, thirteen, a piano accordionist, are increasingly popular. Anthony also plays the piano, saxophone, and clarinet. Ziwich, a professional musican with a degree from the University of Indiana, plays about 140 gigs a year with his band, the International Sound Machine. One of his many recordings was a tribute to Yankovic.

Frankie Spetich has been an accordion institution in Barberton for years. Dr. Tony Adamle, the football player who once captained the Cleveland Browns, played in Spetich's button box group until his death. Del Sinchak and Eddie Vallus are still going strong in Youngstown. Dick and Jack Tady and Sam Pugliano lead the Pittsburgh contingent. Al Battistelli is a Lorain virtuoso. When he played solo at the the Button Box Bash auction, a listener in the audience bid a thousand dollars to hear him play the William Tell Overture. To many fans, retired Jake Zagger of Warren was the finest of all button entertainers. Others vote for Bobby Zgonc, from Pittsburgh, or Clevelander Ron Likovic. The Captain and His Crew, led by retired Cleveland police detective Kenny Zalar and featuring smiling Kathy Hlad, are currently the most popular button box group.

The SNPJ Circle 2 Chorus, directed by Polka Hall of Fame president Cecilia Dolgan, has been putting on the yearly Button Box Bash at the Slovenian Society Home every April since 1983. It lasts all day with a dozen cheesebox groups taking turns on the two stages. More than a thousand people attend.

Radio shows are hosted by Dale and Denny Bucar, sons of veteran polkacaster Eddie Bucar, Val Pawlowski, Joe and Gene Fedorchak, Del Sinchak, Jack Tady, Sam Pugliano, Sharon Ujcich, Pauline Anderson, Joe Godina, and Ray Zalokar, in addition to Petkovsek and Ostry. Locally produced "247 Polka Heaven.com" has a worldwide audience on the Internet. "Polka Polka Polka," produced by Cleveland musician Phil Srnick, is seen on Adelphia cable TV in several cities. The *Polka News*, published in St.

Charles, Michigan, and the *Polka Times*, Pittsburgh, are monthly newspapers that serve readers all over the country. Cleveland's hundred-year-old *American Home* newspaper, published three times monthly, is a leading beacon for all things Slovenian, including polkas.

The Polka Hall of Fame Museum, located in Euclid, Ohio, is open five days a week and attracts about four thousand visitors a year. The accordions of Yankovic and Pecon are on display, along with many other artifacts. The museum has one of the largest collections of polka albums in the world. About two hundred albums are sold every month in the gift shop. In addition, polka historians such as Don Sosnoski, Joe Godina, Brian Juntikka, Bob Roth, and Chuck Debevec have vast personal collections of Yankovic records. Some, including Ostanek, have every record Yankovic ever made. Hoping for the big hit, musicians continue to produce their own polka albums, which sell anywhere from one thousand to five thousand copies. Hundreds of polka bands crisscross the nation.

When real estate man George Knaus and his brother-in-law, Joe Petrich, turned ninety-one in May 2005, they were the guests of honor at a huge polka party at the Slovenian Society Hall. Both men are thin, tall, and agile. The six-footers danced a polka together as the Pecons performed, just to give everybody a laugh. Petrich used to be a minor league baseball player and is an excellent pianist/accordionist. He and Knaus have the energy of forty-year-olds. It is scary to imagine the vigor they must have had in their twenties.

On the same night, Lynn Marie Rink flew in from Nashville to perform at the nearby Beachland Ballroom before another big crowd. She and Kathy Vogt, a button accordionist from St. Catharine's, played some stylish duets that drew huge cheers from the youthful audience, which usually listens to rock.

On a Wednesday in February 2006, throngs again descended on the Slovenian Society Home in Euclid for a benefit for Jake

Zagger's wife, Jackie, who was seriously ill. It was so crowded people had trouble getting to the bar. Numerous bands played all day and night. Even Zagger took the stage, with his old friend, Tony Trontel, also playing. The event, promoted by Bob Kravos Jr., raised ten thousand dollars.

Sometimes the polka beat is heard in unexpected venues, such as Nighttown restaurant, a jazz emporium in Cleveland Heights. A posh private communion party for the granddaughter of prominent attorney Charles Ipavec was held at Nighttown, with accordionist Wayne Tomsic and banjoist Joe Reboudo banging out polkas amidst the servings of shrimp and filet mignon. It was Nighttown's polka baptism.

To the accordion players and their followers, the Americanized Slovenian melodies are symbols of a better, safer era. They bring back memories of a million good times. The players and their audiences owe a debt to Yankovic. Had he never come along, polkas in America might be completely dead. He brought a lot of joy to a lot of people. That is his legacy.

Acknowledgments

I want to thank my wife, Cecilia, for conducting the interviews with Pat Yankovic and Ida Yankovic, the second and third wives of the Polka King, and for suggesting alterations and additions to the manuscript. Special thanks to Chuck Debevec, Joe Godina and Bob Roth for the massive task of compiling the Yankovic discography. Historian Don Sosnoski was always there to handle questions and clarify occurrences. I am indebted to Bobby Yankovic for his candid recollections and to Frank Yankovic Jr., Andrea McKinnie and Tricia Peters for their valuable insights into their father's story. Many thanks to Beth Yankovic Ianni for having the courage to talk about the death of her husband, Johnny. It was a pleasure to interview the musicians, disc jockeys and friends of the polka community, including Karen Anderson, Marion Belle, Ann Birsa, Ed Blazonczyk, Ed Blazonczyk Jr., Jay Broderson, Steve Brunton, Helenrae Budzilek, Denny Bucar, Anthony "Tops" Cardone, Bobby (Kolka) Chick, Georgie Cook, Mike Dragas, Joe Fedorchak, Dick Flaisman, Norman Fuerst, Sutton Girod, Ed Grosel, Eddie Habat, Kathy Hlad, Dorothy Hock, Brian Juntikka, Rose Keba, Dick Koss, Jim Kozel, Grant Kozera, Bob Kravos, Bob Kravos Jr., Fred Kuhar, Gene March, Jimmy Maupin, Joey Miskulin, Frank Moravcik, Frankie Mullec, Walter Ostanek, Ed Ostry, Carl Paradiso, Jeff Pecon, Art Perko, Tony Petkovsek, Eddie Platt, Steve Popovich, Frank Piccorillo, Lynn Marie Rink, Ron Sluga, Richie Vadnal, Brian Sklar, Ray Smolik, Jimmy Sturr, Jerry Suhar, Lou Trebar, Gloria Rado, Jeff Winard, Gail Witlicki and Dave Wolnik. Thanks to the National Cleveland-Style Polka Hall of Fame for contributions from its vast store of photos, and to all others who contributed photos, including the *Plain Dealer*, Ohio's largest newspaper.

Above all, thanks to Frankie Yankovic, for all the good times and memories.

Frank Yankovic Discography

This discography was compiled by Chuck Debevec, Joe Godina, and Bob Roth, all collectors of Yankovic's music. Debevec lives in Rush City, Minnesota; Godina in Hermitage, Pennsylvania; and Roth in Elgin, Illinois. They are separated by hundreds of miles but are united in their love for Cleveland-style polkas and Yankovic's melodies. Debevec and Godina are of Slovenian heritage. Roth is of German extraction. They got to know each other through e-mail in their hunt for Yankovic songs. All were attempting to put together their own discographies of the Polka King's music. When they heard this book was in production, they combined forces and undertook the Herculean effort of assembling this impressive package. Debevec, a retired computer electronics engineer, tracked down the 78s, 45s, and long-playing albums in the discography. Godina and Roth put together the CDs, cassettes, videos, and films. Godina is a retired construction worker and polka disc jockey on Sharon, Pennsylvania, radio. Yankovic was a friend of his family and bought him a set of straps for his accordion when the boy was only five years old. Roth is a retired mathematics teacher and was one of Yankovic's accordion players. He is an avid writer and analyst of Yankovic recordings. To this day, Debevec, Godina, and Roth have never seen each other, communicating only through e-mail.

Following is a list of recordings made by Yankovic. Due to the many labels issuing and reissuing his material, the list is necessarily incomplete. The recordings are listed in the approximate order in which they were released, based on available information and, in some cases, educated guesswork. There will be some overlapping of the various categories.

Included are:
78 rpm singles and album sets
45 rpm singles and album sets
45 rpm extended play [EP] albums
33 1/3 rpm long play [LP] albums
CDs
videos
films

Not included are:
8-track tapes
cassette tapes that duplicate material on LPs
most CDs that duplicate material on LPs

The year given is the year released, unless otherwise noted:
R indicates year recorded.
X indicates estimated year.

The catalog numbers of 78 rpm records are shown in italics.

§ indicates multiple-artist records.
[M] indicates monaural version.
[S] indicates stereo version.
[. . .] indicates missing information.

1. SELF-PRODUCED RECORDINGS

Frank produced two single records, his first, in 1938, on his own Yankee label. The artist name "Slovene Folk Orchestra" was used on the record labels, to avoid trouble with the musicians' union, of which Frank was not yet a member. The following year he produced two more singles, this time on the Joliet label and this time under the name "Jolly Yugoslavs." At a recording session in 1942 he recorded ten or twelve more tunes, eight of which were released in 1947, after they were acquired by Continental Records. On February 2, 1944, while on leave from the service, Frank recorded thirty-two numbers, which were released on the Jolly label.

Yankee *421* 1938 Zidana marela (Silk Umbrella); Oj zmiraj vesel (Always Happy)
Yankee *422* 1938 Zivijo Slovenci (Hurray Slovenes); Slovene Waltz Medley: Jaz pa dekle mam - Adijo, adijo - Daj, daj srcek nazaj

Joliet [. . .] 1939 Free Spirit of Slovenes; Joliet Illinois Waltz
Joliet [. . .] 1939 How Good for Me; Girl in the Garden

Jolly *500* 1944R My Honey Polka; Give Me My Heart Back
Jolly *501* 1944R Jolly Polka; Vadnal Waltz

Jolly *502* 1944R Don't Forget Me Polka; Yankovic Polka
Jolly *503* 1944R Be Mine Be Mine Polka; Slovene Waltz
Jolly *504* 1944R Don't Flirt with My Gal; Kukavica Waltz
Jolly *505* 1944R Jolly Fellows Polka; Herkulovic Waltz
Jolly *506* 1944R Be Happy; Bye Bye Baby
Jolly *507* 1944R Wifey's Chirping Voice; Playful Boys
Jolly *508* 1944R Three to the Left, Three to the Right; Orphan Waltz
Jolly *509* 1944R Cherry Polka; My Honey Is Wandering in Tirole
Jolly *510* 1944R Happy Minutes Polka; Venetian Waltz
Jolly *511* 1944R Daisy Polka; Jingling Tingling Polka
Jolly *512* 1944R Golden Stars Polka; Detroit Polka
Jolly *513* 1944R Where Is That Fly?; Summer Night Waltz
Jolly *514* 1944R St. Clair Polka; I Know of a Sweet Little Girl
Jolly *515* 1944R Clap and Turn; Yours Polka

2. Continental Issues

Don Gabor acquired the rights to all of Yankovic's self-produced recordings, including some that were recorded in 1942 but not previously released. He issued and reissued them on Continental and several other labels. In some cases the titles were mixed up, and in others the songs were retitled. Some of the tunes were shortened by cutting off parts from the beginning or end.

Continental *C-413* 1947Detroitska Polka; Dizzy Day Polka[1]
Continental *C-414* 1947Don't Flirt with My Gal; Herkulovic Waltz
Continental *C-415* 1947My Wife's Chirping Voice; To the Left, to the Right
Continental *C-416* 1947Darling, Who Will Take My Place; My Darling— When You Go Wandering
Continental *C-417* Summer Night; I Know of a Sweet Little Girl
Continental *C-418* Daisy Polka; Jingling Tingling Polka
Continental *C-420* Clap and Turn; Venetian Waltz
Continental *C-422* ŠPod Hrastom Polka[2]
Continental *C-1201* Be Happy; Bye Bye Baby
Continental *C-1203* Happy Minutes Polka; My Honey Polka
Continental *C-1204* Yankovic Polka; Fly Polka
Continental *C-1205* Jolly Fellows Polka; Yours Polka
Continental *C-1206* Cherry Polka; Golden Stars Polka
Continental *C-1214* St. Clair Polka; My Honey is Wandering in Tyrol
Continental *C-1219* Playful Boys Polka; Orphan Waltz

[1] Both selections were mistitled. "Detroitska Polka" is actually "Happy Minute Polka" and "Dizzy Day Polka" is the 1942 version of "Jolly Fellows Polka."

[2] Retitled; the original title is "How Good for Me," recorded in 1939. The flip side is "Ne gremo domov" by the Lausche Trio.

Continental *C-1220* §Jolly Polka[3]
Continental *C-1231* Don't Forget Me; Vadnal Waltz
Continental *C-1237* Patriot Polka[4]; Joliet Waltz
Continental *C-1238* In the Plains; Girl in the Garden
Continental *C-1239* Give Me My Heart Back; Cuckoo Waltz [Kukavitza]
Continental *C-1240* Jolly Polka; Slovene Waltz
Continental *C-1249* What's-a Gonna Be [Daisy Polka]; Mountain Wedding Polka [Jingling Tingling Polka]
Continental *C-1254* Tinker's Song [Bye Bye Baby]; Whistling Sweethearts Polka [Golden Star Polka][5]
Continental *C-1279* §Poppy Polka[6]

Continental *Album No. 49* (78 rpm 3-record set) *Frank Yankovic in Polka Time*[7]
Happy Minutes Polka; My Honey Polka; Yankovic Polka; Fly Polka; Jolly Fellows Polka; Yours Polka
Buckingham B-45-002 Daisy Polka; Detroit Polka
Remington *15003* Bye Bye Baby; My Honey Polka
Buckingham B-45-004 My Wife's Chirping Voice; Clap and Turn
Buckingham B-45-005 Jingling Tingling Polka; My Honey Polka
Remington *15006* Happy Minutes Polka; Cherry Polka
Continental C-45-006 Happy Minutes Polka; Cherry Polka
Buckingham B-45-007 To the Left, to the Right Polka; Golden Stars Polka
Remington *15009* Golden Stars Polka; My Wife's Chirping Voice
Continental C-45-009 Golden Stars Polka; My Wife's Chirping Voice
Continental C-45-011 Fly Polka; Dizzy Day Polka
Continental C-45-012 Jingling Tingling Polka; Yankovic Polka
Remington 1017 To the Left, to the Right Polka; [...]
Remington 036 Herkulovic Waltz; Daisy Polka
Continental C-45-036 Herkulovic Waltz; Daisy Polka
Continental 038 Playful Boys; Jolly Polka

[3] The flip side is "Too Fat Polka" by Jimmy Dale and His Prides of the Prairie.

[4] Retitled; the original title is not known.

[5] Continental Records dubbed vocals over Yankovic's instrumentals and released them under different titles on C-1249 and C-1254. The original titles are shown in brackets. The vocalists were Scotty MacGregor and Patsy Garrett. Two others that were dubbed are "Boarding House Polka" [Playful Boys Polka] and "Just Too Bad" [Cherry Polka]. All six are also on the Palace LP "Candy Polka," which is listed below.

[6] This is a retitled selection. The flip side is "Slovene Polka" by the Lausche Trio.

[7] An album set, comprised of C-1203, C-1204, and C-1205. The album has, on the inside cover, a sketch depicting Frank and his three band members and a short biography. Song titles are not listed on the album, but each record has "International Album No. 49" on the label.

Remington 1061 Fly Polka; Daisy Polka
Remington 1062 Jolly Polka; Playful Boys
Remington 1063 Dizzy Day Polka; Golden Stars Polka
National N452[8] Clap and Turn; Slovenian Waltz

Remington RB-906 (45 rpm 3-record album set) [. . .]
Bye Bye Baby Polka; Yankovic Polka; To the Left, to the Right Polka; My
  Honey Polka; Cherry Polka; St. Clair Polka

Remington [. . .] [45 rpm EP] *Dance Polkas*
My Wife's Chirping Voice; Golden Stars Polka; Cherry Polka; Happy
  Minutes Polka

Remington RB-921 [45 rpm 3-record album set] *In Polka Time*
Daisy Polka; Fly Polka; Jolly Polka; Playful Boys Polka; Dizzy Day Polka;
  Golden Stars Polka
Plymouth PEP-7 [45 rpm EP] *Polka Parade*[9]
Jolly Fellows; Golden Stars Polka; Be Happy Polka; To the Left, to the
  Right

Plymouth POP-100-14 [10" LP] *Polka Hits*
Bye Bye Baby; To the Left, to the Right; Be Happy Polka; My Honey
  Polka; My Wife's Chirping Voice; Golden Stars Polka; Cherry Polka;
  Happy Minutes Polka

Playhouse PL 2014; Remington RLP-1014 [10" LP] *Polka Melodies*
Be Happy; Bye Bye Baby Polka; To the Left to the Right Polka; My Wife's
  Chirping Voice; My Honey; Golden Stars Polka; Cherry Polka; Happy
  Minutes Polka

Pontiac PLP-514 [10" LP] *Let's Polka*
Be Happy; Bye Bye Baby Polka; To the Left to the Right Polka; My Wife's
  Chirping Voice; My Honey; Golden Stars Polka; Cherry Polka; Happy
  Minutes Polka

Remington RLP-1026 [10" LP] *Polka Time*
Detroit Polka [Happy Minutes Polka]; Daisy Polka; Jolly Polka; In the
  Plains [Free Spirit of Slovenes]; St. Clair Polka; Playful Boys
Polka; Joliet [Girl in the Garden]; Don't Forget Me

Remington RLP-1029 [10" LP] *Yankovic in Polka Time*

Cadillac [. . .] [10" LP] [. . .]

---

[8] There is no artist name on the label of this release.

[9] The artist name is given as "Plymouth Polka Orchestra."

Continental CEP-3 [45 rpm EP] *Polka Parade*
Jolly Fellows Polka; Golden Stars Polka; Be Happy Polka; To the Left, to the Right Polka

Palace PST-695 *Candy Polka* [10]
Just Too Bad; What's-a Gonna Be?; To the Left-To The Right; Mountain Wedding; Oak Tree Polka; Tinker's Polka; Boarding House Polka; Happy Minutes Polka; Whistler's Polka; Candy Polka; Be Happy [To the Left-To The Right]; Chirping Voice [Be Happy]

Palace PST-704; Masterseal MSLP-5009; Paris 6; Paris DG-132; Paris PL-66-1343 § *Polka Party* [11]
Bye Bye Baby Polka; To-the-Left-To-the-Right Polka; Be Happy Polka; My Honey Polka; My Wife's Chirping Voice; Golden Stars Polka; Cherry Polka

Palace PST-818 *Let's Polka* [12]

Masterseal MS-92 *Polka Festival* [13]
Jingling Tingling; Clap and Turn; Yankovic Polka; Fly Polka; Yours Polka; Dizzy Day; Don't Flirt; Detroit Polka; Daisy Polka; Jolly Polka; In the Plains; St. Clair Polka; Playful Boys; Joliet Polka

Altone 235 *Polka Festival*
Jingling Tingling; Clap and Turn; Yankovic Polka; Fly Polka; Yours Polka; Dizzy Day; Don't Flirt; Boarding House Polka; Happy Minutes Polka; Whistler's Polka; Candy Polka; Be Happy; Chirping Polka

---

[10] Marketed as a children's record. It contains six songs overdubbed with vocals. Yankovic's name is on the record label, but not on the record jacket. The song listed as "Be Happy" on side 2 is actually "To the Left-To the Right," which is also on side 1.

[11] Side 2 has eight selections by Victor Zembruski.

[12] The artist name on the record jacket is "Frankie Yankovic and His Polkateers" and there is a picture of Yankovic on the front. Possibly it is a multiple-artist recording.

[13] Both this LP and Altone 235, which follows, have the same title and cover. Side 1 of the Altone version has the same selections as side 1 of the Masterseal version, but side 2 has the same selections as side 2 of Palace PST-695 "Candy Polka" (listed above).

3. OFF-BRAND LABELS – TRANSCRIPTION REISSUES

Three of Yankovic's songs—Rolling Rock Polka, Waukegan Polka, and Clinker Polka, which he originally recorded as transcriptions for Standard Radio Transcription Services Inc. in 1950—somehow found their way onto multiple-artist LPs on various labels. Different titles and even different artist names were used in place of the correct ones in some cases. Most contain additional songs attributed to Yankovic, but which are actually by some other orchestra. There are undoubtedly more records. The correct titles of retitled songs are shown in brackets. Albums listed are 12" LPs, unless otherwise noted.

Royale 1838 [10" LP] Novelty Polkas[14]
    Rocking Polka (Rolling Rock Polka); Justa Polka (Clinker Polka)

Allegro 1719 § *Toe Tappi' Tempi*

Rondo R-2003 [M], RS-2003 [S] § *Polkas by Frankie Yankovic and the Jolly Men*

Rondo R-2023 [M]; RS-2023 [S] § *Polka Greats*

Rondo-lette A20; Galaxy 4820§ *Lawrence Welk Plays for Dancing*
    Rolling Rock Polka; Jolly Fellows Polka [Waukegan Polka]

Galaxy 2DP-733 *Polka!*

Design DLP-205; Spectrum DLP-205 § *Polka Favorites for Everyone*
    Rolling Rock Polka; Jolly Fellows Polka [Waukegan Polka]

Design DLP-904; Spectrum SDLP-904 § *Three of a Kind*
    Rolling Rock Polka

Pickwick AK280 § *The Polka Kings*
    Rolling Rock Polka; Jolly Fellows Polka [Waukegan Polka]

Trolley Car TC-5016 § *14 Great Polka Hits*

Longines Symphonette Society 93993 § *Polka Party, Vol. 1*
    Rolling Rock Polka; Jolly Fellows Polka [Waukegan Polka]

---

[14] There are three artists on this record. Their collective name is given as "Royale Polka Players."

4. CAMAY LABEL

These are soundtracks from the short-subject movies Frank made for Snader Telescriptions in 1950.

Camay CA-3021 [M], CA-3021S [S] § *Polka Parade*[15]
    Marianne; Just Because; Blue Skirt Waltz; Hokey Pokey Polka; Acapulco Polka

5. COLUMBIA AND ASSOCIATED LABELS

All in this section are on the Columbia label, unless otherwise noted.

All on the Harmony and Columbia Special Products labels are reissues.

Albums listed are 12" LPs, unless otherwise noted.

The singles had several different series of catalog numbers. Some records were released in more than one series.

10000 series: reissues of polka recordings
12000-F (foreign) series: mostly polka recordings by various nationalities
25000-F series: Slovenian releases; this series was begun in the 1920s
30000-40000 series: popular releases
50000 series: Columbia Hall of Fame Series

45 rpm records had the same catalog numbers as the 78 rpm versions, with an added "4-" prefix. In 1950 and 1951 there were some releases with a "3-" prefix, possibly 33 1/3 rpm singles.

Different series were also used for Yankovic's LP releases. Some LPs were released in both the CL-6000 and FL-9500 series.

CL-6000 series: popular releases in the 10-inch format
FL-9500 series: "foreign" releases in the 10-inch format
CL-2500 series: Columbia's "House Party" series in the 10-inch format
CL- series, beginning at CL-600: popular releases in the 12-inch format
CS- series: stereo releases in the 12-inch format

12276-F, 10001 1946 Ohio Polka; Clairene Waltz
12277-F, 10002 1946 Cherry Polka; Twilight Waltz
12293-F, 10003 1946 Three to the Right, Three to the Left; Vadnal Waltz
12302-F, 10004 1946 Be Mine, Be Mine Polka; Summertime Waltz
12313-F, 10005 1946 Shandy Polka; Happy Hour

---

[15] Side 2 has five soundtracks by Johnny Vadnal. The release date of the album is not known.

12314-F, 10006 1946 Cafe Polka; Hurray Slovenes
12321-F 1946 Jolly Polka; Cheer Up Sweetheart
12325-F, 10007 1946 Bye Bye Baby; Oh Please, Give Me Back My Heart
12339-F, 37581, 10008 1947 Strabane Polka; Rendezvous Waltz
12342-F, 37813, 10009 1947 Three Yanks Polka; Dreamer's Waltz
12347-F, 37848, 10010 1947 Clinker Polka; Cocktail Waltz
12351-F, 37948, 10011 1947 Andy's Jolly Hop Polka; Rolling Rock Polka
12359-F, 4-12359-F, 38072, 10012, 4-100121948 Just Because; A Night
  in May
12362-F, 38103, 10013 1948 The Page; The Accordion Man
12365-F, 10014 1948 Flute O'Phone; Jo Ann
12376-F, 10015 1948 Oh Marie; On the Beach
12381-F 1948 The Iron Range; Linda's Lullaby
12390-F 1948 Euclid Vets; My Honey Is Wandering
25193-F[16] 1948 Gostilniška Polka; Živijo Slovenci
25194-F[17] 1948 Zivahna Polka; Srecen bodi, srcek moj
*25195-F*1948 Židana marela; Moja decla
12394-F, 4-12394-F, 10016, 4-100161949 Blue Skirt Waltz; Charlie Was
  a Boxer
12395-F, 10017 1949 Bar-Room Polka; Whoop Polka
12399-F, 10018 1949 (You'll Be Sorry) From Now On; Rosalinda Waltz
12414-F, 10019 1949 St. Bernard Waltz; Bye Bye My Baby
12417-F, 10020 1949 Milwaukee Polka; Susie
12420-F 1949 Christmas Polka; There'll Always Be a Christmas
12427-F, 10021 1950(Cleveland) Polka Town; Honey
12429-F, 10022 1950 The Girl I Left Behind; Clink Clink Polka
12441-F, 10023 1950 You Are My One True Love; Hu-la-la-la-la
12447-F, 4-12447-F, 10024, 4-10024 1950 Tic-Tock Polka; When Banana
  Skins Are Falling
12453-F, 10025 1950 How Many Burps in a Bottle of Beer; Smiles and
  Tears
12480-F, 10026 1950 Yankovic Polka; I've Got a Date with Molly
25196-F 1950 Moja baba je pijana; Gremo na Štajersko
37374[18] 1950X Ohio Polka; Summertime Waltz
38799, 3-38799 1950 Hoop-Dee-Doo; Night After Night
38824, 3-38824 1950 When You're Away; I'm Gonna Get a Dummy
38884, 3-38884 1950 Beer Barrel Polka; Marianne
38923, 3-38923 1950 Acapulco Polka; Red Lips Waltz
38984, 3-38984 1950 Beloved, Be Faithful; Hokey Pokey Polka

---

[16] Same as 12314-F, except that the titles are in Slovenian.

[17] Same as 12321-F, except that the titles are in Slovenian.

[18] Reissue of the 1946 releases from 12276-F and 12302-F.

39010[19] Comb and Paper Polka; Pumpernickel
39046, 3-39046 1951 The Petite Waltz; The Polkarina
39116, 3-39116, 4-39116 1951 My Girl Friend Julayda; The Waltz That
　Made You Mine
39143, 3-39143, 4-39143[20] 1951 Comb and Paper Polka; You Are My
　Sunshine
39255, 3-39255, 4-39255[21] §1951 Pumpernickel
12524-F, *39269*, 3-39269, 4-39269 1951Frances, Darling Frances; Emilia
　Polka
12525-F, *39327*, 4-39327 1951 Shenandoah Waltz; Play Ball
4-12527-F1951 Just Because; Charlie Was a Boxer
12531-F, *39350*, 4-39350 1951 Just Because (International Version);
　Charm of Your Beautiful Dark Eyes
12532-F, *39351*, 4-39351 1951 Ely Polka; Way Up the Hudson
39476, 4-39476 1951 Pretty Polly Polka; Rose of Old Monterey
39532, 4-39532 1951 Tchin Boom Da Ra; Who'd Ya Like to Love Ya
50060, 4-50060 Blue Skirt Waltz; Just Because

　All of the following LPs and EPs, up to and including B-9741, consist of
previously recorded material, except as noted.

CL-6057 [10" LP] § *Popular Favorites*
Blue Skirt Waltz

C-204 [78 rpm 4-record set], CL-6116 [10" LP] § *Everybody Polka!*
　I'm Gonna Get a Dummy; How Many Burps in a Bottle of Beer

CL-6304 [10" LP], FL-9505 [10" LP] *Frankie Yankovic Dance Parade*
　(1951)
　Yankovic Polka; You Are My One True Love; Hu-la-la-la-la; Polka
　Town; The Girl I Left Behind; I've Got a Date with Molly; Honey;
　Milwaukee Polka

F-4 [78 rpm 4-record set], CL-6307 [10" LP], FL-9513 [10" LP] *Frankie
Yankovic's Original All-Time Hits* (1951)
　Cafe Polka; Hurray Slovenes; Rendezvous Waltz; Strabane Polka;
　Happy Hour; Shandy Polka; Clairene Waltz; Ohio Polka

[19]　This single, with Doris Day as the featured artist, is listed on settlet.fateback.
　　com, which has listings of 78 rpm records for various labels. It is not listed in a
　　Columbia Records discography from 1959, nor in the Columbia Records Com-
　　plete Catalog 1952–1953. The songs were also released on 39143 and 39255.

[20]　Doris Day is the featured artist.

[21]　Doris Day is the featured artist. Yankovic accompanies her on one side only. The
　　flip side is "I Can't Get over a Boy Like You" with orchestra conducted by Axel
　　Stordahl.

F-11 [78 rpm 4-record set] *Frankie Yankovic–The Polka King*
Andy's Jolly Hop Polka; Rolling Rock Polka; Bar-Room Polka; Whoop
Polka; Tic-Tock Polka; When Banana Skins Are Falling; Yankovic
Polka; I've Got a Date with Molly

F-23 [78 rpm 4-record set], F4-23 [45 rpm 4-record set], B-358 [45
rpm EP 2-record set], CL-6314 [10" LP], FL-9528 10" LP] *Frankie
Yankovic Polka Parade* [22] (1951)
Beer Barrel Polka; Copper Range Polka; Tchin Boom Da Ra; Who'd Ya
Like to Love Ya?; Hoop-Dee-Doo; Lucy Polka; My Wife Is Happy; Ely
Polka

F4-24 [45 rpm 4-record set], B-359 [45 rpm EP 2-record set], CL-6315
[10" LP], FL-9529 [10" LP] *Frankie Yankovic's Waltz Parade*
Blue Skirt Waltz; Honey; Night after Night; When You're Away;
Charm of Your Beautiful Dark Eyes; The Petite Waltz; Beloved, Be
Faithful; Red Lips Waltz

F4-25 [45 rpm 4-record set], B-360 [45 rpm EP, 2-record set], CL-6303
[10" LP], FL-9503 [10" LP] All-Time Hits
Just Because; St. Bernard Waltz; Bye Bye My Baby; Charlie Was a
Boxer; Bar-Room Polka; Whoop Polka; Rosalinda Waltz; You'll Be
Sorry from Now On

12561-F 1952 Waukegan Polka; Orphan Waltz
39594, 4-39594, *50084*, 4-50084 1952 Christmas Chopsticks; The Merry
Christmas Polka
39630, 4-39630 1952 The Blond Sailor; Only You
39649, 4-39649 1952 Ten Swedes; Gerald's Polka
39694, 4-39694 1952 The Butcher Boy; Smile, Sweetheart, Smile
10087 1952 Pojdi zmenoj; Slovenian Waltz Medley

B-426 [EP, 2-record set], CL-6296 [10" LP] *Dancing with Frankie
Yankovic*
Waukegan Polka; Gerald's Polka; Crying Polka; Mark Polka; June
Waltz; Shenandoah Waltz; Orphan Waltz; Remember Dear

B-1570 [EP] *America's Polka King*
Just Because; Tic-Tock Polka; Beer Barrel Polka; Hoop-Dee-Doo

39870, 4-39870 1953 Golden Pheasant; Tony's Polka
39884, 4-39884 1953 Torna a Surriento; Be Happy
39960, 4-39960 1953 Felicia No Capicia; Josephine Please No Lean on
the Bell

---

[22] "Lucy Polka" and "Ely Polka" were not previously released.

10097, 4-10097 1953 Moja baba je pijana; Moje decla
10104, 4-10104 1953 So Long Darlin'; Fall in Love

B-1652 [EP] *Frankie Yankovic's Waltz Favorites*
   Blue Skirt Waltz; When You're Away; Beloved, Be Faithful; Fall in Love

B-1674 [EP] [...]
   Blue Skirt Waltz; When You're Away; Beloved Be Faithful; Red Lips
   Waltz

B-1676 [EP] [...]
   Just Because; St. Bernard Waltz; Rosalinda Waltz; From Now On

B-1682 [EP] *Frankie Yankovic's Polka Favorites*
   My Girl Friend Julayda; Golden Pheasant; Emilia Polka; Tony's Polka

40012, 4-40012 1953 Alpine Climber's Ball; Skylark Polka
40075, 4-40075 1953 Valley Spring Polka; One More Dance
40114, 4-40114 1953 Mark Polka; Remember Dear

B-1753 [EP] *Dance the Polka*
   Tony's Polka; Pretty Polly Polka; Golden Pheasant; So Long Darlin'

B-1962 [EP] [....]
   Waukegan Polka; Gerald's Polka; [two more selections]

40171, 4-40171 1954 Until You Came to Me; Duluth Polka
40203, 4-40203 1954 Crying Polka; Sunset Valley Polka
40247, 4-40247 1954 Once-a-Year Day!; June Waltz
40282, 4-40282 1954 Pittsburgh Polka; Neapolitan Nights
40352, 4-40352 1955 Nightingale Polka; Joliet Waltz
40418, 4-40418 1955 I Don't Wanna Mambo Polka; Village Inn Polka
40506, 4-40506 1955 Hey! Mr. Banjo; Pretty Music

CL-638 *Polka Party*
   Tic-Tock Polka; My Girl Friend Julayda; Blue Skirt Waltz; Neapoli-
   tan Nights; Village Inn Polka; Bye Bye My Baby; Beer Barrel Polka;
   Hoop-Dee-Doo; June Waltz; The Whirlaway Waltz; Emilia Polka; Just
   Because

B-1992 [EP] *Frankie Yankovic's Polka Party*
   Blue Skirt Waltz; Neapolitan Nights; June Waltz; The Whirlaway
   Waltz

CL-2524 [10" LP] *Polka, Anyone?* (1956)
   Pittsburgh Polka; Alpine Climbers Ball; I Don't Wanna Mambo Polka;
   Nightingale Polka; Joliet Waltz; Once-a-Year Day!

CL-2580 [10" LP] *Just Another Polka!* [23]
   Just Another Polka; San Antonio Rose; Yes Sir, That's My Baby; Margie; Let a Smile Be Your Umbrella; There Is a Tavern in the Town

CL-728 § *All-Star Pops*
   Hey, Mr. Banjo

B-2087 [EP] § *All-Star Pops*
   Hey, Mr. Banjo

B-2548 [EP] *Frankie Yankovic and His Yanks*
   Just Because; Tic-Tock Polka; Blue Skirt Waltz; Beer Barrel Polka

B-2575 [EP] *Frankie Yankovic and His Yanks*
   Emilia Polka; Hoop-Dee-Doo; My Girl Friend Julayda; Pittsburgh Polka

B-2622 [EP] *Frankie Yankovic and His Yanks*
   Just Another Polka; Milwaukee Polka; Golden Pheasant; Tony's Polka

40520, 4-40520 1956 The Goodnight Waltz; Dance, Dance, Dance
40552, 4-40552 1956 My Mary Polka; Andrea's Waltz
40637, 4-40637 1956 The One Note Polka; Sing a Yodeling Song
40678, 4-40678 1956 The I.O.U. Polka; The Flemish Polka
4-40722 1956 Johnny's Polka; Beautiful Rose
4-40740 1956 Polka Pal Polka; Wondering Waltz
40816, 4-40816 1956 Chicagoland Twirl Polka; Diane Waltz

CL-974 *It's Polka Night* (1956)
   Oh, Marie; Alpine Climbers Ball; Tic-Tock Polka; Nightingale Polka; Three Yanks Polka; Just Another Polka; Duluth Polka; Pittsburgh Polka; Milwaukee Polka; Joliet Waltz; (Cleveland) Polka Town; Ohio Polka

B-9741 [EP] *It's Polka Night*
   Duluth Polka; Nightingale Polka; Pittsburgh Polka; Ohio Polka

40902, 4-40902 1956 Bunny Polka; The Bluebird Waltz
4-40950 My Favorite Polka; Let's Be Sentimental

CL-1038 *TV Polkas* (1957)
   Valley Spring Polka; My Mary Polka; You Are My One True Love; Polka Pal Polka; The Girl I Left Behind; Johnny's Polka; Cafe Polka; Chicagoland Twirl Polka; The One Note Polka; The I.O.U. Polka; The Goodnight Waltz; Sunset Valley Polka

---

[23] Selections on this LP were not previously released.

B-10381 [EP] *Polka Pal Polka* (1957)
Valley Spring Polka; My Mary Polka; You Are My One True Love;
Polka Pal Polka

B-10382 [EP] *Cafe Time* (1957)
The Girl I Left Behind; Johnny's Polka; Cafe Polka; Chicagoland Twirl
Polka

B-10383 [EP] *Sunset Valley Polka* (1957)
The One Note Polka; The I.O.U. Polka; The Goodnight Waltz; Sunset
Valley Polka

4-41026 1957 Squeeze Box Polka; Must We Say Goodbye

CL-1146 *Polkas in Hi Fi!* (1958)
Liechtensteiner Polka; Baby Doll Polka; Joe's Polka; A Long, Long
Polka; A Thing of Beauty; Tie a String Around Your Finger; Old Okla-
homa; Robbie's Polka; Put a Light in the Window; Debbie's Waltz; The
Happy Wanderer; Roving Lullaby

B-11461 [EP] *Polkas in Hi Fi! – Volume I* (1958)
Liechtensteiner Polka; Baby Doll Polka; Joe's Polka; A Long, Long
Polka

B-11462 [EP] *Polkas in Hi Fi! – Volume II* (1958)
A Thing of Beauty; Tie a String Around Your Finger; Old Oklahoma;
Robbie's Polka

B-11463 [EP] *Polkas in Hi Fi! – Volume III* (1958)
Put a Light in the Window; Debbie's Waltz; The Happy Wanderer;
Roving Lullaby

4-41112 1958 Tie a String Around Your Finger; Old Oklahoma
4-41169 1958 Robbie's Polka; A Thing of Beauty
4-41232 1958 Chop Suey Polka; Roseann Polka [Frankie's Polka][24]

CL-1281 *Polka Hop, Yankovic Style* (1959)
Frankie's Polka; Cross Key Polka; Eddie's Polka; Carol's Waltz; Milan's
Polka; Karen Ann Polka; Roseann Polka; Lovey Dovey; Over the Three
Mountains Waltz; A Night in May; The Whirlaway Waltz; Strabane
Polka

---

[24] This was supposed to be a recording of "Roseann Polka" but "Frankie's Polka"
was substituted by mistake.

B-12811 [EP] *Polka Hop, Yankovic Style – Volume 1* (1959)
Frankie's Polka; Cross Key Polka; Eddie's Polka; Carol's Waltz

B-12812 [EP] *Polka Hop, Yankovic Style – Volume 2* (1959)
Roseann Polka; Karen Ann Polka; Lovey Dovey; Milan's Polka

B-12813 [EP] *Polka Hop, Yankovic Style – Volume 3* (1959)
The Whirlaway Waltz; Over the Three Mountains Waltz; A Night in
May; Strabane Polka

4-41303 1959 Roseann Polka, No. 2 [Frankie's Polka][25]; Over the Three
Mountains Waltz
4-41338 1959 Eine Kleine Cha Cha Cha; Ya Ya Wunderbar
4-41412 1959 The Happy Polka; The Next Time Around
4-41457 1959 Rosa Rosa Nina; Moonlight Waltz
4-41565 1959 My Darling Ann; Town Tap Polka
4-41657 1959 Carol Ann Polka; St. Louis Polka
4-41806 1959 Red Wing; I've Got a Wife
4-41960 1959 Bruno's Polka; P.T.A. Polka
4-42010 1959 You and Me; Kringleville Polka
4-42181 1959 Pocatello Polka; Anniversary Waltz

CL-1358 [M], CS-8165 [S]; Columbia Special Products EN13087 *The
All-Time Great Polkas* (1959)
Beer Barrel Polka; Helena Polka; Hoop-Dee-Doo; Hu-La-La-La-La;
Clarinet Polka; Just Another Polka; Just Because; Tic Tock Polka;
Liechtensteiner Polka; Barbara Polka; My Girl Friend Julayda; Penn-
sylvania Polka

B-13581 [EP] *The All-Time Great Polkas, Volume 1* (1959)
Beer Barrel Polka; My Girl Friend Julayda; Hu La La La La; Helena
Polka

B-13582 [EP] *The All-Time Great Polkas, Volume 2* (1959)
Clarinet Polka; Just Another Polka; Just Because, Tic-Tock Polka

B-13583 [EP] *The All-Time Great Polkas, Volume 3* (1959)
Liechtensteiner Polka; Barbara Polka; My Girl Friend Julayda; Pennsylvania Polka

CL-1443 [M], CS-8293 [S] *The All-Time Great Waltzes* (1959)
Blue Skirt Waltz; Over the Waves; Three O'Clock in the Morning; My
Wild Irish Rose; Skaters' Waltz; Beautiful Ohio; You Can't Be True

---

[25] This was issued in an attempt to rectify the error on 4-41232, but Columbia
only repeated the same mistake.

Dear; When It's Springtime in the Rockies; Let Me Call You Sweetheart; Now Is the Hour; You Tell Me Your Dream, I'll Tell You Mine;
Missouri Waltz

B-14431 [EP] *The All-Time Great Waltzes* (1959)
Blue Skirt Waltz; Beautiful Ohio; You Can't Be True, Dear; Missouri
Waltz

CL-1551 [M], CS-8351 [S] *Friendly Tavern Polkas* (1960)
Friendly Tavern Polka; Tinker Polka; Emilia Polka; Rock and Rye
Polka; Too Fat Polka; Under the Double Eagle; Rain Rain Polka; The
Woodpecker Song; I Love to Polka; Strip Polka; Bye, Bye, My Baby;
Jolly Lumberjacks

CL-1620 [M], CS-8420 [S] *Happy Polkas & Dreamy Waltzes* (1961)
Cherry Polka; Ohio Polka; Clinker Polka; Three Yanks Polka; Iron
Range Polka; Page Polka; Dreamers' Waltz; Twilight Waltz; Honey-
moon Waltz; Linda's Lullaby; Sleepy Baby; Accordion Man Waltz

CL-1738 [M], CS-8538 [S] *America's Polka King* (1962)
I'm Looking Over a Four Leaf Clover; Baby Face; When You Wore a
Tulip; Linger Awhile; Ferryboat Serenade; Itsy Bitsy Teenie Weenie
Yellow Polkadot Bikini; Heartaches; June Night; I've Been Working on
the Railroad; Have I Told You Lately That I Love You; La Dolce Vita;
Sioux City Sue

CL-1804 [M], CS-8604 [S] *The Greatest Polka Sound Around* (1962)
I've Got a Wife; You and Me; Pocatello Polka; Eine Kleine Cha Cha
Cha; Roseann Polka; St. Louis Polka; Red Wing; Ya Ya Wunderbar;
Rosa Rosa Nina; Bruno's Polka; Kringleville Polka; New York Polka

CL-1952 [M], CS-8752 [S] *Your Favorite Polkas* (1963)
Milwaukee Polka; Chicagoland Twirl Polka; Duluth Polka; My Wife
is Happy; Sunset Valley Polka; Rolling Rock Polka; I've Got a Date
with Molly; Valley Spring Polka; Oh Marie Polka; Spring Time Polka;
Euclid Vets' Polka; Musicians Come and Play

CL-2001 [M], CS-8801 [S] *Who Stole the Keeshka?* (1963)
Who Stole the Keeshka?; The Old Family Album; Jolly Polka [Polka
Pal Polka]; Skylark Polka; Top of the Hill Polka; Dance Dance Dance;
The Engagement Waltz; Two Hearts in Three-Quarter Time; Rosa-
linda Waltz; Felicia's Waltz; Swiss Valley Waltz; Wunderbar

4-33050[26] Just Because; Blue Skirt Waltz
4-42527 Silk Umbrella Polka; My Sweetheart Polka

---

[26] This is a reissue in another series—possibly the Columbia Hall of Fame.

4-42652 Top of the Hill Polka; Engagement Waltz
4-42680 Who Stole the Keeshka; The Old Family Album
4-42838 1964X Josef Palianski; Polka Marie
4-43117 Ja sam Majko; Baby Doll Polka

CL-2095 [M], CS-8895 [S] *Dancing 'Round the World* (1964)
  Never on Sunday; Whoo-pie Shoo-pie – Gray Horse Polka; Two Gui-
  tars; O Marie – Luna Mezzo Mare – Tarantella Italiana; Ja sam majko;
  Let's Go to Styria – On the Mountain; Irish Washerwoman – MacNa-
  mara's Band; Sukiyaki; Hawaiian War Chant; Hava Nagila; The Petite
  Waltz; Mexican Polka – El Rancho Grande; Du du, Leigst Mir im
  Herzen – Ach du Lieber Augustin – Ein Zwei Sofa; Osman Aga

CL-2201 [M], CS-9001 [S] *Dance! Dance! Dance!* (1964)
  Beaver's Polka; Slovenian Home Polka; Ricky's Polka; Silk Umbrella
  Polka; Shanty Polka; My Sweetheart Polka; Rendezvous Waltz; The
  Prune Song; Put Your Little Foot; There Where the Flowers Bloom;
  My Darling Ann; We Can Remember Those Days

CL-2253 [M], CS-9053 [S]; Columbia Special Products 11186 *Christmas
Party* (1964)
  Jing-a-Ling; Merry Christmas Polka; Blue Christmas; Rudolph, the
  Red-Nosed Reindeer; Jingle Bells Polka; Christmas Polka; There'll
  Always Be a Christmas; Christmas Chopsticks; Christmas Lullaby;
  Medley: The First Noel – It Came Upon the Midnight Clear – Away
  in a Manger – We Three Kings of Orient Are; Medley: O Come, All Ye
  Faithful – Good King Wenceslas – Ihr Kinderlein kommet; Medley:
  Joy to the World – Deck the Halls with Boughs of Holly – God Rest Ye
  Merry, Gentlemen

4-43173 1964 Jing-a-Ling; There'll Always Be a Christmas
[...]1964 Christmas Chopsticks; The Merry Christmas Polka

CL-2335 [M], CS-9135 [S] *Happy Time Polkas* (1965)
  Copper Range Polka; Golden Pheasant Polka; Ely Polka; Jolly Polka;
  Happy Time Polka; Hurray Slovenes Polka; Mark Polka; Andy's Jolly
  Hop Polka; The Girl I Left Behind; Marianna; In Brazil They're Nuts
  About the Polka; Mary Lou

CL-2423 [M], CS-9223 [S] *Polkas & Waltzes Just for Fun* (1965)
  In Heaven There Is No Beer; Billows' Polka; Smile Sweetheart Smile;
  Toy Accordion; When Banana Skins Are Falling; Teach Me How to
  Yodel; The Last Time I Saw Henry; Barking Dog Polka; Dancing with
  Alice; Alpine Climbers' Ball; Peanuts; Broken Wine Glass

4-43400 The Last Time I Saw Henry; Dancing with Alice

CL-2480 [M], CS-9280 [S] *Movie-Time Polkas* (1966)
Those Magnificent Men in Their Flying Machines; Forget Domani;
Supercalifragilisticexpialidocious; Life Goes On; Get Me to the Church
on Time; Do-Re-Me; Pie in the Face Polka; A Spoonful of Sugar; Lara's
Theme; The Lonely Goatherd; With a Little Bit of Luck

CL-2487 [M], CS-9287 [S] *Greatest Hits* (1966)[27]
Blue Skirt Waltz; Just Because; Beer Barrel Polka; Pennsylvania Polka;
I Got a Wife; Happy Time Polka; Milwaukee Polka; Hoop-Dee-Doo;
Too Fat Polka; Who Stole the Keeshka?; The Last Time I Saw Henry

[...]Happy Time Polka; Milwaukee Polka

Harmony HL-7389 [M], HS-11189 [S] *Polka Time* (1966S)
Clarinet Polka; Ferryboat Serenade; The Woodpecker Song; Tinker
Polka; When You Wore a Tulip; Barbara Polka; Linger Awhile; June
Night; When It's Springtime in the Rockies; Three O'Clock in the
Morning

CL-2562 [M], CS-9362 [S] *Beers 'n' Cheers* (1967)
Let's Go Skiing; Blue Eyes Crying in the Rain; Schnaps; Slovenian
Waltz Medley; Jaz pa na gremazako; Johnny's Polka; Uncle Jake's
Polka; Ravine Waltz; Miami Polka; Ann's Waltz; Indian Hills Polka

4-43596 1967XCheers, Beers and Tears; Saigon Sally
4-43672 There's No Joy Left Now in Milwaukee; Blue Eyes Crying in the
Rain
4-43863 Let's Go Skiing; Teach Me How to Yodel
4-45555 Who Stole the Keeshka; Too Fat Polka

CL-2759 [M], CS-9559 [S] *Saturday Night Polka Party* (1967)
Tiddly Winks; Charm of Your Beautiful Dark Eyes; Nightingale Polka;
Billy's Polka; June Waltz; The Oompah Polka; Drina; When You're
Away; Ravine Waltz; Morning Glow; I Ain't Down Yet

Harmony HL-7455 [M], HS-11255 [S]; Columbia Special Products
[. . .] *Hoop-Dee-Doo* (1967X)
Just Another Polka; Let a Smile Be Your Umbrella; Yes Sir, That's My
Baby; Margie; San Antonio Rose; There Is a Tavern in the Town; The
One Note Polka; The Flemish Polka; Blue Skirt Waltz; Hoop-Dee-Doo

CS-9685 *Polka My Way* (1968)
Polka Town; Saigon Sally; Incline Polka; Gerald's Polka; A Night in
May; Theme From "The Yellow Rolls-Royce"; Waukegan Polka; Pie in

[27] Reissued selections

the Face Polka; Mark Polka; Theme From "Jules and Jim"; Red Lips Waltz; Village Inn Polka

Harmony HS-11375 *Favorite Polkas and Waltzes*
Dance, Dance, Dance; The Engagement Waltz; Skylark Polka; Rosalinda Waltz; Top of the Hill Polka; The Old Family Album; Swiss Valley Waltz; Polka Pal Polka; Felicia's Waltz

Harmony H-30409 *Blue Skirt Waltz*
Blue Skirt Waltz; Life Goes On; June Waltz; Ann's Waltz; Lara's Theme; Rendezvous Waltz; Milwaukee Polka; Johnny's Polka; [more selections]

Harmony H-31255 *Just Because and Other Favorites*
Tick Tock Polka; Linger Awhile; Village Inn Polka; Heartaches; I'm Looking Over a Four Leaf Clover; June Night; Beer Barrel Polka; Just Because; [more selections]

Harmony H-32431; Columbia Special Products 13516 *The Dancingest Polkas Around* (1973)

6. Various Labels – New Releases

Those listed in this section are new releases, unless otherwise noted.

Dyno DLP-1107 *An Evening at Yankovic's* (1968)
Strabane Polka; Old Oklahoma Waltz; Baby Doll Polka; Whirlaway Waltz; Broken Reed Polka; Wandering Waltz; Whoop Polka; Remember Dear; Happy Minutes Polka; Suzy Waltz; So Long Darlin'; Mary Jo Waltz

RCA Victor LPM-3915 [M], LSP-3915 [S]; RCA Victor ANL1-1036 [S] *Polka Variety* (1968)
The Happy Time; Trollie's Polka; You Are My One True Love; Leeann Waltz; Pete's Polka; Hey Baba Reba; Cabaret; Yankovic's Polka; Blue Eyes Crying in the Rain; Carol Ann Polka; Bar Room Polka

RCA Victor 47-9469 1968X Hey Baba Reba; Bar Room Polka

RCA Victor LSP-4033 *Yankovic's Favorite Polkas* (1968)
Pretty Polly Polka; Blue Skirt Waltz; Ten Swedes; Cross Key Polka; Can't We Talk It Over; Honey; My Favorite Polka; Just Because; Beautiful Rose; Who'd You Like to Love Ya?; Pittsburgh Polka

RCA Victor LSP-4087; RCA Victor ANL1-1922 *A Yankovic Dance Party* (1969)

Happy Hour Waltz; Sweetheart Waltz; Pretty Music; You Are My Sunshine; St. Bernard Waltz; Town Tap Polka; Old Time Flavor; Charlie Was a Boxer; Secretary Polka; Morning Glow; The Good Night Waltz

RCA Victor LSP-4182 *Polka Dots* (1969)[28]
Three Yanks Polka; Flutophone Polka; Those Were the Days; Jo Ann Waltz; Have Another Drink on Me; Robbie's Polka; Baskovic Polka; She's a Good Little Girl; Mary Jo Waltz; Chip on Your Shoulder; St. Louis Polka

RCA Victor LSP-4252 *Polka Time* (1970)
Clink! Clink! Another Drink; Moonlight Waltz; I'm Gonna Get a Dummy; Oh Carol Dear; Do Your Own Polka; Summertime Waltz; Strip Polka; Somewhere My Love; Get Closer to Your Partner; Cocktail Waltz; One O'Clock Polka

RCA Camden ACL1-0575 § *Beer Barrel Polka Party*[29]
Charlie Was a Boxer; Strip Polka

Dyno/Rim SLP-1 § *All Star Polka Spectacular*
Baby Doll Polka

V SVLP-8009 *Just for You* (1970)
St. Clair Polka; Tick Tock Polka; Beloved Be Faithful; Broken Reed Polka; Blue Eyes Crying in the Rain; Geraldine Waltz; Just Because Polka; Rolling Rock Polka; Clairene Waltz; Roseann Polka; Liechtensteiner Polka; Happy Wanderer Polka

V V-506 Tick Tock Polka; Blue Eyes Crying in the Rain
V V-507 Geraldine Waltz; Happy Wanderer
V V-508 Liechtensteiner Polka; Just Because

KL KLP-15 (with Jimmy Maupin) *Try It – You'll Like It* (1971)
I Love to Polka; My Wife is Happy; Morning Glow Waltz; Oh Marie Polka; Ely Polka; Helen Polka; Tony's Polka; Cheer Up Sweetheart; Teach Me How to Yodel; Happy Slovene; Old Oklahoma Waltz; Iron Range Polka

KL KS-41 Teach Me How to Yodel; Morning Glow Waltz
KL KS-129 Happy Slovene Polka; Oh Marie Polka

Western World Music WL-501 *The Greatest Requests* (1972)

---

[28] This record and LSP-4252, which follows, were probably recorded at the same time.

[29] Reissued material.

Just for You; Jolly Lumberjack; That's Why You Remember; Dance Dance Dance; Gone Away Waltz; Milwaukee Polka; My Mary; Top of the Hill; You're My Girl; Bye, Bye, Baby; Accordion Man; Moja dekla

Western World Music 5505 You're My Girl; That's Why You Remember
Western World Music 5508 Just for You; Gone Away Waltz
Western World Music 5509 Beer from Iron City; Accordion Man Waltz

Helidon FLP 04-037 *Bye Bye My Baby* (1974)[30]
Moje dekle; Maricka moja [My Mary Polka]; Slovenski valcki [Slovenian Waltz Medley]; Gostilniska polka [Café Polka]; Modro krilo [Blue Skirt Waltz]; Samo zato [Just Because]; Bye Bye My Baby; Vrh hriba [Top of the Hill Polka]; Cez tri gore [Over The Three Mountains Waltz]; Vre, vre, vre; Sonce zaslo je ze; Ciribiribela

ABC ABCD-873 *Frank Yankovic's Favorite Polkas* (1975)
Polish Power; Sing Da-Ye-Nu; Let's Go Skiing; She's a Good Little Girl; Just Because; Acapulco Polka; Have a Happy; And Away We Go; Polish Polka; Champagne Taste and a Beer Bankroll; The Square Dance Polka; Helena, My Helena; One-and-a-two-a Polka; The Skiiers Polka; The Old Barber Shop Quartette; Tick Tock Polka

ABC ABC-12081 1975 Polish Power; Sing Da-Ye-Nu

Telemark S-6410 *Party Time Polkas and Waltzes* (1975)
She's a Good Little Girl; Let's Go Skiing; Everybody Polka; Acapulco Polka; Jolly Polka [Jolly Lumber Jacks]; Johnny's Polka; If I Had My Life to Live Over; The Skating Song; An Old Fashioned Waltz; Wedding Waltz; Sheila's Waltz; The Accordion Man Waltz

Telemark [. . .][31]Johnny's Polka; Jolly Lumberjack

7. Various Labels – Reissued Material

All of the recordings in this section consist of reissued material.

Pickwick 3285 *25 Polkas*

K-Tel NC-420 § *25 Polka Greats*
Too Fat Polka; Pennsylvania Polka; Under the Double Eagle; Emilia Polka; Ohio Polka

---

[30] A Slovenian issue. English titles are shown in brackets.

[31] Telemark was a company that produced dance records. There were probably more singles issued on this label than the one listed here.

Commonwealth Music BU4980 *20 Greatest Hits*

Tee Vee TV-1010 *Super Polkas, Volume 1*
Beer Barrel Polka; My Girl Friend Julayda; Everybody Polka; Just Another Polka; Just Because; Liechtensteiner Polka; I Got a Wife; Helena My Helena; Let's Go Skiing; Melody of Love

Tee Vee TV-1020 *Super Polkas, Volume 2*

Tee Vee TA-1029 *Super Polka* (1978)
Beer Barrel Polka; My Girl Friend Julayda; Everybody Polka; Just Another Polka; Just Because; Liechtensteiner Polka; I Got a Wife; Helena My Helena; Let's Go Skiing; Melody of Love; Who Stole the Keeshka; You Are My Sunshine; Have A Happy Polka; Hoop-Dee-Doo; She's a Good Little Girl; Pennysylvania Polka; Clarinet Polka; Champagne Taste Beer Bankroll; Tick Tock Polka; Blue Skirt Waltz

Murray Hill 943485 *66 All Time Polka Hits*
Beer Barrel Polka; Liechtensteiner Polka; Pennsylvania Polka; Just Another Polka; Clarinet Polka; [more selections]

Tele House CD 2034 [4-record set] § *Polka Party*[32]
Milwaukee Polka; Broken Reed Polka; Strabane Polka; St. Clair Polka; Rolling Rock Polka; Cafe Polka; Just For You; My Mary Polka; Dance, Dance, Dance; The Pizza Polka; One-and-a-two-a Polka; Champagne Taste and a Beer Bankroll; Helena, My Helena; The Jackie Gleason Polka [And Away We Go]; Lorelei Polka; Teenage Polka; The Square Dance Polka; The Old Barber Shop Quartet; Tick Tock Polka; Just Because

K-Tel [. . .] § *Polka's Greatest Hits*
Three Yanks Polka; Johnny's Polka; Blue Eyes Crying in the Rain

[. . .] [. . .] *50 Years of Frankie Yankovic*
Pennsylvania Polka; My Melody of Love; Too Fat Polka; Blue Skirt Waltz; Liechtensteiner Polka; Beer Barrel Polka; Just Because; Cleveland, a Polka Town; Milwaukee Polka; Bar Room Polka; Hoop-Dee-Doo; Baby Doll Polka; Beer Drinking Song; Blue Eyes Crying in the Rain; Tic Toc Polka; Who Stole the Keeshka; Cafe Polka; Zivili brace, zivili sestra; That Silver Haired Daddy of Mine; In Heaven There Is No Beer

---

[32] This also consists of reissued material, no other listings for "The Pizza Polka," "Lorelei Polka," "Teenage Polka," or this version of "The Café Polka." They were probably originally issued as singles.

8. Polka City Label

All of the recordings in this section consist of reissued material, except as noted.

Polka City PC-370 [2-record set] *60th Birthday – 40 Greatest Hits* [33] (1975)
Just Because; Three Yanks; Hoop Dee Doo; Old Oklahoma Waltz; Ohio Polka; Emilia Polka; Liechtensteiner Polka; The Girl I Left Behind; In Heaven There is No Beer; Cafe Polka; Who Stole the Keeshka; You're My Girl; Too Fat Polka; Broken Reed Polka; Strip Polka; Somewhere My Love; Tic-Toc Polka; Helena Polka; Julida Polka; Linda's Lullaby; Blue Skirt Waltz; Dance Dance Dance; Top of the Hill; Just Another Polka; You Can't Be True Dear; Beer Barrel Polka; Yankovic's Polka; Milwaukee Polka; Whirlaway Waltz; Pennsylvania Polka; Accordion Man Waltz; I've Got a Date with Molly; Bar Room Polka; Susy Waltz; Baby Doll Polka; My Mary Polka; 3 O'Clock in the Morning; Happy Wanderer; Barbara Polka; Cleveland the Polka Town

Polka City PC-372 [2-record set] § *The World's Greatest Polka Package*
Just Because; Julida Polka; Blue Skirt Waltz; Three Yanks Polka; Just Another Polka; You Can't Be True, Dear; Who Stole the Keeshka?; Too Fat Polka

Polka City PC-701 *The Polka King* (1976)
Strabane Polka; Wondering Waltz; Bye Bye My Baby; Remember Dear; Sonce Zaslo; I'm a Sailor; Married; Jolly Lumberjack; Over Three Hills; My Sweetheart; Gone Away Waltz; Just for You

Polka City PC-706 § *Polka Party*
Dance Dance Dance; Blue Skirt Waltz

Polka City PC-707 § *Polka Special*
Top of the Hill; Just Another Polka

Polka City PC-708 § *Polka Holiday*
You Can't Be True Dear; Beer Barrel Polka

Polka City PC-709 § *Polka's Greatest*
Yankovic's Polka; Milwaukee Polka

Polka City PC-710 § *Polka Fun*
Whirlaway Waltz; Pennsylvania Polka

---

[33] This was originally titled "60th Anniversary—40 Greatest Hits."

Polka City PC-377 [2-record set] *I Stopped for a Beer* (1977)[34]
  Old Milwaukee Polka; Dreamer's Waltz; You'll be Sorry; The Rose of
  Old Monterey; Jolly Fellows Polka; Summer Night Waltz; Three to
  the Right, Three to the Left; Smile Sweetheart Smile; Roseann Polka;
  My Honey Is Wandering Through Tirole; Bruno's Polka; My Melody
  of Love; I've Got a Wife at Home; I'll Wait for You; Frances, Darling
  Frances; Linda's Lullaby; Paloma Blanca; The Wedding Waltz; Sunset
  Valley Polka; Beloved, Be Faithful; Lovey Dovey Polka; Twilight Waltz;
  My Girl Friend Julayda; I Stopped for a Beer

One "M" ML-1102 You'll Be Sorry; I'll Wait for You
One "M" ML-1103 Old Milwaukee Polka; Summer Night Waltz

Polka City PC-378 [2-record set] *Featuring the Great Johnny Pecon*
  (1977)
  Hoop-Dee-Doo; Cafe Polka; Honey Waltz; Clinker Polka; Marianne;
  Happy Hour Waltz; I've Got a Date with Molly; Iron Range Polka;
  Summertime Waltz; Hu La La La Polka; Milwaukee Polka; Gerald's
  Polka; Smiles and Tears Waltz; I'm Gonna Get a Dummy Polka; Felicia
  No Capicia; JoAnn Waltz; How Many Burps in a Bottle of Beer; Moje
  Decla; The Waltz That Made You Mine; Play Ball Polka; Bye Bye Baby
  Polka; Andy's Jolly Hop Polka; Red Lips Waltz; Golden Pheasant
  Polka; Petite Waltz; Charlie Was a Boxer; Clairene Waltz; Euclid Vets
  Polka; Dreamers Waltz; Frances, Darling Frances; Hokey Pokey Polka;
  Tony's Polka; Night After Night Waltz; Flute O'Phone Polka; Jose-
  phine, Please Don't Lean on the Bell; Bar Room Polka; Vadnal Waltz;
  Hurray Slovenes Polka; When You're Away Waltz; Zivahna Polka

Polka City PC-379 [2-record set] § *The World's Greatest Waltzes*
  Somewhere My Love; You Can't Be True Dear; Beloved Be Faithful;
  Blue Skirt Waltz; My Melody of Love; Three O'Clock in the Morning;
  Old Oklahoma Waltz; Whirlaway Waltz; The Girl I Left Behind; Susy
  Waltz; Accordion Waltz; The Wedding Waltz

Polka City PC-381 [2-record set] *40 Polkas and Waltzes* (1978)
  Just Because Polka; The Accordion Man Waltz; Oh! Marie Polka;
  Beloved Be Faithful; The Page Polka; The Butcher Boy; Rendezvous
  Waltz; On the Beach Polka; Way Up the Hudson; Clink Clink Polka;
  Yankovic Polka; Cheer Up Sweetheart; When Banana Skins Are Fall-
  ing; Rosalinda Waltz; Ohio Polka; Shenandoah Waltz; Strabane Polka;
  Ten Swedes; Cocktail Waltz; Jolly Polka; My Girl Friend, Julayda;
  Blue Skirt Waltz; Cherry Polka; St. Bernard Waltz; Polkarina Polka;
  Twilight Waltz; Rolling Rock Polka; The Girl I Left Behind; Ely Polka;

[34] New release. Recorded by One "M" Records.

Tick Tock Polka; Be Happy Polka; You Are My One True Love; Shandy Polka; Torna a Sorrento; Be Mine Be Mine Polka; Susy Waltz; Zidana Marela; Give Me Back My Heart; Whoop Polka; Emilia Polka

Polka City PC-386 [2-record set] *40 Great Waltzes* (1978)

Polka City PC-390 [2-record set] *Everyone's Favorites* (1979)
I've Been Working on the Railroad; Hava Nagila; With a Little Bit of Luck; Those Magnificent Men in Their Flying Machines; You Can't Be True Dear; Mexican Polka & El Rancho Grande; Put Your Little Foot; The Happy Wanderer; When It's Springtime in the Rockies; Itsy Bitsy Yellow Polka Dot Bikini; When You Wore a Tulip; The Woodpecker Song; Shenandoah Waltz; Supercalifragilisticexpialidocious; Too Fat Polka; O Marie, Luna Mezzo Mari, & Tarantella Italiana; Mary Lou; Du, du, liegst mir im Herzen & Ach du lieber Augustine; Have I Told You Lately That I Love You; Linger Awhile; Do Re Mi; Just Because; You Are My Sunshine; Let Me Call You Sweetheart; Never on Sunday; Dance, Dance, Dance; I'm Looking Over a Four Leaf Clover; Baby Face; Clarinet Polka; Hava Nagila; Sukiyaki; Three O'Clock in the Morning; Heartaches; Come Back to Sorrento; With a Little Bit of Luck; Hawaiian War Chant; Get Me to the Church on Time; A Spoonful of Sugar; Those Were the Days; My Wild Irish Rose; Somewhere My Love; Mexican Polka – El Rancho Grande; Irish Washerwoman – MacNamara's Band

Polka City PC-392 § [2-record set] *Polka's Greatest Bands* (1979X)

Polka City PC-396 [2-record set] *The Great One* (1979)
Silk Umbrella Polka; Ferryboat Serenade; June Night; Frankie's Polka; Forget Domani; Pretty Music; Robbie's Polka; Old Time Flavor; Over Three Hills Waltz; Carol's Waltz; Morning Glow; Life Goes On; My Favorite Polka; Shanty Polka; Slovenian Home Polka; Beaver's Polka; Karen Ann Polka; Joe's Polka; Pittsburgh Polka; Jaz pa na gremazako; Tie a String Around Your Finger; Once-a-Year Day!; A Thing of Beauty; The Lonely Goatherd; Pie in the Face Polka; Milan's Polka; Debbie's Waltz; Town Tap Polka; Rendezvous with You; Let's Go Skiing; Ricky's Polka; Schnaps; Eddie's Polka; There Where the Flowers Bloom; My Sweetheart Polka; Cross Key Polka; Pretty Polly Polka; La Dolce Vita; Secretary Polka; A Long Long Polka

Polka City PC-400 [2-record set] *40 Hits I Almost Missed* (1979)
Red Raven Polka; Blue Bird Waltz; Oh, Suzannah Schottische; Vienna Forever; Homecoming Waltz; Holzauction Schottische; Wooden Heart; True Love; Life in the Finnish Woods; Johnny's Knockin'; Skal Skal Skal; Apples, Peaches, Pumpkin Pie; From a Jack to a King; Orphan Waltz; Iron Range; Tennessee Waltz; Drinking Champagne; Minneapolis Polka; Edelweiss; Barbara Polka; No Beer Today; Cuckoo

Waltz; Red Wing; EI EI EI O Polka; Neapolitan Nights; Al a Ne; Que
Sera; Tinker Polka; Ranger Waltz; Jolly Polka; You Light Up My Life;
Tavern in the Town; All I Need Is You; Jingle Tingle; My Happiness;
On the Beach; Tanta Anna; Copper Range; Eins Zwei G'Suffa; Hurray
Slovenes

Polka City PC-403 [2-record set] *Polkas for Dancing* (1980)
I Love to Polka; Peanuts Polka; Dancing with Alice; Happy Time
Polka; Chip on Your Shoulder; Have Another Drink on Me; She's a
Good Little Girl; Get Closer to Your Partner; In Brazil They're Nuts
About the Polka; Indian Hills Polka; One O'Clock Polka; Billows
Polka; Do Your Own Polka; Springtime Polka; New York Polka; Ravine
Waltz; The Last Time I Saw Henry; Miami Polka; Broken Wine Glass;
Uncle Jake's Polka; Teach Me How to Yodel; Toy Accordion; Barking
Dog Polka; Baskovic Polka

Polka City PC-407 [2-record set] *My Very Best* (1981)
Blue Eyes Crying in the Rain; Carol Ann Polka; Polka Town; Two Gui-
tars; Village Inn Polka; Ya Ya Wunderbar; Cabaret; Polka Pal Polka;
Saigon Sally; Waukegan Polka; Leann Waltz; The Old Family Album;
You and Me; Trollie's Polka; That's Why You Remember; Mark Polka;
Skylark Polka; Ja sam majko; Pocatello Polka; Grayhorse Polka; Eine
Kleine Cha-Cha-Cha; My Wife Is Happy; Cheer Up Sweetheart; Rosa
Rosa Nina

Holiday HR-101; Polka City [. . .] *Christmas with the Yankovics* [35]

Polka City PC-212 *The Best of Frankie Yankovic*

Polka PC-214 *Polka's Best*
Just Because; Julida Polka; Blue Skirt Waltz; Julida Polka

Polka City PC-8001 *Dance Little Bird* (1982)
Dance Little Bird; Blue Skirt Waltz; Dance Dance Dance; Just Another
Polka; You Can't Be True Dear; Beer Barrel Polka; The Sweet Nearness
of You; Milwaukee Polka; Pennsylvania Polka; Accordion Man Waltz;
Three O'Clock in the Morning; Happy Wanderer

Polka City 4500[36]Dance Little Bird; The Sweet Nearness of You

Polka City PC-8002 § *Really Hooked on Polkas* [37]

---

[35] A reissue of Columbia CS-9503 "Christmas Party," but with the songs in a different sequence.

[36] New release. The songs are also included on PC-8001.

[37] New release. It features continuous playing.

Hoop-Dee-Doo – Too Fat Polka – Liechtensteiner Polka – Just Because
– Baby Doll – Melody of Love – Wooden Heart – Springtime Polka
– Strip Polka – Pennsylvania Polka – Helena Polka – Beer Barrel
Polka – Tic Toc Polka – Red Wing – Who Stole the Keeshka – Happy
Wanderer – Apples, Peaches, Pumpkin Pie – Just Another Polka – In
Heaven There Is No Beer – Clarinet Polka – Rain Rain Polka – Three
Yanks Polka – She Told Me[38] – Julida Polka – Bye Bye Baby – EI EI EI
O.

Polka City PC-8004 *Turned On Polkas and Waltzes Too* (1983)[39]
Hoop-Dee-Doo – Too Fat Polka – Liechtensteiner Polka – Just Because
– Baby Doll – Melody of Love – Wooden Heart – Springtime Polka
– Strip Polka – Pennsylvania Polka – Helena Polka – Beer Barrel
Polka – Tic Toc Polka – Red Wing – Who Stole the Keeshka – Happy
Wanderer – Apples, Peaches, Pumpkin Pie – Just Another Polka – In
Heaven There Is No Beer – Clarinet Polka – Rain Rain Polka – Three
Yanks Polka – She Told Me[40] – Julida Polka – Bye Bye Baby – EI EI
EI O; Blue Skirt Waltz – Du du, Leigst Mir im Herzen – Rendezvous
Waltz – Blue Eyes Crying in the Rain – Somewhere My Love – Give
Me Back My Heart – Twilight Waltz – Over Three Hills – You Can't Be
True Dear – Only You – My Darling Ann – Anniversary Waltz – Prune
Song – My Honey Is Wandering – Rosalinda Waltz – Neapolitan
Nights – Beautiful Rose – I'll Wait for You – You Are My One True
Love – Let Me Call You Sweetheart – When You're Away – Red Lips
– Smile Sweetheart Smile

Polka City PC-1009 § *Happy Birthday*
Yankovic's Polka; Beer Barrel Polka; Pennsylvania Polka; Whirlaway
Waltz; Milwaukee Polka

Polka City PC-1010 § *They Don't Get No Better*
Dance, Dance, Dance; Blue Skirt Waltz; Top of the Hill Polka; Just
Another Polka; You Can't Be True, Dear

Polka City PC-1011 § *Polka's Greatest Hits*
My Mary Polka; Three O'Clock in the Morning; Happy Wanderer;
Barbara Polka; Cleveland the Polka Town

Polka City PC-1012 § *Polka's Greatest Bands*
Accordian Man Waltz; I've Got a Date with Molly; Bar Room Polka;
Susy Waltz; Baby Doll Polka

---

[38] "She Told Me" is not listed on the record jacket or label.

[39] Continuous playing on both sides. Side1 is identical to the Yankovic side of PC-8002. Side 2 is a new release.

[40] "She Told Me" is not listed on the record jacket or label.

9. Various Labels

All in this section are new releases.

Peppermint Presents PP-1314 § *The Best of Polka Time U.S.A.* (1984X)
Beer from Milwaukee

Cleveland International CI-10001; Smash 422-830105-1 *I Wish I Was 18
Again* (1984)
    I Wish I Was 18 Again; Blue Eyes Cryin' in the Rain; Silver Haired
    Daddy of Mine; I Wanna Call You Sweetheart; I'll Always Love You;
    Who Stole the Keeshka; Goodbye Sarajevo; Only You; Play, Play Your
    Accordion; My Melody of Love; The Grandfather's Song

Cleveland International CI-10002; Smash 422-830396-1 *Christmas
Memories* (1984)
    Old Fashioned Christmas Polka; A Christmas Wish; What Christmas
    Means to Me; Blue Christmas; Christmas Chimes; There'll Always
    Be a Christmas; Christmas Doll; Christmas Memories; Christmas in
    Europe; Silent Night

Cleveland International [...]Old Fashioned Christmas Polka; There'll
    Always Be a Christmas

Smash 888196 Old Fashioned Christmas Polka; Christmas Chimes

Cleveland International CI-10003; Smash 422-830024-1 *70 Years of Hits*
(1985)
    Ziveli brace, ziveli sestra; Hey Little Sweetheart; Blue Skirt Waltz;
    Cleveland, a Polka Town; Corrida No. 1 – Serenata Nortena; Just
    Because; Beer Drinking Song; Beer Barrel Polka; The Slovenian Waltz
    Medley; Looking Back

Smash 422-830407-1 *America's Favorites* (1986)
    Tic Toc Polka; Pennsylvania Polka; Baby Doll Polka; Milwaukee Polka;
    Bar Room Polka; Cafe Polka; Liechtensteiner Polka; Hoop-Dee-Doo;
    In Heaven There Is No Beer; Too Fat Polka

Mercury[41] 422-832854-1 *Live in Nashville* (1987)
    Hu La La; Baby Doll; We Left Our Wives at Home; The "Music Row"
    Oberek; The Strip Polka; Top of the Hill; Who Stole the Keeshka; In
    Heaven There Is No Beer; The Key's in the Mailbox; No Beer Today

WRS WRP-10008 § *Polka Stalgia, Volume 2* (1988)
    The Girl I Left Behind

---

[41] The record jacket has Smash and Polygram; the label has Mercury.

K-Tel 648-1 *Let's Have a Party* (1990)
Let's Have a Party; Say Thank You Dear; Toe Tappin' Happy Polkas; Let's Be Sentimental; Do I Want You?; Alpine Climber's Ball; Thanks For Making Us So Happy; Do You Ever Miss Me?; Tell Me Now; Shine, Little Sunny, Just Shine

GNP Crescendo 842 I'm Dreaming; Henrietta Polka

10. Guest Artist Recordings

Frank also performed with other artists on a few records.

King 833 (1963R) *All-Stars of Polkaland, U.S.A.*[42]
Just Because; Red Handkerchief Waltz; Henrietta Polka; Blue Skirt Waltz; Liechtensteiner Polka; Silk Umbrella Polka; You Are My One True Love; Sugar Loaf Waltz; Helena Polka; Beer Barrel Polka; Rosalinda Waltz; Too Fat Polka

BelAire BA-3034 *Polka Music Is Here to Stay*[43] (Ed Blazonczyk)
Polka Music Is Here to Stay

HG HG-5030 (1985X) *Beer Barrel Polkas:*
Grant Kozera and His Band Featuring Frankie Yankovic
Beer Barrel Polka; My Darling Ann; Silk Umbrella Polka; When You're Away; Dance Dance Dance; Skylark Polka; In Heaven There Is No Beer; Diane Waltz; Barking Dog Polka; You Can't Be True Dear; Clinker Polka; The Waltz That Made You Mine

WRS WRP 10007 *Polka Stalgia, Volume 1*[44] (Walter Ostanek)
Joann Polka

11. Cassette Tapes

Three cassette tapes of Yankovic's earliest releases were issued in 1990. The series was not available on LP records.

Sunshine SNC 109 [Cassette] *The Early Years, Volume 1* (recordings from 1938 to 1942)
Silk Umbrella Polka; Hooray Slovenes Polka; Waltz Medley; Free Spirit of Slovenes; How Good for Me; Girl in the Garden; Don't Flirt with My Gal; Herkulovic Waltz; My Wife's Chirping Voice; Three to the Left,

---

[42] An orchestra composed of polka stars: Bob Kames, Frankie Yankovic, Georgie Cook, Gene Heier, Joe Potzner, Louie Bashell, Romy Gosz, and Valentine Kujawa.

[43] Vocal by Frank Yankovic.

[44] Vocal by Frank Yankovic.

Three to the Right; Darling, Who Will Take My Place?; Happy Minutes Polka; Jolly Fellows Polka; Dizzy Day Polka

Sunshine SNC 110 [Cassette] *The Early Years, Volume 2* (recordings from 1944)
My Honey; Give Me My Heart Back; Zivahna Polka; Vadnal Waltz; Don't Forget Me; Yankovic Polka; Slovene Waltz; Kukavica; Jolly Fellows Polka; Herkulovic Waltz; Be Happy; Bye Bye Baby; Playful Boys; Orphan Waltz

Sunshine SNC 111 [Cassette] *The Early Years, Volume 3* (recordings from 1944)
Cherry Polka; My Honey Is Wandering in Tirole; Happy Minutes Polka; Venetian Waltz; Daisy Polka; Jingling Tingling Polka; Golden Stars Polka; Detroit Polka; Where Is That Fly?; Summer Night Waltz; St. Clair Polka; I Know of a Sweet Little Girl; Clap and Turn; Yours Polka

12. COMPACT DISCS

(List compiled by Bob Roth and Joe Godina)
There are many compact disc releases on the market, mostly reissues of the LPs that were available previously. Here is a listing of some notable exceptions.

K-Tel 648-2 (1990) *Let's Have a Party* [45]
Let's Have a Party; Say Thank You Dear; Toe Tappin' Happy Polkas; Let's Be Sentimental; Do I Want You?; Alpine Climber's Ball; Thanks for Making Us So Happy; Do You Ever Miss Me?; Tell Me Now; Shine, Little Sunny, Just Shine

GNP Crescendo GNPD 2217 (1993) *America's Polka King Frankie Yankovic, One More Time*
Milwaukee Polka; Let's All Dance the Pittsburgh Way; Just Because; I'm Dreaming; Whoop Polka; Happy Mountaineer; Blue Eyes Crying in the Rain; Henrietta Polka; I Wish I Was 18 Again; Café Polka; Beer Barrel Polka; No Beer Today; You Are My One True Love; Top of the Hill Polka; Blue Skirt Waltz; From a Jack to A King; Slovenian Waltz Medley; Baby Doll Polka; Save the Last Dance for Me; In Heaven There Is No Beer

Cleveland International (1996) *Frank Yankovic & Friends, Songs of the Polka King, Volume 1* [46]

---

[45] Although listed under LPs, the LP version was limited because it was released during the transition period from LP to CD.

[46] Features guest appearances by various polka and country stars.

Just Because; Who Stole the Keeshka; Hoop-Dee-Doo; Blue Skirt
Waltz; Too Fat Polka; Cleveland the Polka Town; The Beer Barrel
Polka; In Heaven There Is No Beer; The Bar Room Polka; Zivili Brace,
Zivili Sestra; For Old Times Sake

Cleveland International (1997) *Frank Yankovic & Friends, Songs of the
Polka King, Volume 2* [47]
The Night Frank Yankovic Came to Town; The Pennsylvania Polka;
Hey Little Sweetheart; My Melody of Love; Milwaukee Polka; That
Silver Haired Daddy of Mine; I Wanna' Call You Sweetheart; Baby Doll
Polka; Play, Play Your Accordion; The Yankovic Medley

A 'n' D Music CD 004 § (1997) *Kanada, Slovenija, Amerika* [48]
Bye, Bye My Baby; Smiling Eyes; Broken Heart; It Thrills Me So

Soundies 630.734.3044 [2-CD set] The Complete Standard Transcrip-
tions [49]
Beer Barrel Polka; My Sweetheart Polka; She Told Me She Loved Me;
Honey, Why Can't You Be Sweet to Me?; Vegas Polka; Strabane Polka;
Silk Umbrella Waltz [50]; Cleveland Polka; When You're Away; Tick
Tock Polka; Three Yanks Polka; Cafe Polka; Oh Marie; Rolling Rock
Polka; Clinker Polka; Blue Skirt Waltz; Just Because; Josephine, Please
No Lean on the Bell; The Girl I Left Behind; A Night in May; Night
After Night; Pretty Polly Polka; Charm of Your Beautiful Dark Eyes;
Tchin Boom Da Ra; Orphan Waltz; Ely Polka; Rose of Old Monterey;
Frances Darling Frances; Nights of Splendor; Gerald's Polka; Butcher
Boy; Emilia Polka; Waukegan Polka; Come Back to Sorrento; Copper
Range Polka; Tony's Polka; Felicia Polka [51]; Jolly Fellows Polka; So Long
Darling; Fall in Love; Smile Sweetheart Smile

Peppermint PR5043 (1999) *Smile*, The Joey Tomsick Orchestra
A Tribute to the King

Below are more of the many compact disc releases on the market; all are
reissues of the LPs that were available previously. There are too many to
list, as manufacturers rerelease mixes of different tunes with different
packaging. This is just a sample of what is available.

---

[47] Features guest appearances by various polka and country stars.

[48] Artists include Frank Yankovic, Walter Ostanek, and Alfi Nipic. Produced in
Slovenia by Dejan Nipic.

[49] Yankovic recorded these forty-one tunes for Standard Radio Transcription
Services, Inc., in 1950.

[50] "Silk Umbrella Waltz" is mistitled; it is actually a polka.

[51] "Felicia Polka" is actually "Felicia No Capicia" and is not a polka.

The All Time Great Polkas: Frankie Yankovic Plays in Person (reissue of
   Columbia LP)
Frankie Yankovic and His Yanks' Greatest Hits (reissue of Columbia LP)
Frankie Yankovic and His Yanks: Happy Wanderer (reissue of the Co-
   lumbia LP but now on the Sony label)
The Polka King Remembered: An Evening at Yankovic's (reissue of Dyno
   LP; CD number is CD-1107)
MCA records MCAD-31179 *Frank Yankovic and His Orchestra, Greatest
   Polkas and Waltzes, Volume 1*
MCA records MCAD-31180 *Frank Yankovic and His Orchestra, Greatest
   Polkas and Waltzes, Volume 2* [52]
The Polka King: 48 Polkas and Waltzes
60th Anniversary Greatest Hits, Volume 1
Polygram Records *America's Favorites, the Polka King Plays Party Re-
   quests*
Ross Records 6672-2 Laserlight Records 12226 *Frankie Yankovic: Dance
   Little Bird*
Polygram Records *Christmas Memories*
RCA 07853-67933-2 *Greatest Polka Hits*
Cleveland International Records HER 2007-2 (2000) *Live in Nashville*
Cleveland International Records HER 2005-2 (2000) *70 Years of Hits
   with Frank Yankovic*
Cleveland International Records HER 2006-2 (2000) *I Wish I Was 18
   Again*
Columbia/Legacy CK 87178 *The Best of Frank Yankovic Polka King* [53]

Columbia/Sony CD 6857 *Doris Day Happy Hits*
   Comb and Paper Polka (Yankovic with Doris Day)

Bear Family (Germany) UPC No.: 79005115609 (1993) *It's Magic* (Doris
   Day)
   The Comb and Paper Polka; Pumpernickel; You Are My Sunshine

(2002) *Button Box Hits*
One Last Time with Walter Ostanek and the Western Senators
Frank Yankovic Greatest Hits, Volume 2
K-Tel 3112 *Toe Tappin' Polkas*

---

[52] Portions of the two CDs above were originally released as *Frank Yankovic's
   Sixteen Favorite Polkas*, ABC Records LP ABCD-873, recorded February 1975.

[53] "Comb and Paper Polka" (Yankovic with Doris Day).

13. Video

A sample listing of some of the video available.

VHS (1993) *One More Time* (3 volumes)[54]
Whitestar 1714 VHS (1995) *Frank Yankovic America's Polka King*[55]
Czech Video VHS (1992) *Frankie Yankovic and Friends*

14. Films

Snader Telescription Films[56]
1201 *Acapulco Polka*
1202 *Hokey Pokey Polka*
1203 *Blue Skirt Waltz*
1204 *Marianne*
1205 Just Because Polka

15. Major Yankovic Band Lineups

1930s
Al Naglitch, piano
Jim Hocevar, guitar
Bill Dunlavey, saxophone
Lee Novak, drums
Frank Skufca, banjo

Early 1940s
Joe Miklavic, banjo
John Hokavar, bass
Al Naglitch, piano

1946–49
Johnny Pecon, chromatic accordion, vocals
Georgie Cook, banjo
John Hokavar, Adolph "Church" Srnick, and Stan Slejko, bass
Al Naglitch, piano

1950–1954
Anthony "Tops" Cardone, accordion
Buddy Griebel, piano
Carl Paradiso, banjo, vocals
Al Leslie, bass

---

[54] Produced by Universal Productions International, Inc., Milwaukee, Wisconsin.

[55] PBS TV special.

[56] Made in Hollywood in 1950 to be shown in movie theaters, not commercially available.

1950s
Richie Vadnal, accordion
Emmette Morelli, piano, solo vox
Ron Sluga, banjo, vocals
Pete Rogan, bass

1950s
Joe Sekardi, accordion
Emmette Morelli, piano, solo vox
Eddie Teener, banjo, vocals
Pete Rogan, bass

1960s
Mike Zitkovich, accordion
Ray Smolik, piano, solo vox
Pete Rogan, bass
Roger DiBenedict, banjo
Joey Miskulin, accordion
Roger Bright, piano and accordion
Chuck Davis, steel guitar and banjo
Lou Kish, bass

1970s
Jeff Winard, accordion
Jay Broderson, banjo
Denny Bonek, bass
Bobby (Kolka) Chick, drums

Polka Varieties TV band
Joey Miskulin, accordion
Dick Sodja, piano
Ron Sluga or Rudy Vincent, banjo
Adolph "Church" Srnick, bass
Jack "Porky" Ponikvar or Billy Zallar, drums

1980s
Joey Miskulin, accordion
Bobby Yankovic, banjo
Dave Wolnik, drums

Other musicians who spent significant time with Yankovic were accordionists Jimmy Maupin, Grant Kozera, Herb Eberle, Bob Kravos Jr., Anthony "Corky" Godec, Eddie Stampfl, Jim Kozel, Don Lipovac, Fred Ziwich, Dan Peters, Eric Noltkamper, Frank Moravcik, Steve Kucenski, Bill Wardle, and Don Kotzman; pianists Frank Piccorillo and Ron Roetter; banjo players Joe White, Bob Haaker, Buzz Bradley, Harry Mays, and Denny Anderson; bass men Marty (King) Kukovich, Stan Mozina, George Carson, and Mike Dragas; and drummer Buddy Kumel. Hundreds of others played with Yankovic for shorter periods.

Index

A "P" in the page number listed below indicates a photograph located in the photo section beginning after page 116.